REGEN

HOW TO RESTORE YOUR HEALTH AND REBUILD YOUR BODY WITHOUT DRUGS OR SURGERY

By Joel Jay Baumgartner M.D.

Bestselling Author and Global Leader in Regenerative Wellness

Bonus Recipes and Meal Plans!

This book includes detailed recipe books and additional meal plans at:

www.JoelBaumgartnerMD.com

Thanks to my beautiful wife, Debbie, for your love and support and to my three amazing children - Teddy, Corrielle and Faith - for being my reason to make the world a better place. I love you all!

PREFACE

I'm in college working as a nurse's aide in my home town nursing home. There's a patient, Barb, who is like a body still alive but with no one home. Barb had multiple strokes. The doctors have no solution for her other than to have her bodily functions constantly cared for. My job is to take her down to lunch, feed her, bathe her and put her to bed.

One day, out of boredom, I start telling Barb about my day. I get what I expect, absolutely no response. But it becomes my habit to talk to Barb whenever I'm caring for her.

Three days into this, I say, *"Hey Barb, there's this really cute redhead named Jen. I want to ask her out but I'm...I'm really nervous."*

And I see it....

Barb turns her head towards me.

"There is someone in there!"

Things progressed fast from there. Soon Barb was squeezing my hand, feeding herself, and telling me stories about her late husband Joe and her three kids.

By the end of the summer, I'd say, *"Barb, let's see what's on the radio? Want to dance?"* Then I'd stand her up, and we'd rock back and forth and I'd say, *"I love you..."* ... *"I love you too,"* she'd whisper.

My experience with Barb prompted me to become a doctor. A healer. It taught me to look past the "symptoms" and "prescriptions"- to always seek the deeper solution. All Barb needed was to be truly cared for again.

Fast forward to when I'm 32, after I've completed med school, after a 3-year family medicine residency, after I've done fellowship in nonsurgical orthopedics and sports medicine, and while I'm working as a physician for a large hospital based medical clinic.

I'm seeing 25-30 patients a day with pressure to see more and make money for the "system". Patients with chronic pain conditions and arthritis are all on narcotics, anti-inflammatories, muscle relaxants, antidepressants and cortisone shots. The negative side effects and risks are rarely discussed. Then, after multiple invasive procedures and surgeries, many patients aren't healed, and the pain persists.

I can see firsthand that the traditional medical care, big box hospital system I'm in is broken. But I still remember how I felt with Barb's "awakening" and I'm determined to restore health and heal the body without drugs or surgery.

So, in 2008, I took a big risk and quit my job to create my own clinic. My chance to live out my quest to redefine healthcare. I feel like Jerry Maguire, leaving to follow my instincts and fulfill my PURPOSE... **"True health is achieved by creating truly healthy people."**

My first two hires were former patients, Susan, a nurse with expertise in Hormone Therapy and Functional Medicine, and JR, a personal trainer who got great results with his clients by helping them make lifestyle changes.

With the three of us onboard, Rejuv Medical was born! **Functional Medicine, Fitness and Regenerative Medicine.**

Today Rejuv Medical is a team of 80 employees. We're proud and humbled that together we've redefined healthcare, lead the way in regenerative medicine, and been awarded three consecutive years for Central Minnesota's Best Specialty Physician (An award given to me, but truly shared by my team).

I love my profession as a doctor, physician and a healer. And even though it's 20-something-years later, that summer with Barb is still very much a part of me. It's my touchstone to the potency of truly caring for your patients and addressing the root cause of their diseases and degeneration.

Table of Contents

INTRODUCTION

Natural forces within us are the true healers of disease. — **Hippocrates**

The other day, I took my family to our local county fair. It was electric with sounds, sights and "smells". Families gathering for some down-home Minnesota fun, taking their chances on games and tasting the newest deep fried delectable. After about five minutes of observing the families passing by, I started to notice a pattern. Parents were walking around with a stressed, tired, forlorn look on their weathered faces, followed by agitated, unhappy kids walking with the same body habitus as their parents. They were overweight, lethargic and unhealthy. They represented the trend we live in, where unhealthy lifestyle choices are affecting the health of the entire family.

As our population "grows" so does the plethora of chronic diseases that are stealing the longevity and luster of life. We live in a world where technology is advancing exponentially. Despite all the technology innovation, the health of our society is declining. It is time to tap into the research and technology that can reverse disease and degeneration. We need to focus on lifestyles that promote long-term health to create families who thrive and reverse the current health trends.

In health care, we need to get away from a new pill for every symptom and the many unneeded, invasive procedures and surgeries eating away our health care dollars. The use of dangerous high-dose cortisone injections and chronic pain medications are having detrimental effects on our joints and bodies. It is time we, instead, look at changing our lifestyles as a first line of defense against disease and focus on regenerative orthopedic procedures that can heal and reverse our pain, injuries and degeneration. It is exciting to know that we have the ability to truly reverse disease and heal our bodies. We can make changes in our lives and make healthcare decisions that will rejuvenate our bodies and impact the health of generations to follow.

To make positive change and heal our bodies, we need to have specific goals. First, we need to optimize our health to create a healing environment. Next, we need to initiate healing at the site of degeneration with Prolotherapy, Platelet Rich Plasma (PRP) or Stem Cell procedures that are proven to have positive effects. After initiating healing, we need to avoid degenerative influences that slow or impair the healing process and, finally, we need to maintain that healed area once our goals are achieved. This process can reverse degeneration and rebuild our bodies, enabling us to enjoy all that life has instore for us.

I have developed the C.F.A.N. model for optimal healing. When those puzzle pieces are put together, you create a picture for healing and disease reversal without unneeded medications or premature surgeries.

In the **C.F.A.N.** model for optimal health and healing, the **C** stands for cell health. This includes what we put in our body nutrition-wise, whether we engage in healthy exercise daily, the balance of our internal hormones and micronutrients, and how we deal with life stressors and sleep. The **F** represents functional movement. To have healthy functional movement we must have proper core strength, flexibility, balance and healthy fascia. Without healthy functional movement, our bodies are more prone to injury, breakdown and degeneration.

Next, the **A** is for the articulation. This is the joint, the joint capsule, the joint cartilage and the ligaments that hold the joint together. An example would be the knee, which has cartilage on the inside that, when healthy, aids in range motion and function. These structures, when injured or unstable, lead to arthritis from abnormal wear patterns in the joint.

Until recently, the only treatments available for chronic pain and degeneration were cortisone injections, pain medications or surgery. Fortunately, advancements in regenerative orthopedics have given us the tools to actually REGENERATE the broken body. Regenerative procedures like Prolotherapy, PRP (Platelet Rich Plasma) and Stem Cell injections can reverse these degenerative processes without the side effects of cover-up medications or risks of invasive surgeries. The cells used are from you own body and have a powerful impact on healing and regeneration through the stimulation of the body's natural healing response. The body can heal itself!

Finally, the **N** is for nerve health. A healthy nervous system is critical for proper function and musculoskeletal movement in the body. Every nerve that leaves the spine eventually passes by and has an effect, either positive or negative, on the muscles, ligaments, tendons and joints they innervate. They have a direct effect on the function as well as the ability of that joint to repair and heal after an injury.

Also critical for success is the neuropsychiatric connection. We need a positive outlook and have the skills to set goals based on our core reasons for change. It all starts with the brain by making the decision to change.

Through optimization of each of the elements of the **C.F.A.N.** model, true health and healing is obtainable and a new model for healthcare emerges, changing the landscape of medicine from disease control to disease prevention and reversal. This new vision of healthcare empowers us to heal and regenerate without having to settle for cover-up medication, harmful injections or unneeded surgeries.

An NFL Story

In the NFL, it is pay for play. Those athletes compete at a high level of intensity with the risk of injury lingering with every battle. They sacrifice the long-term health of their joints for the immediate task at hand. They play to WIN... and at ALL COSTS. They are popping anti-inflammatory medications to get through the game and are having multiple cortisone injections to enable them to return to play. They pay the price years later, when their bodies are broken down from the years of abuse.

Last summer, a former NFL football player came to see me with knee pain and the inability to engage in high-impact training and running because the pain in his knee. He had had a few bang-up injuries in competition and, subsequently, had orthopedic surgery to "clean it up". He made it through his competitive years relying on cortisone injections to get him through his seasons. The cumulative effect of his meniscal "cleanup", cortisone injections and daily anti-inflammatory medications left him with a knee broken down with arthritis. He could no longer run, perform or engage in the physical activities he once excelled at. He asked, *"Can you help?"* He had heard about Stem Cell procedures and asked if they could help him with his knee arthritis and pain. He wanted to again use his body and continue his passion for fitness and activity. The good news for him: the answer was "yes."

His x-rays and MRI (Medical Resonance Imaging) revealed the source of his pain and inability to run. He had a full thickness loss of cartilage over the inside surface of his knee and under his knee cap. He also had thinning and instability of one of the stabilizing ligaments in his knee. We performed an ultrasound-guided Stem Cell procedure, distributing the stem cells over the areas of cartilage loss in his knee. We also injected PRP into his meniscus as well as the stabilizing ligaments that support his knee. He was already eating very healthy and taking care of his body, so he had a good head start on the healing process. Many patients we see are not eating healthy or exercising.

Around the second month after his procedure, he was out walking his dog. He hadn't tried running but, unfortunately for him, it started to rain hard. He thought, "*well, I can either get soaked or I can test out my knees*". He ran all the way home without pain and without any swelling or pain the next day. He is now running, doing Olympic weight training, and is much more active than he was prior to his procedure. He is able to play with his children, run with the dog and wakes up the next day ready to hit the road running again. Regenerative injections have returned to him a quality of life that he had previously lost. He continues to eat healthy, exercise and enjoy life as it was meant to be lived.

Sally's Story

Sally is an energetic, loving and enthusiastic woman who, despite the aches in her knees and back, is always smiling and laughing through her pain. She has the right attitude. She is in her mid-50s and was planning on using these years to travel, spend time with her grown children and, hopefully, enjoy grandkids someday soon. Before she saw me, she'd been treated by her orthopedic surgeon. She was getting cortisone shots every three months and taking daily Ibuprofen just to suffer and limp through the day.

Her doctor said, "*let's continue this for a few more years until you are a little bit older and then we can do a knee replacement.*"

I hear words like that every day from my patients. She did not want to suffer any longer nor continue to put cortisone into her body and was not very excited about her only option in the end being a knee replacement.

A friend of hers had been reading on advancements in orthopedics and told her about research being done using stem cells for arthritis conditions. She called us and made an appointment to discuss her options. After our consultation, for the first time in years, she had hope. At the end of office visit, her tears of pain were replaced by tears of joy... but we had some work to do. Over the last five years, through the combination of menopause, being inactive and the over-consumption of "comfort foods", she had gained about 50 pounds of excess weight. This was not helping her diabetes and it was definitely contributing to the breakdown and pain in her spine and knees. So, our first focus was to improve her cell health. We needed to get her body healthier so that she would have an optimal healing response with her spinal PRP and knee stem cell procedures. With the thought of having less pain and her core motivation for change being the vision of running and playing with her grandchildren, she embraced the challenge to overhaul her health. We taught her how to eat healthy whole foods, helped her set personal health goals and showed her how to exercise and strengthen her body around her broken down joints.

Two months later, she was already transforming. She had seen our nurse practitioner for her hormone and menopause issues. She had lost 35 pounds, was enjoying walking again, and was eating healthy. Her husband was excited about her changes and was supporting her on this journey while changing his health as well. She was sleeping better without hot flashes and her energy was improving after getting her body back in balance again. Then, she had a PRP procedure to her spine, followed by stem cells, to target the arthritis and meniscal tears in her knee.

Three months after her procedures, she still has a contagious smile, is exercising daily, eats healthy and enjoys cooking delicious recipes. She is over 50 pounds down and feeling the energy she had in her 30s. I hear stories like this one every day and it fuels my passion to create a new healthcare model that focuses on disease prevention and treatments that reverse chronic disease and heal painful degeneration in our bodies.

I love what I do. I have the opportunity to go to work and make a true difference. Through innovation and technology, and the research and advancement in regenerative orthopedics, we have the ability to return peoples' quality of life; to decrease chronic pain; and to reverse the degeneration of the joints and spine. We can **REGENERATE**!

My Story - REGENERATE

Big Brother, Mom, the Military, Dad, the Twins, Barb, Susan, JR and a bit of FAITH

Our current healthcare model is broken, expensive and is not changing the health of our society. Patients are suffering from chronic disease and body degeneration without options to escape. They are hopeless and broken.

FLASHBACK

I'm 32 years old. A young, energetic, altruistic physician working in a large healthcare model. I am seeing as many patients a day as I could squeeze in; I am stuck in a model of prescribing medications to cover up their symptoms, while injecting their joints and spine with cortisone. I'm often referring to expensive surgeries or procedures that drove profits for the large system, but those procedures and surgeries are often very risky to my patients and they often return still in pain and with disability.

The large healthcare system I worked for then made the decision to pull out of town, leaving me without a secure job in 60 days. At that time, my wife and I and our two children had planted roots in our community, but we had to make a decision. I could move to the new city with my current employer, have a stable job and continue as part of this large healthcare system - or I could start my own clinic leaving me vulnerable, insecure and at risk. I had a responsibility to provide for my family, but I also had a great responsibility as a physician to help and to heal those who entrusted me with their health. I was scared and broken thinking about my fate. I had to make a decision.

BROKEN

One of the earliest memories I have of myself is as a shy, insecure and small-in-stature little boy. It is 1980 and I am in second grade, living Denver, Colorado, after moving to a new town and school every few years - my dad was an officer in the military. I am the middle child, with my older brother being three years older and my sister being five years younger. My brother is big for his age, athletic, and a sports enthusiast who excelled in both academics and sports. Being only three years behind him, he is my hero and someone I look up to and respect.

At our neighborhood school, my shyness kept me from talking much. I, often spent the day hiding my "wet" pants because I was too embarrassed to talk to the teacher to ask if I could use the bathroom. I wanted to learn more, ask questions and interact with my friends, but I went entire days without talking to teachers. My lack of confidence and ability to talk and ask questions caused me to fall behind in school and have few good friends.

My family loved me, and I was secure in my home, but my inward insecurity developed from the on-the-move military lifestyle I grew up in, combined with my smaller stature and shy demeanor. My dad was a military doctor, so we ended up moving to another town about every two years. From preschool to fifth grade, I attended six different schools and had moved through four different states. I never had the same group of friends for more than a few years and lacked a stable platform or identity.

Now, my mom, Ellen, was an intuitive mother. Early on, she noticed that my brother and I were different both in stature and personality. My brother was larger and excelled in team sports, like basketball and football, so she purposely put me into different individual sports, like gymnastics and tennis, so I didn't compete with his accomplishments. She wanted to avoid me being compared to the success of my brother in his team sports.

Finally, after years of moving around, the last city we moved to was Dickinson, North Dakota. Dickinson was a small, rural North Dakota town - a place where football was king. So here I was, starting fourth grade as a tennis player and a male gymnast, in a small rural country town. I was the only male gymnast in the entire town and had to train with the girls' team until we petitioned to get a men's team going when I was in 6th grade.

Also, as a young kid, I was very creative and could create things, so I discovered I excelled in art. I would spend hours taking a white piece of paper and creating it into a "masterpiece". During that time in my life, I found an identity through being good at art and being good in the individual sports of gymnastics and tennis.

I learned how to be a fighter, work hard and succeed through my own means. I learned how to survive on my own by being outside the box and not following the status quo. Back then, I was outside what was considered normal for a North Dakota kid. I was made fun of because I was "different" - "*Guys do not do gymnastics*". Now come on, we all know now that a male gymnast is one of the most powerful, strong athletes and, pound for pound, can rival the strongest football player - but others didn't see me that way.

It really was not COOL to be a creative, somewhat quiet, tennis player and gymnast.

Over time, I grew to be ok with what I was, despite not fitting into the mold of my 'normal' peers. Little did I know that all of this was developing my character and comfort level to be outside the box and not always part of the mainstream. It created in me not only a physical strength but a mental integrity that would serve me well in the future.

Another vivid memory I have is me at around five or six years old. I remember walking upstairs to my dad's office where he would be at his desk, reading medical journals with the lights off and the door closed. I remember a draft coming from underneath his door - I would put my nose to the floor and lay there listening to Paul Harvey on his radio. I could smell his signature Aramis cologne from under the door. It was comforting to know he was there.

He was a busy physician. He would often be gone to the hospital in the morning when we woke up. He would come home for dinner and head back to the hospital in the evenings for rounds and patient care. It's funny because, at that time in my life, the last thing I wanted to be was a physician because of the lifestyle it required and the sacrifices that a medical family makes.

REBUILT

My dad retired from the military and, through junior high and high school, we never moved again. In junior high, I started to hit my stride. I was successful in gymnastics and tennis and still found joy in the creativity I could express through art. Those who once found me different now found me fun and unique. I also found out that I could make people laugh, and I was actually a likable person. I was ok with being good at things others were not.

I still suffered some deep insecurities and felt I needed to prove to others that I had worth, that I was talented, smart and an athlete. I often saw myself then as an insecure little kid who was different from the other kids around me. I realize now that those experiences growing up have shaped me into I am today. My mother's wisdom in putting me into activities where she knew I would excel gave me the will to fight hard, stick to my guns and be the best I can be using the talents and gifts God gave me. Traveling from town to town and school to school without a stable friend base taught me to be independent and resilient. It gave me legs to not only stand on, but a will to create, fight, work hard and the goal to become "someone".

In high school, I continued to pursue art, tennis and gymnastics. I did well in school and had a few core friends. They enjoyed my uniqueness and artistic side and continued to build me up to give me confidence in who I was as "someone". Thank you, Aaron and Ali, for being my best friends and part of the development of who I am and who I was to become today.

In high school, I wasn't part of any one group but was "friends with everyone." I didn't want to judge or exclude, and I would go out of my way to accept others who were "different" or didn't fit the status quo. I knew what it felt like to be shamed and pushed around for being who you are - and it was time to stand up to it.

Then I met April and Vanessa, who truly were different. They were short, German, identical twins with very low voices and thick curly big red hair. They were ridiculed and shamed every day in our school; teased and bullied by the "cool crowd". "*Hey, here comes Eek and Meek*" ... "*Eek Eek Eek*" was a daily dialogue they would hear. They were freshmen when I was a senior.

As a senior, I knew I was unique and I was now confident in who I was. I related to these two girls who were different and unique in their own special way. The truth is they were kind, funny, loving, real people. They had emotions and feelings. I remembered what it was like to have no friends, to feel insecure and to not have an identity. I wanted to protect them... so, they would meet me at my locker and I would walk them to their classes. We would talk about their classes, their dogs or their new scotty dog-shaped earrings. We talked about everything and nothing, like regular friends do. I gave them an identify. No one made fun of them or bullied them when we walked together. I was their friend, but they gave me more then I think they will ever know. They planted a seed in me that would later grow into part of who I am today. In fact, it was part of who I was even back then... a genuine, nice and caring person. It actually made me very accepted throughout my school. I was a person that was known to genuinely care for others.

My senior year, I was voted most influential in our senior class, voted in as Student Body President and voted on as Homecoming Royalty. I was unique, but that was ok. What I learned then was that it wasn't that I was a gymnast, a tennis athlete, or being an artist that made me so special. What I realized about myself was that one of my greatest gifts was that I felt empathy, that I had a heart for people and a passion to help those who are hurting.

I went on and graduated from Dickinson High School, confident in who I was as a person, proud of myself for who I had become, but heading to college with no idea as to what to do with my life. I was fearless, or maybe just naïve. I walked onto the University of North Dakota (UND) diving team and made the team after never have been on a diving team in my life. I convinced the coach to give me a try since I had a strong gymnastic background. I also tried out for an opera without ever having had a voice lesson. I absolutely did NOT get a role in the show, but it demonstrated that I was up for any challenge. Fear would not hold me back. I had a deep sense that I could do anything. My key Bible verse then was, "*I can do all things through Him who strengthens me,*" Philippians 4:13.

It was then when I started to realize I needed to do something to help people. I had the gift of empathy and compassion. I started college and graduated as a Visual Arts major. It was great - I had four years to really develop the creative side of myself. I fully enjoyed my studies and excelled during those years. I would spend every day creating art and channeling my creative energy in unique ways. But I questioned how I could I truly help people with my creativity.

DISCOVERY

During my college sophomore summer, I had three jobs. One was teaching art in the local prison. Another was teaching art to the elderly in assistive living and the third was working as a nurse's aide in a local nursing home. The third job change my life forever. At the nursing home, I would get to work by 6 a.m. to get the residents out of bed, take them to the restroom, clothe them, bathe them, feed them and put them back to bed. Each one of the residents had a story... a life lived... a life lost. Every one of them loved someone and had someone who, at one time, loved them back. They were all approaching the end of their journeys.

Something inside me was awakened through this experience when I met a lady named Barb. My job was to take her down to lunch, feed her, bathe her and put her to bed. Barb sat alone in a wheelchair, constantly rocking, and wore gloves on her hands so she would not pick at her face. She was legally blind and never spoke. I spent the first week of my job simply doing my job. I was bored with it all so, over time, I thought, *"Well, I have nobody else to talk to I might as well talk to Barb."*

I would tell her about my day or a girl I liked. I would tell her stories about my summer and how I went waterskiing over the weekend. I would tell her about a dance I went to the weekend before and who I danced with that evening. After a few days of talking to Barb, she started to turn her head towards me. She was actually listening, so I started asking her questions about herself and about her late husband Joe. She started to smile and slightly giggle at some of my funny stories. Soon Barb was feeding herself without her gloves on and stopped obsessively picking at her face. Something inside Barb had been restored. She had been rejuvenated.

One of my favorite memories toward the end of that summer was with Barb. Every time I put Barb to bed, I would turn on the radio and we would slow dance through an entire song. Even though Barb couldn't see me fully, she would stare at me with a big toothless smile. At the end of our dance, I would tuck her into bed, pull her covers up to her chin and kiss her on the cheek while whispering, "*I love you, Barb.*" She would always respond in her soft grandma voice, "*I love you too.*"

Barb's transformation changed my life. She gave me a purpose and made me realize I am special, and that I can have a profound influence on people just by caring for them deeply. I'm thankful to this day for the gift Barb gave me.

That was the summer I decided I was made to be a doctor. I added pre-med to my art degree. I was focused and determined. I saw medical school as a way to truly have impact and change people's lives for the good.

I had also developed a faith in God. With that faith, I knew I was created exactly the way I was... caring, funny, smart, creative and outside the box - for a higher purpose. Whether I got accepted to medical school or not, I knew I could have a positive effect on many people's lives.

It was a bit ironic that I had chosen the same path my dad had taken, despite my aversion to that lifestyle as a kid. But, in retrospect, I also saw the profound influence my dad had on his patients and the love they mutually shared for each other.

To this day, he is still practicing medicine and influencing the lives of his patients in a deep and meaningful way.

So there it was… I now knew my purpose, my mission and my WHY! All of who I had been molded into though my life had prepared me to become someone who would have a positive influence on those who entrusted me to care for them. "I am going to become a physician. I want to change people's lives!"

Now I was a senior in college. I had worked hard for four years, received good grades on all my courses, competed as a collegiate diving athlete, and then I applied to medical school. It was the week when the life-changing, decisive letter from medical school was to arrive in the mail. That letter would decide my fate. Would I be a starving artist, or would I get accepted into medical school?

I called my dad on the phone and said, "*Dad, I have the medical school letter in my hand and I'm going to* open it. *Are you ready?*" I opened the letter and it read, "*Dear Mr. Baumgartner, Congratulations you have been chosen to be a part of the medical school class of 1995.*" "*Dad, I think I am in... I am in - I am going to be a doctor!*" So, faith and God had made the decision for me. My purpose in life was to help others in a deep and meaningful way. I was going to be a doctor, a physician, a healer.

MEDICAL SCHOOL

Medical school was a challenge, but I had been trained to be fearless, fight hard and excel. I was in the top of my medical school class. I enjoyed the challenge but felt empty without the freedom and creativity that art school had given me. It was all books, lectures, lab and tests - week in, week out. I gave up a large part of who I was to study.

The first two years were difficult. I often questioned myself - why am I doing this? Do I really enjoy this? Is this really what I want to do with my life? After two years, we started doing rotations in clinics and hospitals. This was when I, again at last, had the opportunity to interact and have a positive influence on people and my patients. It confirmed that this is what I was meant to be - I was meant to be a healer.

At graduation, we all took the Hippocratic oath, "*FIRST DO NO HARM.*" Unfortunately, the further I got into practicing medicine, the more I realized that our current healthcare model was broken. We're allowing people to become unhealthy and live a life like Barb, broken down and degenerated.

I did a family medicine residency, thinking this would be the best way to truly help the most people. The more I got into the established healthcare model, the more I realized I was just putting patches on things, covering symptoms with more medications and cortisone, and often creating more side effects from the treatments I was giving.

Wanting once again to do more, I went from family medicine to apply, and got accepted, into a fellowship in nonsurgical orthopedics and sports medicine. This was aligned with my interest in the human body, anatomy, and sports and fitness.

During my fellowship, we focused on medical treatments that aimed at healing the body and not just covering up symptoms with pain medications or cortisone shots. I realized true health comes from creating healthy people and that the existing healthcare model truly needed an overhaul if we were to make profound change in our patients' lives. The current model of healthcare needed redefining, innovation and creativity. I was groomed for the challenge.

During this time, I married my best friend. My wife and I grew our beautiful family by three children through the gift of adoption (Teddy, Corrielle and Faith). And I started my first real job as a physician working for a large hospital-based medical clinic with the goal of growing their orthopedic and sports medicine department.

There was no room there for creativity, innovation or thinking outside the box. I was seeing 25-30 patients a day, with pressure to see more, to get them through the system and make money for that system. The patients I was seeing for their chronic pain conditions and arthritis were all on narcotic medication, anti-inflammatories, muscle relaxants and antidepressants. Many were receiving multiple cortisone shots a year in an attempt to cover up their painful conditions. The negative side effects on the cartilage and risks of those injections were rarely discussed with them. Most had multiple surgeries and invasive procedures and were still suffering from pain and disability.

I found myself in a healthcare model where I didn't feel I was making lasting change in the health of my patients. I would see them over and over again for medication refills, and they would leave with both of us frustrated, wishing we could do more. The system was broken.

Despite all the advances in science and technology, my patients' treatment options were the same as twenty years ago. The cost of all the medications and surgeries were driving healthcare costs up and insurance premiums were escalating as a result. Going to work for me at that time was becoming unfulfilling and did not support my core reason for becoming a physician. We were supposed to be healers. We took the Hippocratic oath to "first do no harm," yet the side effects of the multiple medications given, the narcotics, the cortisone injections and multiple surgeries were starting to do more harm than good. Deep down, I knew there was a better way to treat my patients, but I was strapped by the constraints of the system I was employed in that was supporting my family. There was no room to be a pioneer or think outside the box.

It was then – now nine years ago - that a divine intervention took place. I believe all things happen for a reason.

The large hospital system I was working for decided they no longer wanted to have a clinic in my town. All the physicians and staff got a 60-day notice; after that time, we were either on our own or could move to the Twin Cities and work for the large hospital system there.

I wanted to stay in the town I was in and not move my family. I had friends and my new family had taken root. That meant I only had two viable options. The first option was to interview with another medical clinic in town, have a stable job and continue in a job similar to my last employment. The other option was to stand alone, be independent and start my own clinic. The second option was unstable, uncertain and vulnerable. But it also meant the chance to have freedom and the ability to be creative, to problem-solve and redefine healthcare by creating a model of medicine that deeply cared for my patients and could really change their lives in a profound way. My visionary creative mind was reignited.

MISSION AND PURPOSE

My patients deserved more. All I needed was someone to believe in me and that person was Susan. Susan was a nurse and patient of mine. She said, *"Joel, you are special, and I know you can do this."* Man, she gave me a sense of purpose and a confidence that I was created for something big. She stood by me and was my nurse at my first clinic location. Rejuv Medical was born. We had just two employees.

It was tight financially, and downright hard for many months. I wasn't paying myself and I was down to one house payment before hitting rock-bottom. At one point, we lost all our insurance contracts because we were too outside the box with our PRP and functional medicine approach.

Rejuv was knocked down, but never were we defeated.

Then the tide changed. We started getting paid for our services. Month-by-month, we started to create a movement in our community with what we were doing. We hired a front desk person to manage patient scheduling so we could spend more time with the patients. It was heading in the right direction, but my vision was not yet complete. My patients were having less pain through PRP and Stem Cell procedures, but we were not getting to the root causes of their degeneration and disease. I needed to create a system that would make my business more stable while, at the same time, restoring my patients' health through changing their lifestyles.

Health and fitness became how I optimized my medical and orthopedic outcomes, while attracting new patients to my business. I couldn't do this alone, so I asked one of my patients - who was also a star personal trainer at the local gym - to join me in my quest to create a new healthcare model to really change the health of our patients. Enter JR and our enhanced ability to restore my patients' lifestyles through fitness and nutrition, and now to market my clinic as the model of healthcare that aims to truly restore health to patients. JR was Rejuv's 4th employee addition - and the rest is history.

THE NEW MODEL OF HEALTHCARE: REGENERATIVE ORTHOPEDICS, FUNCTIONAL MEDICINE and MEDICAL FITNESS

Regenerative Orthopedics, Functional Medicine and Medical Fitness became the three founding pillars of Rejuv Medical and our new model of healthcare. At our clinic, through our **INNOVATIVE** and **INTEGRATIVE** approach, we can **OPTIMIZE** your outcomes.

INNOVATION is used through the technology and science behind regenerative procedures, like PRP and Stem Cells. Our unique diagnostic, cell processing and comprehensive injection technique is what sets us apart from other clinics.

Next, we **INTEGRATE** Functional Medicine and Medical Fitness to **OPTIMIZE** our health and healing outcomes.

CONCLUSION

I have a purpose and passion. I am not the shy, introverted little boy too scared to ask a question. I was created by God to shine bright and make a difference in the lives of those I serve. I have been given gifts and talents that are meant to be shared with the world to create healing, acceptance and health. I am a strong, independent pioneer with a purpose and a vision. **I Am Redefining Healthcare**.

Healthcare is a broken system. Our society is living with pain, chronic disease and physical body degeneration. Unhealthy lifestyles have broken us down to steal our zest, passion and vitality and leave us broken and degenerated. The current healthcare model aims to mask symptoms with drugs, pain medications, damaging cortisone injections or surgery. The current system is expensive with all the prescriptions, diagnostics, hospitalizations, procedures and surgeries. Our health insurance premiums are increasing, and our health outcomes are decreasing.

The problem is most people do not know there are other options to treat their deteriorating bodies. They feel hopeless, out of control, cornered and defeated. They are told they either have to live with it, take more medications, or have surgery. I personally have been in pain and out of commission myself - I know the frustration and apathy felt when you are not able to live in a body that is pain-free and functioning optimally.

There is HOPE that we can reverse your chronic diseases through lifestyle changes, supplementation and functional medicine. We can then regenerate physical pain, arthritis and brokenness with innovative treatments like PRP and Stem Cell procedures. I have helped thousands of people regain their lives through restoring their health and rebuilding their bodies. Know this - you have options with your healthcare. You do NOT have to live hopeless, in pain, tired, helpless, broken down and degenerated.

This is where Rejuv was born. From my own origin of brokenness and vulnerability to a realization of a true calling and purpose, I created Rejuv to fill the gap in our broken healthcare system. We truly can REGENERATE our patients' bodies.

This model first **Restores** patients' lifestyle through fitness, nutrition, sleep, and stress management. Next, we **Rejuvenate** their health through functional medicine. Lastly, we **Rebuild** their bodies using regenerative procedures that focus on healing the body without masking medications or surgery. This triad has changed healthcare.

From there, Rejuv Medical and the C.F.A.N. model was born. My goal is to change healthcare and to teach other physicians this model so more people can reverse chronic disease, heal their body and live their lives to the fullest.

I recently wrote a training book for physicians teaching the complexities of the procedures. It is titled, **Regenerative Injections: The Art of Healing**. Together, we are all health-changers, health innovators. We are **HEALTHOVATORS!**

Through this book, I hope you can learn to take control of your health, be educated on your treatment options, and be empowered to make a change in your life that will not only change your life but the lives of those around you.

SECTION ONE

A LESSON IN HISTORY

CHAPTER 1: HOW DID WE GET HERE?

Wherever the art of medicine is LOVED, there is also a love of humanity. — Hippocrates

To fully understand how we can reverse disease, it is important to be aware of some of the influences that have led to the diseased state we are in as a society. From the day we are born, we are at the mercy of environmental, physical, emotional and nutritional influences. These can either help build the foundation for health or create patterns and genetic preferences that allow disease to either blossom or wither.

We have control over many of these influences as follows.

LIFESTYLE INFLUENCES

First - and possibly the most important influence on health and healing - is body weight. Studies prove that extra body weight directly influences disease and degeneration in our bodies. Nutrition can either feed the fire or snuff out the inflammation that burns in our bodies. We are in control of what goes into our bodies and can influence the effect nutrition has on healing.

Next, our lack of movement and exercise slowly adds to the body weight and allows our bodies to stiffen and age at a faster rate.

Finally, smoking, chemicals, drugs and our liquids of choice will have a direct impact on how our bodies age or heal.

STRESS

Stress can also cause premature aging and disease. It comes in three forms: physical, emotional and environmental. Physical stress would be the pressures in activities of daily life as well as the physical stresses of recreational activity. Without proper rest, physical stress can affect our healing as repetitive micro-injury leads to breakdown.

Emotional stress is the pressure from psychological influences. This can come in the form of a demanding job as well as stress from unhealthy or unsupportive relationships.

Environmental stress affects our bodies, with toxic influences from chemicals in our food and water as well as pollution in the air.

A combination of physical, emotional, and environmental stresses will lead to impaired function and a decreased ability to heal and repair.

ENDOCRINE AND NUTRIENT IMBALANCE

The endocrine system is like an orchestrated symphony with many independent instruments working together to produce a well-balanced song with harmony and energy. If the flute section is out of tune, the entire orchestra sounds off. The endocrine system is a complex interaction between many systems needed to create energy and balance in our bodies. If parts are not functioning fully or are out of balance, the outcome is dysfunction, lack of energy and breakdown in our bodies. It is important to have all systems optimized to create an environment of health and healing.

GENETICS

Yes, we are born with genetic "gifts" passed on. It is what we do with those genetics that affect the final expression of those genes and how they influence us from a health perspective. We can have an influence through epigenetics as to whether those "gifts" are expressed as health or disease. Unfortunately, we cannot be in control of everything that influences our health. Uncontrollable forces will affect our bodies as well include aging, trauma and overuse.

AGING

The slow but certain breakdown of our skin, spine, muscle and joints will happen regardless of whether we live in a bubble or take every opportunity for adventure and living possible. Our spines will weaken, our skin will sag and our organs will slow in function. Now, we can influence them in many positive ways, but we will - at some point - again be dust.

TRAUMA and OVERUSE

We will all experience unforeseen injury and trauma over the course of our lives. Falling off a horse, spraining an ankle, or sustaining a whiplash injury driving to work can all strain the ligaments that give our joints stability. These cumulative events create weakening of our joints and ligament that, over time, contribute to accelerated degeneration and functional decline. Overuse from sports, play or occupation also can create micro-injuries that, over time, contribute to breakdown and degeneration.

The wrong trend is emerging in our healthcare. Chronic disease, pain and arthritis, surgeries performed, and medications written are all on the rise. They parallel the trends seen in body weight in our society.

In the next three years worldwide, over 2.3 billion humans will be considered overweight with 700 million in the obese category. Diabetes, hypertension, heart disease stroke, many cancers, dementia, depression, joint arthritis and most chronic disease have a direct influence on carrying extra body weight.

In the United States, it is predicted that by 2020, 40% of our population will be in the obese category. Obesity is also a problem in our children and adolescent populations. Although it appears obesity trends are leveling off in the childhood population at around 17%, the rates are alarmingly higher than a generation ago, which will lead to an adult population suffering the diseases associated it.

We have a responsibility to the generations to come. This generation of children is the first to live sicker and die younger than their parents. One in three children will develop weight-related diabetes during their lifetime. Now we are seeing teens with older adult-type heart disease and strokes. Childhood obesity has a greater impact on life expectancy than all childhood cancers combined. How is this happening?

We have advanced so much in science and technology. Our schools have special programs and technology in every room, yet our kids are becoming sicker and more apathetic than ever.

This problem is rooted in an imbalance that has crept into our homes, schools and society. We have an increase in calories consumed with a decrease in calories used. Calories are increasing in our snacks, school lunches, fast foods and home meals. Fewer calories are being spent as kids are being entertained on a tablet or video game and not out in nature exploring, playing, competing and creating. We all love technology… or, at least, many of us like the convenience and accessibility of information we obtain from our phones and computers.

But it is the same "advances" that are leading to less movement and activity, slowing down our metabolisms and packing on the unwanted fat stores. TV, computers, video games, tablets and phones have replaced capture the tag, flag football, dancing, creative play. In our schools, we have less physical education, free play time and recess, which is even more dramatic in our high schools. Our children are eating fewer meals at home, less fruits and vegetables and more junk food, fast food, fried food and processed food… if you can even call it "food".

It is also becoming a global crisis. For example, worldwide we now have around 350 million diabetics but, by 2030, it is estimated to climb to 450 million. Over the last 20 years, diabetes has increased 10 times. By 2020, 20 million deaths will be from infections while 50 million deaths will from chronic preventable diseases like heart disease, diabetes and cancers.

Extra weight creates disease in our bodies. Heart disease, Diabetes Type 2, cancers (breast, colon, uterus), hypertension, high cholesterol, stroke, liver and gallbladder disease, sleep problems, arthritis, infertility and menstrual problems are all directly related to extra body weight. Two-thirds of all diabetics have underlying heart disease that can creep in as a silent killer. Diabetes causes loss of sensation in the extremities leading to falls and wounds. It is the leading cause of blindness over age 24 and the leading cause of kidney failure.

Death from stroke or heart attack is four times higher in those with excess body weight. Diabetics carry a four times higher rate of dementia; diabetes is linked to mood disorders and depression. Obesity increases the growth rate of most cancers. It is the leading cause of high blood pressure and liver failure.

This societal crisis is also creating a healthcare crisis. In the next ten years, $3.4 trillion will be spent on obesity-related health concerns. It consumes one in every 6 to 10 health dollars spent. Costs for healthcare are doubling every decade while overweight Americans cost the healthcare system 40% more than the healthy population. Billions of private and government monies are spent every year on new drugs to treat chronic diseases. We cannot support this rising cost - implosion is inevitable if we don't change the ominous trends.

Amazingly, 90% of chronic disease is preventable. Obesity is the leading cause of PREVENTABLE death in the United States and the world. We need to target the root causes of disease and degeneration to truly change our societies' heath and decrease medical costs.

This epidemic will NOT be cured by a new medication. We NEED lifestyle and behavioral habit changes with sustained behaviors that create health and reverse the destructive effects robbing us of our potential and zest. It starts with us, spreads to our family members, involves our community and then these positive changes will affect the world. It starts with a step... an idea... an inspiration... an influence to bring about CHANGE!

SO HOW DID WE GET HERE?

To understand the solution, we first must understand how we got to this point. We can look to technology, our nutrition (or lack thereof), and, finally, exercise habits to understand these trends.

First, with technology, we have created amazing advances that are innovative, creative and advance many aspects of our lives and industry in very productive ways. But those same advances have created an environment for a society to expend less calories than they consume. This pattern, over time, leads to weight gain and disease development.

Electricity	Cars/trains	Light bulb
Sewing machines	Pens	Refrigerator
Phones	Elevators	Oven
Microwaves	Vacuum	Radio
TV	Washing machine	Plastic
Airplanes	Satellites	Computers
Internet	Cell phones	Smart phones

Advances in technology

Along with technology taking away our need to be physical and use our bodies, our nutrition is paralleling these changes at the same time.

EARLY AMERICAN DIET. Let's take a time machine back to the days of the open plains where buffalo roamed free. The early Native Americans were nomads. They had to travel by foot to find food, shelter and safety. They would scavenge for food, hunt and fight for daily survival. They ate wild roaming animals and gathered roots, fruits and vegetables for food and nutrition. They had NO fast food if the deer or buffalo were not available.

PRE-INDUSTRIAL DIET-1800's. Then, in the 1800's, we were able to domesticate animals and plants, eliminating the dependency on hunting and scavenging for food. Farms were able to produce foods in mass quantities, then preserve or can them for later consumption. Sugar, cereal grains, fatty processed meats, oils and salt became readily available. Even with all the available food, jobs that were physically-demanding labor and home chores still burned many calories, snuffing away much metabolic-related disease.

INDUSTRIAL DIET-1930's. Enter electricity and a plethora of conveniences to the household - with refrigerators, we could store dairy and meats longer. Beef was being fattened for slaughter in feed lots. (Before 1850, all beef was lean and free-range or pasture-fed.) Breakfast was dominated germ-free and convenient breakfast cereals over meat or plant-based options. Despite all the changes, meal prep still took about two hours and mom had a garden full of organic vegetables and fruits that took up a good part of the plate at the sit-down family dinner.

STANDARD AMERICAN DIET (SAD) - current day.

Times have changed. What used to take a few hours to prepare now takes minutes. We have fast foods, pre-packaged foods and microwave ovens - all leading to less meal prep time. That is great in that it frees us up to do other activities we enjoy! But the food sources and quality of foods we devour are not fueling us; now they feed the illness that has become part of our households. Our total calories are increasing. Look at these trends:

- 1950's - 1,900 calories
- 2008 - 2,661 calories
- 2016 - 3,750 calories

- 1957 - 1 oz hamburger
- 1997 - 6 oz hamburger

Now we supersize, we go with the double bacon barbeque cheese one-half-pounder burger saying, "*I haven't had a good burger in a long time.*" Just the burger is over 1,000 calories, then add the fries and soda. GULP! Not that we can't have a fun night out, or indulge occasionally, but when these patterns dominate what we are eating, disease is inevitable.

We also have some new western staples in our diets in the form of sugar, refined white flour and vegetable oils. Each year, people consume an average of 150 pounds of sugar. Sugar is laced in all of our foods, even in marketed 'health foods' like cereals, yogurt, 100% fruit juice, sauces and most packaged foods. Soft drinks are an addiction laced with not only sugar but high fructose corn syrup. In 1942, we drank around sixty 12-ounce sodas a year. In 1957, the average-sized drink was 8 ounces and, in 1997, it increased to 32-64 ounces. From 1942 to 2005, production of soft drinks increased 10 times. We have an average calorie intake from sugar drinks of around 500 calories. Remember a specialty coffee can have up to 1000 calories.! Is the sugar high worth the health low?

Teenage consumption of sugary drinks and soda is increasing rapidly. Refined white flour has become an

American staple. Rocketing in the 1950's, flour-based products brought the largest increase in nutrient-void foods after sugar.

Finally, the consumption and addition of vegetable oils to our processed foods has added to the decline in nutritious whole foods. These damaging oils are added to most of the off-the-shelf processed foods we consume. Trans fats and fried food intake has increased dramatically over the last 20 years. Remember, we are addressing the unhealthy fats here, not the healthy fats like olive oil, avocados, nuts and coconut oils.

As our brains and bodies are aging, developing and trying to heal, we need healthy nutrients from nutritious density. Unfortunately, the top three vegetables eaten by children are French fries (25% of all their vegetables), iceberg lettuce (99% water with minimal nutritional value) and ketchup (NOT a vegetable and is half sugar or high fructose corn syrup).

Adults are not doing any better. The Second National Health and Nutrition Examination conducted a survey revealing the following trends. Less than 10% of Americans consume five servings of fruits and vegetables each day; 40% of Americans do not consume daily fruit. 50% of Americans do not consume daily garden vegetables and 70% of Americans do not consume daily fruit or vegetables rich in vitamin C. 80% of Americans do not consume daily fruit or vegetables rich in carotenoids (carrots, sweet potatoes, green leafy vegetables and tomatoes).[19] We need healthy fruits and vegetables for their antioxidant properties and ability to fight free radicals that can attack and damage our DNA, causing premature aging. The goal is a healthy balance. The chapter on nutrition will dive into this fully.

Also contributing to a decline in health is the loss of the family meal. Food eaten away from home has less nutrient dense fruits and vegetables and more processed foods void of nutritional value, leaving the consumer craving more of it to satiate their legitimate hunger. One-third of patients do fast food frequently with one-fifth of meals consumed in the car during a commute. 12% of adult calories are from fast foods. Kids are also eating 25% of their meals away from home, with fast foods being 50% of those meals. There is a benefit nutritionally to eating at home, but also psychosocially. Kids who eat at home have better social adjustment, higher grades and less smoking and drug use than kids eating away from the home.

Snack consumption is also contributing to the health crisis. Studies confirm that much of our daily calorie loads come from unhealthy snack choices. In 1978, 28% of people ate two or more snacks a day, increasing to 45% in 1996. Now, 60% of us are indulging in two or more calorie-dense nutrition-void snacks a day. In obese children, 100% eat at least one unhealthy snack a day, with 36% eating four or more.

CHANGE IN HUMAN BEHAVIOR

As a kid, we would head out the door after school or Saturday morning and play for hours in the field next to my house. I remember digging in the dirt, building forts, organizing play football games, riding our bikes, swimming and having a blast doing it. Kids now spend more time indoors than outdoors, and more time sitting on the couch watching TV or playing video games. Kids average four hours a day in front of a screen, which is more then they spend at school during active learning. They spend less time running, walking or exploring and have less imaginative play.

One of my greatest joys is to watch my children put down the computer and get lost in playing and inventing fun activities stimulating the mind and body. Now kids are much less physically active and so are the adults. 60% of our days are spent doing sedentary activities like our jobs, watching TV, eating or staring at our computer screens.

MORE STRESS WITH LESS SLEEP

Aaaaaaah... big yawn and stretch. I love waking up on a Saturday after a full night's rest feeling refreshed and alive! Sleep regenerates us - we heal and repair during those crucial sleep hours. In 1959, the average number of hours slept per night was eight; now we sleep less than 7 hours a night and are working weekends to bookend a busy work week without rest and down time.

Poor sleep patterns are also related to obesity and other chronic diseases. Sleep is the time when our body releases healing hormones to repair and heal the day's micro-trauma and breakdown. It recharges the brain, so we can think sharply and be caring, passionate, energized contributors to society. 70 million Americans don't sleep well and suffer from insomnia. 10% of us are on prescription sleep medication. The scary data is that those on sleep medications are three times more likely to die early.

Stress is also on the rise and affecting our bodies' ability to heal and repair. We are surrounded by influences that break us down. Poor diets, physical inactivity, inflammatory burdens to the body, poor sleep, demanding family dynamics, unhealthy relationships and increased work demands all contribute to our stress loads. The problem is we do not take the time to unload or remove stresses that bring us down.

A recipe that blends poor nutrition, lack of exercise, uncontrolled stressors, deficient restorative sleep and unbalanced hormones creates a main course of poor health, weight gain and body degeneration. With the abundance of sugars, liquid calories and refined processed foods, the cells in our bodies become resistant to insulin and, accordingly, the body needs more insulin to control all the circulating carbohydrates.

Remember, insulin is a storage hormone. Continued high insulin leads to obesity, muscle loss, inflammation and chronic diseases like heart disease, strokes, dementia and cancers. Most of our current medical treatments, orthopedic surgeries and drug prescriptions are treating risk factors and symptoms but not addressing the root causes of the disease. We need to target the causes and change society's nutrition, lifestyles and environmental influences to turn on the genes for health and longevity. We need to build up people's skills and knowledge, so they can make personal changes that will improve their health, then influence their families and communities.

CHAPTER 2: REGENERATIVE ORTHOPEDICS - A NEW PARADIGM

Progress is impossible without change, and those who cannot change their minds cannot change anything. — **George Bernard Shaw**

PAIN, INJURY AND ARTHRITIS

Extra body weight causes chronic medical diseases, but it also contributes to orthopedic degeneration and arthritis. Joint arthritis, tendon breakdown, low back pain and nerve impingement are all related to extra body weight. Chronic pain and orthopedic concerns burden our medical clinics. Each year, $7.4 billion are spent on drugs for pain while $80 billion of productive work time is lost due to chronic pain. Sadly, 15 million patients seek help for pain issues and $260 billion (a year!) are spent on medications with the top medication being a narcotic for pain control. Of the rest of them, seven out of ten are for high blood pressure, diabetes and acid reflux - all diseases that can be prevented with lifestyle intervention.

I see patients every day who are suffering from pain and arthritis issues, who are on chronic pain medications and told the only thing that we can do next is cortisone injections, surgery or one more pain medication. Those patients come to me looking for hope. They don't want to continue taking medications that cover up the symptoms. They know the pain is not in their head and don't want another antidepressant medication. They would like to avoid surgery if possible. A lot has changed over the last 15 years in how we treat orthopedic, pain and arthritis issues. We now have procedures, like PRP and Stem Cell, that are focused on healing, regeneration and decreasing the need for surgeries, narcotics and cortisone.

We are in a crisis with the abuse of opioid narcotics in the U.S. They all carry a serious risk of overuse, abuse, overdose and death. Overdose from narcotics is now the leading cause of accidental death in the U.S. In March of 2016, the FDA made a statement: "*We need to focus on better non-opioid management options, including alternative treatments.*"

Another problem that is not helping with chronic orthopedic disease management is the overuse of non-steroidal anti-inflammatory drugs (NSAIDS). A 2015 study in the journal Osteoarthritis Cartilage showed that those taking NSAIDS and over-the-counter pain medications were at two times the risk for progressing their knee arthritis to a total knee replacement surgery than those who did not take the medications.[22] The problem here is that many physicians are still using these medications for pain control with orthopedic problems. Another study on NSAIDS and soft tissue injuries, like ankle sprains, concludes that they impair the healing process and prolong repair.

Another and more serious concern lies in the overuse of injected corticosteroids. They are commonly injected into painful joints and the spine. These steroids are not the muscle-building anabolic type of a steroid. In fact, they are the exact opposite. At the doses injected, these steroids are muscle-damaging and are considered a catabolic steroid that lead to further disease and degeneration. In the Orthopedic Journal of Sports Medicine, May 2015, an article reviewing hundreds of corticosteroid studies concluded that at the doses injected into the joints and spine for arthritis and degeneration have DEFINITE detrimental effects. "*They are associated with gross cartilage damage and chondrotoxicity.*"[23] So what is being injected to "help" with the pain is contributing to the destruction of the joint.

A randomized blinded placebo-controlled study in JAMA in 2013 on tennis elbow (tendon degeneration) compared physical therapy to a steroid cortisone injection into the tendon. It concluded at 26 weeks and one year that the cortisone group have greater recurrence and lower complete recovery rates. The injection of cortisone was not only not helpful but impaired the long-term healing in the area injected.[24] Another startling article was in the Journal of Bone Joint Surgery in 2013. It compared 3,000 patients with back pain who had an epidural steroid injection to 3,000 patients who did not receive an injection. It concluded that patients with an epidural steroid injection had an increased risk for spinal fracture by 29% with each injection. In our pain and orthopedic clinics, it is standard care to give up to six of these injections in the spine a year.

Steroids do not help with the problems and, in fact, can cause an accelerated degeneration in the areas injected. Tendon rupture, skin atrophy and ulcer are also associated with these injections. Steroids have a well-documented negative effect on tissue but, just as serious, they cause other side effects that contribute to illness. They cause elevated blood sugars and worsening of diabetes. They cause mood swings and insomnia, increased risk of all fractures, fluid retention, weight gain, increased infection risk, menstrual irregularities, glaucoma and suppressed adrenal function.

A recent New York Times article highlighted the risks of cortisone injections into the spine with permanent neurologic damage and systemic side effects as reasons to NOT receive these types of risky procedures. They also revealed that the drug company who makes the drug in the first place did not recommend use in the spine due to the risks they found during their research of the drug. When injected in the spine, it is considered an off-label use and not what the drug was originally indicated for by the drug company. So, when your physician says, "*let's try a little cortisone shot to see if we can help with your arthritis*," politely answer, "*No, Thank you.*" Instead, ask if they have heard of Prolotherapy, PRP or Stem Cell treatments that can have a positive healing and regenerative effect on the body without the damaging effects of cortisone.

Moving on, after a few failed steroid injections, patients will get the news, "*Well, the next step would surgery. We don't have anything else to offer.*" That is true - surgery is always an option, but it may not always be the next step. We utilize surgery when necessary and appropriate, but the problem here is that many trusting patients are opting for surgery thinking it is the only next step they can try. It is important to be fully informed of what is out there for treatments of arthritis and chronic pain.

A study in the New England Journal of Medicine in July 2013 showed that knee meniscal arthroscope surgery was no better than placebo after a year when compared to physical therapy.[24] Another study showed that meniscal surgery with removal of the meniscus, or a "clean-up surgery", has been shown to definitely accelerate degeneration and arthritis in the joint after the surgery has been performed. Knee meniscus surgery is the most common orthopedic surgery done with over 700,000 procedures done per year, and the cost for surgery ranging from $5,000 -

$20,000 per surgery. This totals at around $4 billion of healthcare costs. The surgery should not be done as often as it is and often should not be the first line of treatment for this problem.

Next, the total joint replacement may be advised. It is a very common option for joint arthritis. With these surgeries, there is an increased risk of blood clots and heart attack after procedure. There is also risk of infection immediately after surgery up to years later. Metal ions are being found in the bloodstream because of the metals used with surgery, which can cause chromosomal instability, reproductive failure, and gene damage in the cells.

Another study showed that, at five years, around 54% of patients had their pain return with around 15% having more severe pain. At times, a joint replacement may be needed, but they should not be the first-line treatment for knee arthritis. Some private insurance companies require their patients to try a Stem Cell procedure before they will pay for a total joint replacement. Those companies that cover the regenerative procedures find they save around 84% of their orthopedic healthcare costs.

What is exciting in the field of arthritis is that there is now research with good evidence showing that procedures like Prolotherapy, PRP and Stem Cell can be helpful with arthritis and even help reverse degenerative cartilage damage. It has become a powerful option for people suffering from debilitating pain, injury and arthritis of the spine and peripheral joints. All three of these procedures aim at healing and regenerating the body vs. covering up the pain. They use the body's natural healing mechanism and are catalysts to start the healing process.

After the injections, the body takes over and starts to heal the injected area. Prolotherapy uses a concentrated dextrose solution that acts as a slight irritant and stimulates the repair process. PRP, Rich Plasma, is created from the patient's own blood after a simple blood draw. The platelets are concentrated in the body's nutrient-rich plasma, then precisely re-injected to the areas of degeneration. Stem cells, which are the most powerful healers in our body, are also cells taken from your own body. The stem cells are harvested from the bone marrow or adipose tissue, which are both rich in stem cells. These cells have a powerful ability to heal and regenerate cartilage, ligament and meniscal tissue throughout our joints and spine. We'll talk more about these effective treatment options and discuss the evidence in a bit.

It is important to get the correct diagnosis and know what the source of your pain truly is, so that the pain (once identified) can be treated appropriately. Science and technology have advanced orthopedic treatment significantly over the last two decades, giving the patient more options that are less invasive and with fewer long-term side effects. The good news is we can now actually heal and repair!

When it comes to aging, arthritis, pain and degeneration, we need to look at the different influences that can heal us and take away the influences that can hinder. I like to look at it like a scale. We can take things off one side and put things onto the other side to shift the balance. We can stop the degenerative influences of smoking, unhealthy nutrition and dietary habits, stress and inflammation, poor sleep habits, medication side effects, and muscle atrophy from lack of movement and exercise. Those can be replaced by healthy, whole, regenerative foods, stress reduction techniques and good sleep hygiene. Inactivity is replaced with medical fitness focused on correcting dysfunctional movement patterns and weakness in our muscles and fascia that protect our joints and spine.

It is time to avoid prescriptions with side effects that interfere with the body's ability to repair and heal. It is time to avoid cortisone injections into the joints and spine that can further damage cartilage and have other systemic side effects. Sometimes the body just needs a tip in the balance to a healthier state, thus allowing the body to heal itself; other times, it needs a procedure, like PRP or Stem Cells, to ignite a healing response. This is the healthcare of the future. This is the ultimate in healthcare reform. This model decreases long-term costs of medications, unneeded surgeries and expensive procedures. It creates a nation that is healthy, educated, vibrant and inspired.

SECTION TWO

The C.F.A.N. MODEL - CELL HEALTH

CELL HEALTH OVERVIEW: INNOVATION-INTEGRATION-OPTIMIZATION

As a whole, we are not heading in the right direction from a health perspective. We are growing more obese as a population, with obesity rates soaring and soon to be close to 40 percent of our population. Chronic lifestyle-driven diseases, like heart disease, hypertension, diabetes, cancer, arthritis, back pain and inflammatory disorders, are plaguing our population.

Patients come in to see me every day with pain, arthritis and body breakdown from the aging process or injury. Many of them have the layer of fatigue and lack of vitality on top of their pain and disability from lifestyle diseases. The disease processes are treated with multiple medications that address the symptoms, but not the root cause of their problem. These medications have their own set of side effects that compound the patient's situation. It is a never-ending cycle of disease, dysfunction, medication and more dysfunction.

If we do not address the root causes of the initial disease process, then we will never create a healthy thriving population. We will age with the pain and disability of chronic diseases. Our bodies will NOT have the ability to repair and REGENERATE even with the advancements in medicine like PRP and Stem Cell procedures. To REGENERATE, we first must get the cell health of our bodies tuned up to perform and tap into the body's innate ability to repair itself.

One problem that is not allowing a global health movement is the outdated recommendations and advice from the government and many medical leadership organizations around nutrition.

Current dietary standards are not based on up-to-date science and research. They still follow recommendations promoting 60% percent of our dietary intake be from carbohydrates, like fruits and vegetables and "healthy" whole grain foods. The current recommendation of around 200-300 grams of carbohydrates a day presents a society that will continue to gain about 1.5 pounds of fat a year. The current system is flawed, broken and not based on research or the physiology, biochemistry and endocrinology of the body. The current recommendations have bias towards the grain, corn and food industries. We need to care less about the food markets profits and more about our own, our families and our community's health.

Current Food Pyramid Recommendations

As you can see with the base of the food pyramid, the majority of food intake recommended is in the form of processed grain-based foods (6-11 servings) - 60% of our dietary calories! These are nutrient-poor foods, highly processed and refined and quickly breakdown in the body to surge the sugar and insulin. Most also contain gluten and other anti-nutrients that can cause inflammation and disease.

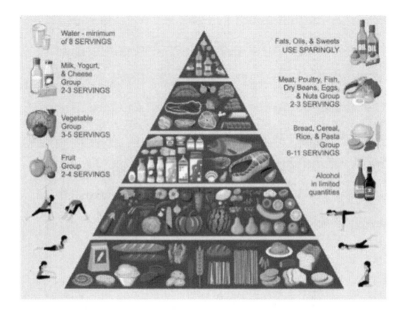

What is a bit disturbing is that this is the "healthy" recommendation. In reality, most people consume much more.

We see that with the standard American diet, where there is a much higher intake of pure sugar foods, snacks, drinks and sodas, sweets and candy "treats" that push average American intake around 300 grams a day. Remember that a hot Starbucks Mocha 20-ouncer has a "delicious" 450 calories and 55 carbohydrates. Use that drink to wash down the medium blueberry muffin with another 61 carbs and 345 calories, and you have a total of 785 calories and 116 carbs. Then, two hours later after the commute to work, you are crashing and craving a treat from the office brownie tray. We need to take control of our health and follow what science, research and that voice deep down inside has always known.

Those large doses of carbohydrates, regardless of the form they come in (sugars, whole wheat grains, fruits or vegetables), will ALL be broken down into simple sugars in the body. The problem is not the fruits and vegetables; it is in the promotion and allowance of such high amounts of grains (cereals, pastas, breads and crackers) with the current food pyramid allowance. They will all spike the insulin and, as we will soon see, an increase weight gain and disease risk. Unless you are an elite athlete, most of us do not need those high-energy carbohydrates daily.

There is a new paradigm and it is starting to gain momentum in many heathy societies focusing on lifestyles to decrease our risk of disease and which can cure many of our epidemic lifestyle-related diseases. As Hypocrites so wisely said, *"Let food be your medicine."*

Now this is the exciting part. Cell health is what underlines all our body's ability to repair and regenerate, and it has a big impact on chronic disease prevention and treatment. It is critical that we understand the different influences that can affect the body in both positive and negative ways. Once you understand cell health and your ability to influence it, you will be empowered to make a positive change in your life!

Over the next few chapters, we will analyze nutrition, exercise, hormones, inflammation, hydration, stress and sleep, and how all these can influence your body in positive and negative ways. We will give you INNOVATIVE strategies to INTEGRATE them into your life as well as how to make new healthy lifestyle habits. We will discuss how our health as a whole has gotten our society to where it is and some of the strategies that are available to us to make positive change. It is time to focus on the future and what we can do to make positive changes in our lives that, in the end, will help the body to heal and, ultimately, REGENERATE. Using the **INNOVATION** of the C.F.A.N. model, we can **INTEGRATE** a strategy to **OPTIMIZE** our body's functions and help turn back the clock, restoring vitality, energy and passion. The first, and possibly the most important, aspect of the C.F.A.N. model is cell health.

I have been practicing regenerative orthopedics for over 12 years. At first, our outcomes were good, but I soon knew we could improve them by increasing the baseline health of our patients prior to their procedures. That's when I made the decision to start improving my patient's health as I approached their pain and degeneration.

Prior to performing a procedure, we started to focus on healthy nutrition, micronutrient supplementation and fitness. What we began to notice is that our patients who made healthy lifestyle changes were responding much more quickly to our procedures and had better outcomes during their follow-ups. I had patients who were coming in for a stem cell regenerative procedure two month after their initial consultation and had lost 30 or more pounds at the day of their procedures. Their pain levels had improved, and they had a profound increase in energy and quality of life without any procedures. I then knew that **CELL HEALTH** is the foundation for healing and that all the different issues that contribute to cell health will be important to optimize the patient's internal environment for healing.

General questions to screen for issues in CELL HEALTH:
- Are you overweight?
- Do you feel fatigued?
- Do you sleep less than 8 hours / night?

- Do you wake up refreshed?
- Do you eat healthy?
- Do you lack exercise?
- Do you feel stressed?
- Do you have any gut issues?
- Do you take time to relax and recover?
- Do you take more medications than you would like?
- Do you get less than 4 servings of vegetables a day?
- Do you drink half your body weight in water ounces a day?

If you have four or more yes answers, you may have an issue with **CELL HEALTH**.

When we talk about cell health, we're referring to the inner health of the individual on a cellular level. How healthy they are on the inside sets the stage for healing and repair to take place once stimulated by regenerative procedures, an injury, or simply as a result of the aging process. This is important to consider when trying to optimize the healing environment prior to regenerative procedures. It is also critical to the outcome after the procedure, because individuals who start out at a healthier level have a much more robust and thorough healing process after the initiation of healing takes place with Prolotherapy, PRP or Stem Cell procedures.

For example, let's compare two individuals. The first individual wakes up in the morning after a restorative 8 ½ hours of sleep, has a healthy breakfast composed of fruits, vegetables and healthy lean protein sources. They then go for a relaxing walk prior to going to work. At noon, they take advantage of the down time and go for a workout followed by a heathy lunch. After a productive and successful workday, they go home to a supportive family, have a healthy dinner, relax a bit playing with the kids and get to bed early so their body has a chance to heal and recharge before the next day.

On the contrary is the overweight man who wakes up after a non-restorative sleep due to his sleep apnea. He rushes downstairs, grabs some coffee and rushes to work. His work day is extremely stressful, and he skips lunch only to work on a presentation while eating a "healthy" granola bar and slurping down more coffee to stay alert. After work, he is starving and heads to a drive-through and pounds his whopper during his long commute home. Once home, he argues with his wife about the dripping sink faucet, goes out back for a smoke, watches TV till midnight and finally falls asleep on the couch.

Even though these examples are on the extreme on both sides, they do show that people can make lifestyle decisions that will affect their health. The first example, when coming in for a consultation, will have a much better outcome with any medical procedure due to their healthy cell health and optimal potential to heal and repair their body.

Fitness and exercise have a great impact on our cell health and the body's ability to heal as well as prevent and treat chronic disease. The lack of exercise and poor nutrition habits is a risk factor for developing chronic diseases including hypertension, heart disease, strokes and many cancers. I like to call this 'medical fitness' because becoming healthy has an enormous impact on long-term disease treatment and prevention. As Hippocrates also said, "*Fitness and exercise truly are the best medicine.*" The best way to change healthcare is to inspire our population to make healthy changes in their daily habits focusing first on nutrition and exercise. Nutrition is the cornerstone and is of critical importance so if this is resonating with you, start with your nutrition.

CHAPTER 3: NUTRITION - YOU ARE WHAT YOU EAT

Let food be your medicine and medicine be your food.
— **Hippocrates**

NUTRITION

Healthy whole foods nutrition is the cornerstone element that is critical in optimizing cell health and creating a healing environment. What we put in our mouths has a powerful potential to augment and push the healing process. It can also reverse the damage of chronic diseases and get at the core issues causing diabetes, hypertension, obesity, heart disease, stroke and decrease the risk of cancer development.

Poor nutrition habits do the opposite and act as fuel to the degenerative inflammatory process and promote the development of chronic disease. On a cellular level, the body needs healthy nutrients, healing proteins and inflammation-modulating healthy fats. When these elements are combined in the right amounts, it sets up the body for optimal healing and disease prevention. With every patient coming to see me at Rejuv Medical for pain and arthritis issues, as well as other medical and functional problems, we always start the discussion on their treatment plan with nutrition. When it comes to weight loss, nutrition is 90% of the story with exercise only being 10%.

A study in 2015 concluded that a higher BMI (Body Mass Index) is associated with a higher cancer mortality risk. This study is the first to show that short-term annual changes in BMI were associated with lower mortality from any type of cancer. In women, higher BMI had higher risk of all cancer mortality, including breast cancer.[114] Healthy eating is critical for the success of any health, wellness or regenerative healing plan.

There are many nutritional plans that someone can adhere to, depending on personal preferences. There is also a plethora of research that seems to support the many different approaches to health. Is fat good or does it clog arteries? Are carbohydrates healthy fuel, or the poison that causes all chronic disease? Should I load up on protein or is there a limit to the amount that is healthy to consume? I agree that it can be very overwhelming and confusing on what the gold standard of nutrition should be for the body.

After years of practicing medicine and utilizing nutrition as a foundation to all our treatments from arthritis to hypertension, I have realized that nutrition is much like a tennis shoe. Nutrition is not one-size-fits-all. We are each different culturally, physically, emotionally, spiritually and genetically. We come from a variety of backgrounds and influences, and what works for one may not be the plan or lifestyle for another.

I used to try to have one eating plan that everyone would follow. It worked for about half my patients, but the others either did not get the results they wanted, or they found they couldn't sustain the lifestyle. I now try to be more individualized and give my patients evidence-based options based on their goals and what they believe will work for them. There are some basic rules that will overlap and apply to all nutrition plans. Let's highlight those universals and then break down the different nutritional options. You can read through the different options and decide what plan works best for you. Also, you can start with one plan and jump to another if you hit a plateau or are looking for additional health benefits. The main thing is finding what fits your lifestyle, beliefs and gives your results that lead to better health and longevity.

UNIVERSAL NUTRITION GUIDELINES

Each of the following is universally beneficial, regardless of individual food plan choices.

1. Hydration - 1/2 one's body weight in ounces.
2. Sleep - 8 hours a day.
3. No sugar, juice or soda.

4. Consume natural, whole, high-fiber foods (goal - 50 grams a day).
5. If consuming animal products, consume seafood, fish, grass-fed meats/dairy or wild game.
6. No highly refined processed grain products.
7. No artificial sweeteners.
8. Organic when possible.
9. Combine with daily exercise.
10. No vegetable or hydrogenated oils/fats.
11. Focus on 2 - 3 well-rounded meals a day as opposed to 6 smaller meals.

We will look in to each one more specifically throughout the book.

There are basically two large categories of nutritional approaches. They both are derived from whole, healthy goods with the above universal guidelines. They basically differ in the amounts and types of foods consumed.

The first is a non-ketosis approach where you consume more carbohydrates and utilize *carbohydrates* as a primary fuel source. The second group will decrease total carbohydrates and utilize *ketones* as a primary fuel source. It relies on the consumption of less total carbohydrates in a day either through eliminating them or fasting and refraining from eating for part of the day. It is possible, as you increase your carbohydrates from a ketosis state, to consume enough carbohydrates that your body will utilize both energy sources.

First, we will present an overview of the two groups. We will follow with some basics on nutrition and then dive into the details of each plan.

NON-KETOGENIC

These plans utilize carbohydrates as the primary fuel source but at a much lower amount of consumption then the standard American diet. The carbohydrates consumed are primarily from healthy fruits and vegetables. At times, the plan may cross over into a ketogenic state during times of lower carbohydrate consumption or longer times between eating. In general, they have slower weight loss rates as the greater amount of carbohydrates will continue to increase insulin levels and prevent tapping fully into fat stores.

For some, these plans are more palatable due to the increased carbohydrates consumption. In all plans, sugars need to be avoided. If a plateau is hit, switching to a lower carbohydrate intake is always helpful. You can always transition into a ketogenic plan as well if you are not making strides towards your goals. The non-ketogenic options include:

- **Rejuv4LIFE-FOUNDATIONAL.** This is a good overall low glycemic index-based nutrition plan. It will promote decreased insulin spikes and improved insulin sensitivity. It eliminates common food sensitivity foods that can impair health and weight loss. It is a good nutrition plan for the general population and a great starting point to making healthy lifestyle changes.

- **Rejuv4LIFE-Plant-Based.** This is a good plan for those with metabolic disease and cancer risk factors. It is a good plan to follow long-term, during detoxification or on a weekly intermittent basis to aide in increasing the protective antioxidants of plant phytonutrients.

- **Rejuv4LIFE-AutoIMMUNE (AIP).** This is an optional plan for those with autoimmune or inflammatory diseases. It is food elimination plan to take away certain foods that can contribute to the inflammation and autoreactivity inflammatory and autoimmune diseases. This option is usually recommended and tracked by a health care professional who is familiar with a functional medicine approach. The AIP can be combined with a ketogenic and/ or intermittent fasting protocol to optimize its effectiveness.

KETOGENIC

These plans utilize ketones from fat stores as a primary fuel source either though a stricter decrease in carbohydrate consumption or by fasting for part of the day. They have good evidence on their effects on metabolic diseases like diabetes and obesity. This is due to the decrease in insulin and increase in insulin sensitivity obtained with these plans. The ketogenic options include:

- **Rejuv4LIFE-ADVANCED-Ketosis.** A good plan to induce weight loss and a good option for restoring insulin sensitivity with Diabetes Type 2 and metabolic syndrome. It may be more difficult to maintain long-term due to carbohydrate dietary restrictions but, for those who adhere to the plan, it can be very successful and satisfying. It can be used for more rapid weight loss induction. Success is based on strict adherence to the plan.

- **Rejuv4LIFE-Intermittent Fasting.** A good plan for those wanting to optimize stem cell production, body healing, hormone optimization and weight loss. It has been found to be a good option for restoring insulin sensitivity with Diabetes Type 2 and metabolic syndrome. It can also be used to induce weight loss, maintain weight loss or break a weight loss plateau. This is not a nutrition guideline but more of a time window of fasting and then a window of eating each day. It can be combined with any nutritional lifestyle to maximize health and intentional outcomes of your plan.

The reality is that all plan groups are interchangeable, and you will most likely flow between them on a weekly basis. I present them individually, so you can see the benefits and structure of each approach. Eating plans and lifestyles are not meant to be rigid rules that must be followed for success, but more as healthy guidelines you can use to structure the style of nutrition that best fits you. There are biologic systems, endocrinology and hormonal influences and nutrition facts that we cannot change so it is important to know the effects different foods have on our bodies. It is also important to know the effects of how we cook our foods and where our foods come from that will affect our health and the outcome of that foods consumption.

So, feel no pressure that you have to do things ONE WAY. Relax and enjoy the learning process and, most importantly, enjoy the outcome that eating the way the optimizes your health will have on your energy, body composition and overall well-being. It is a journey and we need to enjoy the process of finding our own personal health potential.

Before getting into the different nutrition lifestyle options, let's break nutrition down into some basics. In addition to the many micronutrients, vitamins and minerals found in healthy whole foods, we also need to know a little bit about the macronutrients - carbohydrates, proteins and fats and how we can consume them to achieve our ultimate goal of health and disease reversal or prevention.

CARBOHYDRATES

Unfortunately, the carbohydrate has recently gotten a bad reputation. Yes, it's true - carbohydrates in the form of simple sugars, refined fours, liquid sodas and juices, candy and processed foods are not the type of carbohydrates we want to dominate our palate. When consumed in excess, those can lead to insulin resistance and, eventually, a breakdown of our carbohydrate metabolism, weight gain, diabetes and an increase in chronic disease. Healthy carbohydrates from vegetables and fruits can give us many disease-fighting nutrients, great flavor and fiber that has been shown to decrease disease risk.

Let's look at the difference between a simple and a complex carbohydrate. First, a simple carbohydrate, like in the form of white sugar, is absorbed very quickly from the gut and increases the circulating blood sugar very fast. This leads to a spike in insulin levels. If we cannot use the carbohydrate as an immediate fuel, insulin - which is a storage hormone - leads to the storage of the excess energy and can be stored as fat. These include things like table sugars, high fructose corn syrup, processed foods, and energy drinks or sodas. Excess carbohydrates can also be consumed through high glycemic index fruits. The glycemic index of a food is an indicator of how fast a carbohydrate gets absorbed into the bloodstream and subsequently spikes blood sugar levels. Foods with a high glycemic index, over 70, will cause a rapid rise in blood sugar followed by the storage of fat and subsequent weight gain and the risk many chronic diseases.

On the contrary, a complex carbohydrate is a long chain of simple carbohydrates that needs to be broken down prior to being absorbed by the gut. These types of carbohydrates are found in most fruits and vegetables. Legumes and whole grains are high in carbohydrates and may be best to limit their intake if weight loss is a concern. Most grains also contain gluten, which has its own issues that we will highlight soon.

Remember, when foods are overcooked, like over-boiled or fried, it will break up the fibrous bonds between the carbohydrates and increase the glycemic index, making them act more like a simple sugar. The takeaway here is to eat fruit and vegetables in their raw form and, if you are cooking the vegetables, try to lightly stir-fry, steam, or broil them. Foods with a lower glycemic index, less than 55, create a much slower rise in blood sugar and a lower insulin release. These foods are much better for weight loss and weight maintenance, and the high-fiber content has been studied and shown to be beneficial for heart disease, hypertension, cancer prevention and even joint arthritis. High-fiber foods act as a prebiotic and are helpful in maintaining healthy gut flora, which is important for food digestion and immune system support.

There are many diets and fads that will come and go but eating healthy whole foods with attention to the glycemic index will transcend the test of time. A good way to optimize health is to avoid blood sugar spikes that result in insulin spikes, increase adipose and subsequent development of chronic disease. The lower your insulin and blood sugars chronically over time, the less long-term disease. We will look at the effects of high insulin and blood sugars in a bit.

LOW GI FOODS	HIGH GI FOOD
Broccoli 15	Chips 75
Sweet potato 54	Watermelon 72
Banana 54	Golden Grahams 71
Cucumber 15	Rice Krispy's 82
Cherries 22	Rice Cakes 77
Grapes 46	White bread 71
Spinach 15	Baked potato 85

Glycemic Index Chart

It is important to know about the glycemic index so that a person can make smart and informed decisions on the foods they consume. A study in the American Journal of Clinical Nutrition in 2008 showed that eating a diet with lower glycemic index foods leads to decreased chronic disease burden.[36]

It's important to learn to read labels and look at the amount of sugar in a product as well as the amount of fiber. Foods that are low in fiber and have greater than 10 grams of sugar will have a high glycemic index and will spike the insulin, causing more storage of fat if the consumed carbohydrate is not burned off quickly. In general, whole unprocessed foods, especially fruits and vegetables, have a naturally low glycemic index and can be enjoyed without concern.

Let's discuss the importance of keeping a lower insulin level and avoid insulin spiking. Insulin is a hormone made by the pancreas to store energy. It is released in response to circulating sugar and protein in the blood. When insulin levels spike too high, this leads to the storage of excess sugar as energy in the form of fat. Lower and sustained blood sugar levels avoid insulin spikes and create a constant energy source for the body without the energy and sugar crash. This type of blood sugar level is best for longevity and disease prevention. Less processed sugar and refined carbohydrates is key to success.

High blood sugars followed by insulin spikes creates an unwanted and vicious cycle. Insulin drives the blood sugar levels down but, in response, the body craves more sugar and you feel hungry again. The additional sugar consumed drives the insulin levels up, storing excess calories as fat. As more carbohydrates are stored as fat, the extra adipose itself will cause a state of insulin resistance in the body. The higher glucose levels again cause more insulin spikes and the cycle continues with more food, more insulin, more insulin resistance, more sugar storing as fat and more weight gain. This leaves a person feeling tired and hungry and creates more sugar and fat cravings.

Insulin resistance has been shown to be associated with many chronic diseases including sleep apnea, polycystic ovary disease, increased risk for blood clots, heart disease, neurodegenerative disease, increased intra-abdominal fat, elevated blood sugar, hypertension, low good cholesterol, elevated triglycerides, inflammation of the liver, increased risk of calcification of the arteries leading to heart attacks, strokes and peripheral vascular disease. The key to chronic disease prevention is lower insulin levels, improved insulin sensitivity and decreased blood sugars. Dietary and lifestyle changes resulting in loss of body fat is the secret to success.

Remember carbohydrates are not necessarily bad. It is the overconsumption of simple and processed carbohydrates that is creating the problem. There has definitely been an increase in consumption of simple carbohydrates. In the 1800's, the average intake of sugar was 10 pounds a year. Now, we are consuming an average of 150 to 180 pounds of simple sugar a year. That is almost half a pound of sugar a day! A 20-

ounce bottle of soda has 17 teaspoons and the average teen has over 20 ounces a day.

Over the last 30 years, the consumption of high fructose corn syrup has increased dramatically. It has gone from 0% to 66% of all consumed sugars during that time. High fructose corn syrup is a highly processed form of sugar that is associated with weight gain as well as dysfunctions in the gut. Some countries actually don't allow the production of foods containing high fructose corn syrup. Again, make sure you are reading labels and looking for high fructose corn syrup so you can avoid any product containing it. It is found in many sodas, sauces, candy and anything processed with a sweet flavor. The increase in sugar and processed carbohydrates from grains with increased gluten ingestion parallels the increase in disease worldwide.

So we see that, with elevated blood sugar levels, over time our body's cells become resistant to insulin and higher levels are needed to drive the elevated (and toxic, if too high) blood sugar into the cells for storage. The pancreas cranks out more insulin and the cells respond by becoming less responsive and the cycle continues. Eventually, the cells can't take any more sugar due to saturation and then the blood sugar levels in the blood start to become chronically elevated.

This high level of blood sugar is damaging to the body's cells and we see the damage of glycosylation on our blood vessels (arteriosclerosis), organs (kidney, heart, brain), and nervous system (neuropathy). Both acute elevations in blood sugar spikes from a carbohydrate-packed meal and chronic elevations will cause cumulative damage to our bodies and impair healing and regeneration. We CANNOT REGENERATE when our insulin and blood sugars remain elevated. We MUST decrease chronically and avoid acute spikes in blood sugar and insulin if we are to combat chronic disease and promote a healing and regenerative process to occur.

Let's look as some of the consequences of chronically elevated blood sugars. Glucose is a fuel for all the cells in your body when it's present at normal levels but, at high levels, it can become toxic and slowly damage all the tissues in the body. High sugar levels slowly affect the ability of cells in your pancreas to make insulin. The organ overcompensates, and insulin levels stay too high due to the resistance of the peripheral tissue. High levels of blood sugar from metabolic syndrome and diabetes can cause changes that lead to a hardening of the blood vessels or atherosclerosis. The body is harmed by the chronically elevated sugar.

Damaged blood vessels cause problems such as:

- AGEs. These are the byproduct of a chemical reaction when excessive high levels of sugar in the blood react with cells in the body causing long-term damage through glycosylation.
  - Skin wrinkles and damage.
  - Increased heart disease and circulation problems.

- o Increased nerve damage and neuropathies.
- Kidney disease or kidney failure, requiring dialysis.
- Strokes.
- Heart attacks.
  - o Insulin causes increased stickiness of platelets.
  - o Insulin converts macrophages in blood vessel walls to "foam" cells that swell and clot off arteries in the heart and periphery.
  - o Insulin inhibits nitric oxide that causes arteries to be more rigid and increases atherosclerosis.
- Vision loss or blindness.
- Weakened immune system, with a greater risk of infections.
- Erectile dysfunction.
- Nerve damage, also called neuropathy, that causes tingling, pain, or less sensation in your feet, legs, and hands.
- Poor circulation to the legs and feet.

- Slow wound-healing and the potential for amputation in rare cases.

Some of the effects of elevated blood sugar is on its effects on the endothelial (blood vessel walls) cell and its production of nitric oxide. Nitric oxide is a vasodilator. This means it helps our blood vessels relax and open to allow increased blood flow and reduce sheer stress. Without enough nitric oxide, our blood vessels are more susceptible to high blood pressure and our risk for heart disease and atherosclerosis goes up. In our nerves, chronically elevated blood sugar causes the brain and nerves to shrink and impairs function. In the pancreas, it causes the beta cells to shrink and impairs function leading to impaired ability to secrete insulin and control the elevated sugars that are themselves causing global damage.

It is critical that we maintain normal blood sugar levels to prevent long-term consequences. Also, we need to make sure insulin levels do not stay elevated as it too can have negative effects when chronically elevated.

First, insulin is a growth-promoting hormone, and cancer is a problem of unchecked cellular growth. Studies show chronically increased insulin has an effect on cancers like breast, pancreas and prostate.[125]

Other issues with chronically elevated insulin include:

- Obesity (chronic storage of excess carbohydrates and fats).
  - Insulin drives excess carbohydrates and fat into fat cells and causes fat weight gain.
  - Insulin inhibits the fat-burning enzyme lipase and fat can't release its fatty acids into the blood for fuel. So you both store more fat and can't mobilize it for use.
- Insulin resistance and elevated insulin decreases hormone function and synthesis of growth hormone, DHEA and testosterone. Also, hormones stay bound

to SHBG (sex hormone binding globulin) and are not available to the cells for use.

- Accelerated aging. Studies of populations with lower insulin levels over a lifetime live longer and remain the healthiest.
- High insulin blocks thyroid function. High insulin blocks the conversion of T3 to the active form of thyroid hormone-T4.[126]
  - Decreased metabolic rate.
  - Increased fat storage.
  - Decreased energy levels and brain function.
- Increased risk of polycystic ovary syndrome ().
- Increased synthesis of very low density lipoprotein, or VLDL (hypertriglyceridemia). This is a direct link to increased risk of a heart disease and atherosclerosis.[127]
- Hypertension (insulin increases sodium retention by the renal tubules). High blood pressure also increases the risk of heart disease.
- Coronary Artery Disease (increased insulin damages endothelial cells).

- Weight gain and lethargy (possibly connected to an underactive thyroid).
- Interferes with production of critical sex hormones, like testosterone.
- Impairs the body from storing magnesium. When cells become insulin resistant, the body loses magnesium through the urine.

What about the short-term effects of elevated blood sugar from the consumption of sugar-carb packed meals and snacks? These foods generate a fast rise in sugar levels resulting an immediate "high" or rush of energy. That high is countered with an insulin rush that drives the sugar into the cells and, within minutes, you feel a crash and wane of the energy. This low sugar state makes you "hangry" (sluggish, hungry and irritable) - until you get another fix of quick carbs for energy. There are studies showing a link between ADHD (attention deficit hyperactivity disorder) and this rollercoaster effect.

Also, this low-sugar stress on the system also then stimulates cortisol that signals gluconeogenesis and the production of carbohydrates from protein. This results in a catabolic breakdown of your muscle tissue. This is NOT a healthy cycle but is seen by millions daily on the standard American diet (S.A.D.). Rapid rises in sugar also blocks vitamin C from entering cells, preventing the inflammatory protection of the antioxidant.

The best and most effective ways to decrease insulin and blood sugars is through the right nutrition plan, exercise and stress management program. You need to eat healthy carbohydrates from vegetables and some fruits and drop ALL grains, sugars and processed foods. We will address all the ways to do this throughout the book. Stay tuned and prepare to overhaul your health - and change your life.

Next, gluten deserves a punch in the gut as it is another dietary villain, like sugar, that is silently robbing us of our health. Gluten is a protein naturally found in different grains. It is what makes baking dough doughy. It is hidden in many processed foods we consume daily. It can have a serious negative effect on your immune system, brain and gut health. About 1% of the population has a complete inability to digest gluten, which is full-blown celiac disease, but recent research suggests that 10% to 15% of us suffer from intolerance to this problematic protein. This is called **Non-Celiac Gluten Sensitivity** (NCGS).

The problem is most do not associate their symptoms with gluten-containing foods and don't have an accurate diagnosis for their symptoms.

Here is a complete list of symptoms associated with both Celiac disease and NCGS.:

- Abdominal Distention
- Abdominal Pain and Cramping
- Alternating Bouts of Diarrhea and Constipation
- Anemia
- Arthritis
- Attention Deficit Disorder (ADD)

- Back Pain
- Bloating (also called Gluten Intolerance Bloating)
- Bone Density Loss
- Borborygmi (stomach rumbling)
- Brittle Nails
- Canker Sores or Mouth Ulcers
- Constipation (also called Celiac Disease Constipation)
- Stunted Growth and Failure to Thrive
- Dental Enamel Defects
- Depression, Anxiety and Irritability (also called Celiac Depression)
- Dry Hair
- Dermatitis Herpetiformis
- Diabetes
- Diarrhea
- Edema
- Fatigue
- Low Ferritin Symptoms
- Malodorous Flatulence
- Malodorous Stools

- Gluten Ataxia
- Grayish Stools
- Hair Loss (Alopecia)
- Headaches and Migraines
- Hypoglycemia
- Infertility
- Joint Pain
- Juvenile Idiopathic Arthritis
- Lactose Intolerance
- Low Total Cholesterol
- Nausea
- Numbness or Tingling in Hands and Feet
- Osteoporosis
- Peripheral Neuropathy (including either a tingling or sensation of swelling in toes and fingers)
- Sjogren's Disease
- Steatorrhea (high lipids in the stool, which may cause the stool to float)
- Teeth and Gum Problems
- Vitamin and Mineral deficiencies
- Vomiting

- Unexplained Weight Loss
- Urticaria

These symptoms may arise hours, or even days, after you consume gluten. Also, a gluten-free diet has been proven to reduce inflammation and insulin resistance. If you are experiencing a combination of these symptoms, the following foods and products need to be avoided and then concentrate on a gluten-free whole healthy nutrition plan. Take a look at this list and avoid these foods.

Grains and starches that contain gluten:
- Wheat
- Wheat Germ
- Rye
- Barley
- Bulgur
- Couscous
- Farina
- Graham Flour
- Kamut Matzo

- Semolina
- Spelt
- Triticale

Foods that often contain gluten:
- Malt/Malt Flavoring
- Soups
- Commercial Bullion and Broths
- Cold Cuts
- French Fries (Often Dusted with Flour Before Freezing)
- Processed Cheese (e.g., Velveeta)
- Mayonnaise
- Ketchup
- Malt Vinegar
- Soy Sauce and Teriyaki Sauces
- Salad Dressings
- Imitation Crab Meat, Bacon, etc.
- Egg Substitute
- Tabbouleh
- Sausage

- Non-Dairy Creamer
- Fried Vegetables/Tempura
- Gravy
- Marinades
- Canned Baked Beans
- Cereals
- Commercially Prepared Chocolate Milk
- Breaded Foods
- Fruit Fillings and Puddings
- Hot Dogs
- Ice Cream
- Root Beer
- Energy Bars
- Trail Mix
- Syrups
- Seitan
- Wheatgrass
- Instant Hot Drinks
- Flavored Coffees and Teas Blue Cheeses
- Vodka
- Wine Coolers

- Meatballs, Meatloaf Communion Wafers
- Veggie Burgers
- Roasted Nuts
- Beer
- Oats (Unless Certified Gluten-Free)
- Oat Bran (Unless Certified Gluten-Free)

The following are miscellaneous sources of gluten:
- Shampoos
- Cosmetics
- Lipsticks, Lip Balm
- Play-Doh
- Medications
- Non-Self-Adhesive Stamps and Envelopes
- Vitamins and Supplements (Check labels)

The following ingredients are often code for gluten:
- Avena Sativa Cyclodextrin
- Dextrin
- Fermented Grain Extract
- Hordeum Distichon

- Hordeum Vulgare

- Hydrolysate

- Hydrolyzed Malt Extract

- Hydrolyzed Vegetable Protein

- Maltodextrin

- Phytosphingosine Extract

- Samino Peptide Complex

- Secale Cereale

- Triticum Aestivum

- Triticum Vulgare

- Tocopherol/Vitamin E

- Yeast Extract

- Natural Flavoring

- Brown Rice Syrup

- Modified Food Starch

- Hydrolyzed Vegetable Protein (HVP)

- Hydrolyzed Soy Protein

- Caramel Color (Frequently Made from Barley)

These foods and products can do some serious damage to our bodies starting in the gut. Leaky gut from the inflammatory effect of gluten on the gut lining has long been associated with inflammatory foods, including gluten. Scientists have now proven that those with gluten sensitivities and celiac disease have very elevated levels of **zonulin** in their blood. Elevated zonulin further relaxes the lining of the gut, contributing to the cause of leaky syndrome. Zonulin levels can be a diagnostic tool to help identify those at high risk for leaky gut.

Here are the top four reasons to avoid wheat, cereals, bread, pasta, and other gluten-containing foods.

1. Gluten causes leaky gut.

Gluten damages the tight junctions between the cells in your digestive system, allowing small particles of undigested food, bacteria, and even toxins to leak out of your gut lining and enter the bloodstream. Once in the blood, the body's immune system does not recognize the particles and can mount an immune reaction against them. This sets up a multitude of health issues and autoimmune conditions where the body, essentially, attacks itself.

Leaky gut stops your body from absorbing needed micronutrients and inhibits the formation of vitamin B12. Gluten also contains **phytates**, an anti-nutrient that can further block mineral absorption. Anti-nutrients block the absorption of nutrients from the digestive system. Anti-nutrients include:

- **Phytate (phytic acid):** Mainly found in seeds, grains and legumes, phytate reduces the absorption of minerals from a meal. These include iron, zinc, magnesium and calcium.
- **Tannins:** A class of antioxidant polyphenols that may impair the digestion of various nutrients.
- **Lectins:** Found in all food plants, especially in seeds, legumes and grains. Some lectins may be harmful in high amounts and interfere with the absorption of nutrients.
- **Protease inhibitors:** Widely distributed among plants, especially in seeds, grains and legumes.

They interfere with protein digestion by inhibiting digestive enzymes.

- **Calcium oxalate:** The primary form of calcium in many vegetables, such as spinach. The calcium bound to oxalate is poorly absorbed.

Soaking, sprouting and boiling can remove many of these compounds before consumption.

2. Gluten triggers inflammation.

Gluten-induced leaky gut creates inflammation throughout the body. Chronic inflammation adds to every degenerative disease, including arthritis, diabetes, Alzheimer's, cancer, and obesity.

3. Gluten-containing foods are low in nutrients.

Common foods that contain gluten, like cereals, breads, baked goods and pasta, are high in empty carbohydrates and low in vitamins, minerals, and other nutrients unlike vegetables, fruits, nuts, and seeds.

4. Gluten can make you fat and contains other unwanted substances.

Gluten contains anti-nutrient lectins. They are found in all foods, but the highest amounts are found in legumes and grains. It can create pre-diabetes and cause you to store more calories as fat. To make things worse, lectins can trigger leptin resistance, which makes you feel hungrier even after you've eaten a full meal. Some experts hypothesize that it's no coincidence the top eight allergens also contain some of the highest amounts of lectins (including: dairy, egg, wheat, soy, peanuts, tree nuts, fish, shellfish).

Other foods that contain higher levels of lectins include:
- Legumes, such as beans, peas, lentils, and peanuts
- Squash

- Nightshade vegetables, such as eggplant, peppers, potatoes, and tomatoes. Most of the lectins in such foods can be eliminated through peeling and seeding or pressure-cooking.
- Fruit, although in-season fruit is allowed in moderation
- Grains

Combine lectins with leaky gut, inflammation, and the poor nutrient content of gluten-containing foods, and you are set up for weight gain and disease formation. Along with sugars and refined carbohydrates, it is important to avoid gluten foods in your nutrition transformation.

So you can see why gluten, in its many forms, should be completely avoided to optimize your health and regenerative potential.

FATS

Next, let's talk about the "F" word- FAT. For decades, we have gone back and forth on fat, questioning whether we should avoid it or if we should consume it. It is not that all fats are bad, but it is about consuming the right type of fat and avoiding those fats that are not healthy for us.

Fats are very dense in their calorie amounts. One gram of carbohydrates is about four calories while one gram of fat packs about nine calories. Good fats are needed for brain function, hormone production, inflammation control, cellular repair, vitamin absorption and also to help the metabolism and aid in weight loss and weight maintenance. They are critical to making us feel full and controlling the appetite for weight maintenance and weight loss.

Let's first talk about the different types of fats. There are good fats with healthy benefits and then there are the bad fats that are produced through chemical means and can lead to unwanted consequences.

There are basically three types of fats plus the villain trans fats. Fats found in foods are the monounsaturated (MUFA), polyunsaturated (PUFA) fats and saturated fats. Polyunsaturated fats include both omega 3 and omega 6 fats. Saturated fats are found in meats (both beef and chicken) and dairy products as well as from nuts and seeds. The bad fats are in the form of trans, or hydrogenated, fats often found in fried food and junk food and are created through extreme processed chemical methods.

First, let's examine the bad types fats; industrial trans and hydrogenated fats. These fats are found in vegetable oils, margarine, sweets, cake icing, donuts, chips, most snacks as well as deep-fried foods. Hydrogenated fats are processed by heating vegetable oil to very high temperatures with the toxic chemical hexane, which then modifies the fat, creating a more toxic substance. It makes a cheap oil that doesn't spoil. This is good if you want your Twinkie to last 15 years on the shelf, but not good for preserving your body.

Industrialized (artificial) trans fats from processed foods are **toxic**. Studies have strongly linked artificial trans fats to cardiovascular problems, including heart disease. Consumption is also associated with long-term inflammation, insulin resistance and Diabetes Type 2 risk, especially for people who are overweight or obese. Although the amount of trans fats in the modern diet has gone down, the average intake is still dangerously high.

Unfortunately, the labels on junk foods and processed vegetable oils cannot always be trusted. Many "trans fats free" products still contain trans fats. The Food and Drug Administration requires that the trans fats content of food be declared on the Nutrition Facts label to help consumers determine how each food contributes to their overall dietary intake of trans fat but, again, many products still contain them. Many processed foods contain partially hydrogenated oils (PHOs), the major dietary source of industrially-produced trans fats in processed food. It is important to read labels and avoid the toxic industrialized trans (hydrogenated) fats.

What about vegetable oils? They must be healthy since they come from vegetables, right? Well, most of them come from grains or soybeans and, to extract the oils, most vegetable cooking oils go through extreme processing with chemical solvents, steamers, neutralizers, de-waxers, bleach and deodorizers before they are palatable for consumption. The same neurotoxin "solvent" hexane, discussed with the trans fats above, is also used to produce most vegetable oils.

Hexane is a byproduct from gasoline production and is considered a serious occupational hazard and toxic air pollutant. It has been shown that some hexane residue can remain in the oil, and the FDA doesn't require food manufacturers to test for residues. Residue tests done by the Cornucopia Institute in 2009 found hexane residues in soybean oil. I have been in the salad mood lately and was recently at the grocery store looking at dressings. Vegetable oils are found in almost all the dressings. I had to read labels for about five minutes before finding some olive oil-based options. I was surprised and saddened by the fact that they are hidden in many our foods and marketed to the consumer as a healthy fat. There are a few more reasons not to consume too much vegetable oil as follows.

- **Vegetable Oils are Not a "Natural" Fat.**

The term 'vegetable oil' contains the word vegetable, so you might think this equates to a healthy oil. The category of vegetable oils refers to all processed seed oils, like soybean oil, sunflower oil, corn oil, canola oil, cottonseed oil, and safflower oil, as well as a few others. Most are not truly vegetables. Most vegetables oils contain **large** amounts inflammatory fats called omega-6 polyunsaturated fatty acids, which are not healthy when consumed in large amounts.

This does NOT include healthy plant oils, like olive oil or coconut oil. These oils can actually be very good for you.

The U.S. didn't start manufacturing vegetable oils until around a hundred years ago. Between the years 1909 and 1999, the intake of soybean oil increased over a **thousand times** and is now about 7% of calories found in the U.S. diet[93]. As mentioned above, the processing to make these oils uses hexane solvents that produce an unhealthy product. You can choose healthier brands that have been cold-pressed, which will cost more than the cheaply processed vegetable oils, but they still contain an excess of inflammatory omega-6 fats.

- **Vegetable Oils Disrupt the Fatty Acid Balance of The Body's Cells.**

Any time we consume a food or fat, the body will use that nutrient for energy, induce a biologic process or it will be used as part of our structure; nerves, cells, muscle, organ tissue, brain tissue, etc. Omega-6 and omega-3 fatty acids are very biologically active fats and contribute to the cell membrane that covers and protects all of our cells. Humans can't make their own fatty acids, so we need to eat them in the correct balance for optimal function on a cellular level. Too much omega-6 from our diet will become part of our cell membranes, brains, nerves and organ tissue and make them vulnerable to damaging reactions and harmful inflammation. It is critical to get our fatty acids in the right balance for optimal cell function.

Years ago, before all the processed fats and oils consumed our diets, our omega-6: omega-3 ratio most likely was around 4:1 to 1:2. Now with our processed diets and "unnatural" oils, our ratio is as high as 16:1. This balance leads to inflammation, cellular dysfunction and an increase in disease. Omega 6s suppress the insulin receptor gene GLUT4, which contributes to a decreased insulin sensitivity and more fat storage, while omega 3s increase the GLUT4 receptor gene and increases insulin sensitivity and less fat storage.

It was once thought that the more saturated the fat, the unhealthier that fat was for the body. That is not true or based on sound evidence. Another problem with vegetable oils is the relative unsaturation of these fatty acids. Polyunsaturated fats have two or more double bonds, while monounsaturated fats have one and saturated fats have no double bonds. The more double bonds in a fatty acid, the more reactive and unstable it is, which means polyunsaturated fats are inclined to react with oxygen, which can cause chain reactions, like oxidation and free radical damage. This can affect fundamental structures of our cells, like its DNA.

Once consumed, these unhealthy fatty acids will be incorporated into cell membranes, brain and nervous tissue, which increases harmful oxidative chain reactions from the unsaturated double bonds. This equals more room for oxidative stress and more chronic diseases, dysfunction and breakdown. The takeaway teaching here is to vary your diet with a combination of saturated, monounsaturated and polyunsaturated fats, read labels and avoid any types of vegetable oils. Also, increase your intake of omega 3s and limit your intake of omega 6s.

- **Vegetable Oils Contribute to Systemic Bodily Inflammation.**

Eicosanoids, the signaling molecules that are derived from omega-6 and omega-3 fats, are crucial in regulating inflammation throughout the body. The more omega-6s you eat, the more systemic inflammation you will have as a result. Chronic systemic inflammation is not good and is a root cause of many chronic diseases today. In general, eicosanoids made from omega-6s are *pro-inflammatory*, while those made from omega-3s are *anti-inflammatory*.

To summarize, a diet that is high in omega-6 but low in omega-3 increases inflammation, while a diet that has balanced amounts of both omega-6 and omega-3 reduces inflammation and chronic disease risk, including cardiovascular disease, arthritis, depression and even cancer.

- **Vegetable Oils Have High Levels of Trans Fats.**

Another daunting statistic with vegetable oils is that they often contain large amounts of trans fats. In a study analyzing soybean and canola oils found in U.S. grocery stores, they found that about **0.56% to 4.2%** of the fatty acids in them were toxic trans fats[88]. Trans fats are unsaturated fats and tend to be solid at room temperature. Trans fats are very toxic and found to be associated with the risk of multiple diseases, like heart disease, cancer, diabetes and obesity[87]. Many laws worldwide limit or exclude the use of trans fats in foods but, unfortunately, that's not the case here in the U.S. Vegetable oil is in many of our grocery store products, even those marketed as "health food".

- **Vegetable Oils Can Increase Your Risk of Heart Disease.**

There is evidence from both randomized controlled trials and observational studies that vegetable oils can increase the risk of cardiovascular disease. Cardiovascular disease is the most common cause of death in the world. At one time, saturated fats were thought to be a key contributor to cardiovascular disease risk, but newer research shows that they are not.[86] The attention is gradually being turned to the overly processed vegetable oils.

Many randomized, controlled trials have looked at the effects that vegetable oils have on cardiovascular disease. Three studies have found a drastically increased risk[89], while four found no statistically significant effect. If you look at observational studies, you will find a very strong correlation between vegetable oil consumption and an increase in cardiovascular disease risk. The more omega-6s consumed, the greater the risk of death from cardiovascular disease. Even though some studies show that polyunsaturated fats reduce the risk of cardiovascular disease, the problem is that they do not make the separation between omega-3s and omega-6s. They are both considered polyunsaturated fats but have very different effects on the cellular level. When studies do look at them separately, they see that omega-6s actually increase the risk, while omega-3s have a protective effect on cardiovascular risk[90]. All polyunsaturated fats are not equal when it comes to their health effects.

- **Vegetable Oil Consumption is Associated with Other Diseases.**

Because polyunsaturated fats have such a such a strong influence on our bodies' cells on a molecular level, they can have other unwanted and dangerous effects. Although their effects are not well-studied in humans yet, there are both observational studies and animal studies connecting vegetable oils to other serious diseases.

- In one study, increased consumption of omega-6s in breast milk was associated with asthma and eczema in young children[91].
- Studies in both animals and humans have linked increased omega-6 intake to cancer[92].
- One study shows a very strong correlation between vegetable oil consumption and homicide rates[93].
- The omega-6: omega-3 fatty acid ratio (high omega-6 to low omega-3) in blood has been found to be strongly associated with the risk of severe depression[94].

Here is a summary of disorders associated with omega-3 fatty acid deficiency:
- Inflammation (sometimes severe)
- Higher risk for heart disease and high cholesterol
- Digestive disorders
- Allergies
- Arthritis
- Joint and muscle pain
- Mental disorders like depression

- Poor brain development
- Cognitive decline

As you can see, vegetable oil consumption is associated with a wide range of serious diseases.

The increased consumption of vegetables oils, combined with the negative effects of highly refined carbohydrates and sugar, is a big contributor to today's health epidemic. Avoiding vegetable oils and trans fats, and decreasing sugar consumption, is a critical part of avoiding chronic disease risk and part of your healthy lifestyle restoration.

In addition to avoiding vegetable oils, you should attempt to increase your omega-3 to omega-6 ratio. Remember, omega-3 fats have anti-inflammatory properties that help modulate inflammation and aid in the healing process. Omega-3 fatty acids include DHA, EPA and ALA. ALA is found in plants. A study on omega-3 fats showed that a daily tablespoon of ground flax or chia seeds provides adequate ALA for health. A plant-based DHA and EPA source can be found in algae, for which you can take capsules with algae oil. It turns out that fish have higher omega-3s because they eat algae. They have been shown to decrease cardiovascular risk, lower triglycerides and also to decrease the risk of Alzheimer's disease. A good general recommendation to follow is to consume at least 1 to 2 grams of omega-3 fatty acids a day. Special health conditions may require higher doses recommended by your health care provider.

Omega-6 fats are needed for normal cellular function, but they are often over-consumed. Plant oils and foods that contain the following oils should be avoided due to their high omega-6 content.

Certain Vegetable Oils (per tablespoon)
- Safflower Oil (10447mg)
- Grape Seed Oil (9744mg)
- Sunflower Oil (9198mg)
- Corn Oil (7452mg)
- Wheat Germ Oil (7672mg)

- Soybean Oil (7059mg)
- Shortening (4771mg)
- Margarine (3323mg)

Salad Dressings (per tablespoon)
- Mayonnaise (5481mg)
- French Dressing (2927mg)
- Caesar Dressing (4346mg)
- Peppercorn Dressing (3771mg)
- Sesame Seed Dressing (3480mg)
- Light Mayonnaise (3423mg)
- Honey Mustard Dressing (3019mg)
- Italian Dressing (2774mg)
- Thousand Island (2539mg)

Nuts & Seeds (per ounce)
Yes, these have a higher omega-6 content, they also have omega-3s and fiber as well as other micronutrients. They are not considered bad like the vegetable oils and can still be a good source of fat and fuel.
- Sunflower Seeds (9558mg)

- Walnuts (10666mg)
- Sesame Seeds (7064mg)
- Pine Nuts (6967mg)
- Brazil Nuts (6686mg)
- Pecan Nuts (6315mg)
- Pumpkin Seeds (5791mg)
- Peanuts (4055mg) (actually a legume, so also contains lectins)
- Almonds (3785mg)

It is good to still be aware of the omega-6 amounts to help in making good choices. The lists below only show the omega-6s and not the other fats like saturated and trans fats. Let's take a look so we can make more informed shopping and eating choices.

Snacks Made with Omega-6 Rich Fats (per ounce)
- Cheese Flavor Corn Puffs (4809mg)
- Corn Chips (5082mg)
- Barbeque Chips (4183mg)
- Reduced Fat Potato Chips (3366mg)

- Potato Chips (5160mg)
- Cheese Tortilla Chips (3695mg)
- Popcorn (6255mg)-in a bag store-bought or microwave. (Pop your own in coconut oil!)
- Corn Tortilla Chips (2720mg)

Fast Foods Made with Omega-6 Rich Fats (per serving)
- Burger King Onion Rings (16226mg)
- Friday's Chicken Fingers (20916mg)
- Tuna Subway (28208mg)
- Burger King Hash Browns (13504mg)
- Wendy's French Fries (12449mg)
- McDonald's Fillet-O-Fish (6925mg)
- Wendy's Chicken Nuggets (13019mg)
- Popcorn Chicken (5247mg)

Ugh. You can see why deep-fried fast food is not recommended for anyone concerned with a healthy lifestyle. It is NOT a good source of fat. If you have to consume fast food occasionally, order non-fried options and drop the bun. Unfortunately, the meat sources are rarely grass-fed, so they too will have high amounts of omega-6s.

Cookies, Candies, Cakes, Pastries & Muffins (per piece)

- Chocolate Chip Cookies (1048mg)
- Brownies (8446mg)
- Puff Pastry (7856mg)
- Chocolate Cake (2540mg)
- Blueberry Muffins (2163mg)
- Danish Pastry (2069mg)
- Graham Crackers (1943mg)
- Shortbread (880mg)
- Twix Bar (564mg)

Pork Products (per piece) *grain-fed

- Sausage (1569mg)
- Ham (5378mg)
- Bacon (4773mg)
- Ground Pork (3315mg)
- Pork Salami (2780mg)
- Spareribs (2745mg)

- Pork Loin (2156mg)
- Pork Chops (1714mg)

Chicken (per 3 oz) *grain-fed
- Thighs (3161mg)
- Turkey Bacon (5307mg)
- Ground Turkey 15% fat (3185mg)
- Chicken Wing, with skin (3859mg)
- Turkey Meat, with skin (1612mg)

Dairy & Eggs (per tablespoon) *grain-fed
- Butter (341mg)
- Processed Cheese, per oz (1836mg)
- Egg, whole cooked, per egg (594mg)
- Parmesan, per oz (293mg)
- Cheddar Cheese, per oz (280mg)
- Gruyere, per oz (364mg)
- Cream Cheese, per oz (289mg)
- Hard Goat's Cheese, per oz (237mg)
- Whole Milk, per cup (589mg)

Red Meats (per 3 oz) *grain-fed

- Beef (1721mg)
- Lamb (3307mg)

*This shows why it is so important to choose grass-fed over grain-fed animals, egg sources and dairy sources. The non-grain grass-fed animal food will have much less omega-6s and healthier omega-3s.

Omega-3 fats should be consumed and will have a positive effect on overall health. Good sources include (*indicates highest amounts):

- Flax seed and Flax oil*
- Olive oil
- Chia seeds*
- Almonds
- Macadamia nuts
- Walnuts *
- Butternuts
- Brazil nuts
- Cashews

- Hemp seeds
- Cold water fish* -Sardines, Anchovies, Salmon, Tuna, Halibut, Mackerel and Herring
- Algae*

PROTEIN

Next, and also very important in healing, is protein. Protein is made up of different amino acids which are essential for optimal body composition. Amino acids are the building blocks for muscle growth and tissue repair. Protein, in general, is overly consumed and research seems to be showing we do not need as much as we once thought. Actually, too much protein can increase stress to our digestive system and also increase insulin levels. Too much protein will either be excreted as nitrogen waste and tax the kidneys, or the excess protein will stimulate gluconeogenesis to create carbohydrates that, if not used as energy, will (combined with the elevated insulin from the protein bolus) create the stored carbs as fat. So, protein in excess can lead to fat gain. Dang you, biochemistry!

The ideal amount of daily protein for the average sedentary adult seems to be around 56 grams for men and 46 grams for women. Studies are showing the amount of protein needed for repair and daily use is about .5 grams per pound of ideal body weight. If you are active and exercise, there may be a slight increased need for protein and amino acids, but the good news is that exercising makes your body more efficient at using protein, so you really don't need the excessive amounts that many weight lifters and athletes generally consume.

During times of weight loss, protein needs will also be slightly higher, but not excessive. Studies also show that people with injuries or those trying to heal after regenerative procedures may require a slightly higher protein intake to aid in healing the injured tissue. Infants, pregnant women and the elderly also have a higher need, as do athletes and active weekend warriors.

Too much protein will actually stimulate your insulin levels as well and increase your risk for cancer and all the other issues associated with excess insulin, including weight gain and inflammation. Too much protein will also block the utilization of fat in the form of ketones for fuel. If you are trying to lose weight, this is another problem seen with too much protein.

For these reasons, as you will see in the nutrition plan sections on a ketogenic or low-carb plan, you need moderate (NOT HIGH) protein, low carb and high fat to get into the zone for fat burning and weight loss.

Special Needs Protein Populations

Infants. Infants are in a constant state of development as their systems are in constant growth. They need around 1.5 g per kilogram of ideal body weight protein per day. This amount is about double the requirement that of a normal adult.

Athletes. Because of the constant muscle breakdown associated with athletic activity, research seems to conclude that athletes may need a higher protein requirement than the average adult. Bodybuilders require 5% more protein while endurance athletes may need 67% more protein just to maintain their respective muscle mass. A study of athletes showed that the ideal intake of protein to be .94 g per kilogram of body weight[86] - essentially, 1 gram per kilogram of body weight.

It is very helpful that athletes and active individuals have a combination of a protein or amino acids after their workouts to maximize their fitness gains and minimize muscle loss. The muscles are depleted and amino acids need replacement to help with energy storage and healing.

After a workout, a study in 2009 showed that the appropriate amount of protein to be supplemented to maximize recovery after a workout is around 20g. A study in 2013 concluded that post-exercise protein consumption over 20g leads to oxidation and ureagenesis, or excess ammonia, in the body. This means the body is trying to get rid of excess protein and amino acids from the body and not using the extra for good. This could cause harm to the kidneys. In the elderly, the post-workout protein should be around 10g to avoid extra stress to the kidneys. For the very active weekend warrior trying to get bigger, stronger or faster, 1g per kilogram total protein a day with 20g of protein possibly combined with some carbohydrates (like a fruit) after your workout may be ideal. Many vegan athletes who partake in higher-intensity workouts will do a post-workout smoothie with plant-based protein supplements combined with fruit for carbohydrates.

Again, when trying to get the body to burn fat stores and utilize ketones (from fat) as an energy source, studies show that too high a protein intake will impair the utilization of fat. This is in part due to the fact that protein also stimulates the release of insulin (which is a fat STORAGE hormone, not a fat-burning hormone).

The problem is that, when you're on a low carb, ketogenic plan, it can be easy to eat a lot of foods high in protein, because you are decreasing an entire macronutrient group -carbs - from your diet. Many people make the mistake of replacing the carbs with more protein-rich foods. This is where you have to be cautious, as more protein is not always better and, in fact, it can stop you from burning your fat stores for fuel.

A common misconception is that the ketogenic diet is a high-protein plan. To stress this point again, it is actually high-fat, **moderate-protein**, and low-carb lifestyle. The takeaway here is not to eat too much protein (like the old Atkins diet) because it will impair your ability to burn your fat as fuel. High protein essentially turns your diet into a high-carb diet though the conversion of protein into carbohydrates through gluconeogenesis.

Finally, excess proteins drive your hormone systems into a state of continuous growth, through MTOR stimulation (which stands for mammalian target of rapamycin – a gene). This increases cellular division and cellular aging. Enhanced MTOR stimulation has been associated with obesity, cancer, diabetes, insulin resistance, osteoporosis (via urinary calcium loss), kidney dysfunction (due to the stress of excreting nitrogen) and the aging process itself.

On the other hand, decreased MTOR signaling (best done through fasting and calorie restriction periods) is associated with longer life spans. Over-fueling in the form of protein or carbs will lead to increased cell division through MTOR stimulation and increase cancer and chronic disease. Studies also show that increased insulin (through excess carbohydrates AND protein) also stimulates MTOR.

The Bed-Ridden Patient or Post-Regenerative / Surgical Procedure. Research suggests the daily protein requirements for person on bed rest be as high as 1g per kilogram or, on average, around 70 grams of protein per day to preserve muscle mass during healing.

The Elderly. Studies have been looking at this and most recommend a slightly higher increased need for the elderly to avoid muscle wasting. It seems that 1.0-1.2 grams of protein per kilogram is adequate. Note that elderly will have a higher incidence of problems with the kidneys as well and the total amount of protein consumed at a single time should not exceed 15 grams per serving. They will need to distribute their consumption throughout the day.

Pregnant and Lactating Women. Women who are pregnant or lactating have a much higher need for protein because they are "eating for two". The recommended amount for this population is around 71 grams of protein per day.

When it comes to body composition, weight loss and maintaining lean muscle mass, good protein sources can help. If avoiding meat protein, good protein sources include soy, greens, seeds, legumes and rice and raw nuts. When it comes to meat proteins, it is important to make choices with the majority of protein sources coming from smaller animals and seafood and all animals should be free-range grass-fed and organic to maximize omega-3 composition and decrease added hormones and antibiotics. These hormones can make it difficult for weight loss and can interfere in health optimization. Overall, try to decrease your consumption of red meats and larger animals that may contain higher hormones in their fat (even in organic, free-range animals) as this can make it difficult for you to lose weight.

Protein helps slow stomach-emptying and decreases insulin spikes. It also helps maintain fullness (or satiety) and increases the metabolism to decrease fat stores. When consuming a meal, studies show that when you eat the protein source first, it slows down the absorption rates of the carbohydrates, decreasing the glycemic index of those carbohydrate sources. After a hard workout, exercise or injury, it helps with the repair process in building back lean muscle. Note that insulin is released with both carbohydrate and protein intake, so if you are trying to increase your insulin resistance and decrease chronic insulin levels, protein intake should be adequate but not excessive.

SOURCE	FACTS
Seafood	High in healthy Omega-3 fats.
White Meats	Less risk for potential carcinogen risk with white meats compared to red meats. Less hormone influences.
Eggs	Low cost. Perfect protein balance. Good fat.
Legumes	Good protein source. Higher in fiber but contain Lectins (inflammatory/allergenic).
Soy	Low fat. Consumption can decrease cholesterol. Is a natural estrogen and should avoid excessive amounts in children.
Lean Beef	Good source of Iron, Zinc and B12. Potential carcinogen, but possible risk may be related to the cooking process and AGEs. AVOID processed meats if they contain nitrates or other chemicals. Processed meats often have added sugars as well.
Dairy	AVOID milk (lactose sugar) if trying to lose weight. Cheese is both a fat and protein source. Greek yogurt, cheese and cottage cheese if no milk allergy.

Protein sources and nutrition facts

FIBER

Fiber is a food substance found in plants that gives it structure and form. It has no calories or nutrient content but is very important in healthy nutrition. Fiber occurs in both a soluble and insoluble form. They both help with digestion, but they cannot be digested or absorbed by the body. Soluble fibers will bind to the fats in foods and subsequently delay and decrease their absorption. This leads to a lowering of cholesterol and in circulating blood sugar. It is essential for chronic metabolic disease management. Insoluble fibers will enable food to move through the body and be excreted more quickly. It helps with detoxification, hormone balancing and weight loss.

Fiber is also thought to be helpful in the prevention of certain cancers. Fiber is not digestible or absorbable in the small intestine and ends up being partially or fully fermented in the colon. It is a probiotic and acts as an essential nutrient source for healthy bacteria which are also associated with healthy well-being.

Fiber has many essential functions in the body:

- It improves absorption of certain vitamins and minerals.
- It improves digestion and prevents constipation.
- It lowers total cholesterol and triglycerides and increases the good HDL cholesterol.
- It lowers blood pressure.
- It lowers blood sugar and is essential for the treatment of metabolic diseases.
- It coats the intestines and feeds important healthy microorganisms by acting as a prebiotic. Having healthy gut flora is important for many things, from maintaining a healthy weight to boosting immunity.

Studies suggest that fiber is associated with a lower risk of cardiovascular disease, Diabetes Type 2 and mortality. Clinical trials have shown benefits in reducing body weight, blood pressure and an inflammatory marker called the C reactive protein

(CRP). It has also been shown to improve the control of blood sugars.

These protective effects of dietary fiber are most likely caused by its intrinsic property of entrapping sugars and fats to increase your sensation of fullness and to reduce your total calorie intake, reduce cholesterol and improve control of your blood sugars. With its prebiotic function through fermentation in the gut, it helps to stimulate the desirable microbiome to lower infection rates and control systemic inflammation. More evidence is emerging on the importance of healthy gut flora in chronic disease treatment and prevention.

Osteoarthritis is the most common joint disorder for adults over the age of 60. It causes pain and limited physical function and is a leading cause of disability and impairment of quality of life.

A recent study in the Annals of the Rheumatic Diseases in 2017 concluded that findings from two longitudinal studies consistently showed that higher total fiber intake was related to a lower risk of symptomatic osteoarthritis. [86] This conclusion shows that fiber is not only good for metabolic disorders but also helpful for the treatment of orthopedic conditions, including arthritis.

FOOD SOURCES OF SOLUBLE FIBER

Apples	Blackberries	Flaxseed	Pears
Apricots	Broccoli	Grapefruit	Prunes
Artichokes	Brussel Sprouts	Nuts	Psyllium
Bananas	Cabbage	Oat bran	Split peas
Barley	Carrots	Okra	Sweet potatoes
Beans	Chickpeas	Oranges	Quinoa

FOOD SOURCES OF INSOLUBLE FIBER

Bananas	Cauliflower	Potato with the skin	Prunes
Beans	Celery	Lentils	Spinach
Broccoli	Corn	Brussel Sprouts	Brown rice

Nutrition is your cornerstone for health and healing and it also can have influence over your genetics. Epigenetics is a term which means we have control over what genes are expressed. Your genes, which are inherited, control many things including both health and disease expression. Nutritional epigenetics means how we eat affects how our genes are expressed. We can either turn on or turn off the genes that influence the expression of chronic diseases like diabetes, cancer, Alzheimer's disease and obesity.

Even more profound is the concept of trans-generational epigenetics. This means how we eat will not only affect what genes are expressed in us, but also which genes are transferred to our offspring. The choices we make will affect our children's long-term health.

Choosing to eat healthy whole foods will fuel your body to maximize your energy, heal injuries, reverse chronic disease, decrease your need for medications and augment your healing response with regenerative procedures. It will also turn on your healthy genes and suppress the unhealthy genes.

Now that you have a good knowledge base on proteins, carbohydrates, fats and oils, let's take a detailed look at the nutritional plans you can choose from to optimize your health and aid in REGENERATION. We will first explore the non-ketogenic options of the clean eating and the plant-based approach. We will then explore the ketogenic options of a ketogenic lifestyle and intermittent fasting. There is good evidence for all the plans. You need to decide on what plan or combination of plans works best for you. Any plan is a good plan to start with because you can always switch and try another one. Eventually, you will find a plan, or create your own hybrid plan, that works for you, giving you incredible energy and leading to a healthy, vibrant, disease-free body.

NON-KETOGENIC

First, let's look at simple clean eating from a standard and plant-based approach that can be used to restore health and promote healing in the body. These plans have a higher carbohydrate percentage and will not get the body into a state of utilizing the fat stores for energy (ketosis). They may not provide as rapid a weight loss as the ketogenic options below but may be easier for some people and can also be a good maintenance plan. For others, they can achieve successful weight loss when they stay on the **ACCELERATED NUTRITION** carbohydrate level for a prolonged period.

Rejuv4LIFE NUTRITION PLAN

It may seem overwhelming with all the charts and graphs and what seem to be rules to follow with regard to proper amounts of protein, fats and carbohydrates. It really should be very simple - focus on eating healthy, whole foods. I don't believe in diets. What I believe in is a healthy way of life. I believe in changing habits that, over time, become part of who you are every day.

Rejuv4LIFE is a way of life and not a fad diet. The goal is to create an anti-inflammatory and anabolic environment that optimizes healing and improves overall health. The goal is to also maximize fat loss and lean muscle gain. Through this plan, the body will detoxify and retrain the palate to taste food in its whole, healthy and delicious form again. Imagine a ripe, succulent, red, freshly-picked strawberry right off the vine. Close your eyes and open your mouth and slowly bite in to its luscious flesh. What did you taste? You tasted one of the most amazing flavors - and it is not candy, soda or ice cream. That is the goal of this plan. It is to help us taste the amazing, delectable and diverse flavors of real food.

Rejuv4LIFE has three levels of food plans that you can use - they are all clean-eating plans that eliminate sugar and vegetable oils. They maintain the same amount of protein and amount of good fats while the amount of carbohydrates decreases based on your goals and needs. The lower amount of carbohydrates, the more you will stabilize insulin levels and lose more unwanted body fat.

Foundational Nutrition, Accelerated Nutrition and Advanced Nutrition are the three levels, each with decreasing amounts of carbohydrates. All phases focus on healthy clean eating, selecting natural whole foods to both taste delicious and also heal the body.

Each level differs, essentially, in the amount of carbohydrates and types of carbohydrates consumed. Accelerated Nutrition and Advanced Nutrition are a bit more restrictive on the total carbs consumed, totaling around 50-100g a day for Accelerated and 100-150g with Foundational. Less than 50g of carbs would be considered more ketogenic and is considered Advanced Nutrition. That is just fine as well if more rapid weight loss is preferred and will be discussed in the ketogenic section to come.

The goals of these plans are to: detoxify the body, mobilize deep fat stores, increase the body's metabolism, stabilize blood sugars and decrease insulin spikes, retrain the palate to taste foods again in their natural state, and decrease inflammation from inflammatory foods. It is also a time to refocus the mindset and set your personal goals of what you want to achieve during your transition.

With the Foundational Nutrition level, you may have less rapid weight loss, but you will have more food options, making it easier to maintain in the long run. It is a good maintenance level once you have achieved your goals. Your total carbohydrate intake may be increased, but you are still focusing on healthy protein, fat and carbohydrate options. During this time, you may reintroduce limited amounts of grains and dairy (if you choose to consume dairy products) back into your diet as long as weight loss is still happening. You can always return to Accelerated or Advanced (Ketogenic) Nutrition if you hit roadblocks in your weight loss journey or your goals aren't yet achieved.

NON-KETOGENIC

Rejuv4LIFE-FOUNDATIONAL NUTRITION A good overall low glycemic index-based nutrition plan. This plan will result in decreased insulin spikes and improved insulin sensitivity. It is a good nutrition plan for the general population and a good place to start when making changes to your diet.

I will present two **Rejuv4LIFE** options for you to follow. You can also choose a plant-based (whole food plant-based, without animal products) option as well. They will both focus on optimizing health and healing. Any healthy change in our dietary patterns is a good thing for health and disease prevention. Meat and dairy consumption can be a personal issue; curtail use if you feel it fits your lifestyle or if you are having plateaus.

With the **FOUNDATIONAL NUTRITION** level (including the plant-based option), the goal is to start the body's healing as well as detoxify, start to mobilize fat stores and decrease your risk for chronic diseases. It is a good place to start by eliminating sugars and bad fats like vegetable oil.

When starting to make Foundational Nutrition changes, you can also make other healthy lifestyle changes covered in this book. The checklist at the end of this chapter is a great way to get started. It is a time to refocus your health goals and recharge and motivate your mind for personal success. As you continue to decrease your carbohydrate intake, you will have more success with your weight loss and insulin sensitivity.

Here is the basic plan to be followed to optimize your success with your **Rejuv4LIFE NUTRITION PLAN** using either the standard or plant-based options.

1. Consume mostly low glycemic index foods that do not spike your blood sugar and insulin.

Unprocessed whole vegetables and some fruits will have a naturally low glycemic index due to a higher fiber content.

This keeps insulin low and blood sugars steady as well as helps to avoid cravings.

2. Drink plenty of water. Your goals is to drink half your body weight in ounces a day.

This is needed to maintain good hydration and detoxification.

3. Vegetables and Fruits.

Vegetables can be eaten with every meal. AVOID over-cooking so as not to lose nutrients and increase the GI (glycemic index). Fruits can be eaten but focus on low glycemic index varieties and limit fruits if you are not losing weight due to the higher fructose (sugar) contents.

4. Focus on healthy protein sources.

We need protein for repairing our bodies. If you are including meat, focus on organic smaller animals, like chicken, fish and seafood, and limit the days and amount consumed. Avoid over-cooking due to the production of AGEs (advanced glycation end products) which can independently have a risk for cancer. Also, give a plant-based day or two per week a test drive.

5. Eggs.

Eggs can be a source of protein with a complete set of amino acids. The fat is a good fat and will not increase cholesterol.

6. Avoid processed foods.

All processed foods will contain preservatives and chemicals that are not optimal to our health. Processed meats are actually considered a carcinogen with direct links to cancer. Many also have a lot of added sugar.

7. Avoid FAST foods.

If you are out to eat, make healthy choices that fit the guidelines.

8. Avoid dairy if hitting a plateau in your health goals.

Milk, in general has a lot of sugars that cause insulin spikes and can lead to weight gain. Also, remember that dairy can be an inflammatory food for some people.

In addition, dairy decreases thyroid hormone and slows the metabolism. Dairy has been shown to release opioid like substances (casomorphin) which can make it addictive. Non-dairy sources (almond, coconut, rice and soy milk) are available and are a good alternative to dairy milk with equal amounts of fortified vitamin D and calcium.

9. Avoid sugar.

This is an absolute rule. No sugar! Sugar consumption stops weight loss and will be detrimental to health. This includes high fructose corn syrup, corn syrup, juices and soda, dressings and sauces (read the labels). This also includes high-processed grains and wheat flours that have sugar-like effects on the body.

10. Avoid artificial sweeteners or products containing them.

Studies show artificial sweeteners also lead to weight gain. No juices or soda.

11. Avoid alcohol.

Alcohol has been shown to slow down the metabolism and decrease success with weight loss.

12. Eat more fiber.

Fiber helps with weight loss and weight loss plateaus. Consume foods high in fiber such as fruits and vegetables. You can add 15 grams of fiber (combination of soluble and insoluble) as well with a supplement if you are not consuming around 40 grams a day in your food. Aim for twice a day taken before larger meals.

If you have a mostly plant-based diet with your fat and protein, you may not need to supplement with extra fiber. Total fiber intake goal per day, including foods, should be around 50 grams a day. Here are some examples of foods high in healthy fiber:

- 1 large pear with skin (7 grams)
- 1 cup fresh raspberries (8 grams)
- ½ medium avocado (5 grams)
- 1 ounce almonds (3.5 grams)

13. Choose **ORGANIC** when you can.

The fruits and vegetables that you should eat organic are those with a skin. This is due to all the chemicals that remain on the skin used in the production of non-organic fruits and vegetables (i.e., apples, grapes, berries). Also note that you can eat frozen berries which will maintain all the healthy qualities, work great in a smoothie and are much less expensive.

DIRTY DOZEN (EAT ORGANIC ONLY)	CLEAN 15 (OK TO EAT CONVENTIONALLY GROWN)
Celery	Onions
Peaches	Avocado
Strawberries	Sweet Corn
Apples	Pineapple
Blueberries	Sweet Peas
Nectarines	Mangos
Bell Peppers	Asparagus
Spinach	Kiwi
Cherries	Cabbage
Kale/Collard and Greens	Eggplant

Potatoes	Cantaloupe
Grapes	Watermelon
	Grapefruit
	Sweet Potato
	Honeydew and Melon

Foods to Eat Organic

FOUNDATIONAL NUTRITION is a great place to start as you make the decision to live a healthy lifestyle. As you already know, you will start by eliminating all extra sugar and refined carbohydrate sources as well as unhealthy fats like vegetable oil. You will focus on moderate protein intake, a higher healthy fat and lower total carbohydrate intake. This is where you need to be a bit careful. Remember that once you get over 150 grams of carbohydrate intake a day (especially if you are not very active), it will lead to weight gain.

At the **FOUNDATIONAL NUTRITION** level, the majority of carbohydrates consumed during this time will still come from healthy vegetables and small amounts of different whole fruits and non-gluten grains (although it is still best to skip grains all together due to their higher carbohydrate content and less nutrition density compared to vegetables and fruits) to diversify your palate. You can add one serving (1/2 cup cooked) of the following with your breakfast or lunch meal. Try to limit all carbohydrate sources, except vegetables, in the evening hours if your goal is weight loss.

CARBOHYDRATE OPTIONS with FOUNDATIONAL NUTRITION

Fresh/frozen fruits and vegetables. This would be the best option to add back, as fruits can be packed with phytonutrients and antioxidants. They have a higher sugar content so they should be added back in moderation - 1-2 servings per day. You can add more in your diet with a higher activity/exercise level.

Low-Carb Vegetables: You can eat most green veggies without any concern (the following have a very low carbohydrate content and are high in fiber).

- Broccoli
- Cauliflower
- Tomatoes and bell peppers (Night shades can also have lectins in their skin and seeds so, if concerned about lectins, peel and seed.)
- Onion
- Brussels sprouts
- Kale and swiss chard
- Cabbage
- Cucumber
- Eggplant
- Asparagus
- Mushrooms
- Green beans
- Celery
- Spinach

Low-Carb Fruits: These are high in fiber and have less of an effect on insulin. These can be enjoyed during the **FOUNDATIONAL** level (100-150 grams total carbohydrates a day). As long as you are still losing body fat and have a good energy level, feel free to consume 1-2 of these servings a day. If your weight loss plateaus, drop the fruits and focus on vegetables for a week or two and see if you start to lose weight again, or decrease your carbohydrate to the **ACCELERATED NUTRITION** level below. You can also try intermittent fasting to break a plateau.

One note on fruits - they contain fructose as their sugar source. Fructose is considered the most lipogenic sugar (fat-forming) - more on that soon. The following fruits would be the best options to add for their lower glycemic loads, high fiber and because they are packed with powerful antioxidants.

- Grapefruit
- Oranges
- Raspberries
- Kiwis
- Lemons
- Strawberries
- Apricots

Low-Carb Grains and Legumes:

Brown or Wild Rice is an option to use as it has more fiber than white rice and a lower glycemic index, but vegetables would be a preferred option - try making cauliflower rice instead. An interesting thing about rice (and potatoes) is that, once the starch is cooked and then cooled, the starch and carbohydrate has a minimal effect on insulin. Eaten warm or hot, the glycemic index is high. So, if you are having rice or potatoes, consume cold. Quinoa can be a part of your **FOUNDATIONAL NUTRITION** plan if needed and is a seed, not a grain.

- Sweet Potatoes/Yams

- Wheat, bulgur, barley, rye, spelt, oats and other grain-containing products like crackers, cereal, pasta, all breads, tortilla and would be a less desirable option due to the empty calories of most grains, as well as the unwanted gluten and other antinutrients found in them. Continue to avoid if weight loss is still a goal.

- Legumes have a higher protein and fiber content, but their skins contain antinutrients that can prevent absorption of needed micronutrients. If you do decide to eat legumes, make sure you properly soak and prepare them to decrease levels of phytic acid, lectins and saponins. When prepared properly, they do have good nutritional value. Note: they do have a high carbohydrate load despite their fiber so, if weight loss is a goal, they may not be helpful if you hit a plateau or want a faster weight reduction result. It is important that if you have trouble with weight loss, inflammation and pain, or autoimmune disease to be checked for a gluten sensitivity, then avoid it and products containing it if you have an issue.

If you are on a FOUNDATIONAL NUTRITION level and are eating a limited amount grains, here is a list of gluten- free grains. However, remember that carbohydrates in the form of real foods, like fruits, vegetables, nuts and seeds, are nutrient-dense and are a superior option. I list these here as a carbohydrate option but, like all grains, they have limited nutritional value compared vegetable and fruit sources and should only be consumed if you are at your ideal body weight.

If you are trying to lower your total carbohydrate amounts to get into some healthy fat burning, AVOID all grains including these gluten-free varieties.

- Buckwheat
- Millet
- Wild Rice
- Amaranth
- Quinoa
- Sorghum
- Corn
- Teff

When you eat enough healthy fats with your meals, you will not be as hungry between feeding times and should require less snacks. If you are hungry, consume a nutrient-dense snack with good fats included to increase satiety. Examples would be a handful of nuts or seeds, vegetables and nut butter, vegetables and guacamole or a healthy protein bar (read ingredients and be cautioned on the added sugar of many brands).

Once you have reached your weight loss goals and your blood sugar and cholesterol levels are controlled, then you can adjust your total carbohydrates to possibly include more fruits and/or whole grain foods. Once over 150 grams of carbohydrates, your activity level would have to increase to burn the extra carbohydrate energy and avoid it being stored as fat.

During your maintenance phase, your food sources are still healthy whole foods, but you may be consuming more carbohydrates in the form fruits or gluten-free grains. This phase would be for the very active individual, athlete and those at an ideal body weight with good insulin sensitivity and health. If your weight starts to increase, you can decrease your carbohydrate consumption and go back to a **FOUNDATIONAL** or **ACCELERATED NUTRITION** level of carbohydrate intake to get back at your desired weight goal.

Throughout this journey of changing your health habits, you may go through times when your nutrition is not optimal. Focus on maintaining a normal portion size with these meals. Stay guilt-free because you have earned it! We all need to learn to embrace and enjoy our journey to health. Once you are back on the bandwagon, try to stay consistent with your eating habits.

ACCELERATED and ADVANCED (Ketogenic) NUTRITIONAL PLANS

ACCELERATED=50-100 grams of carbs a day
ADVANCED= less than 50 grams of carbs a day for maximal weight loss and fat burning

ADVANCED NUTRITION is a great method of eating for weight loss, metabolism resetting, insulin and blood sugar decrease, and for insulin sensitivity. Once your carbs get low enough, your body will need to start to mobilize its fat stores for energy. With the breakdown of stored fat, your body creates ketones from the fat to use as energy for the brain and muscles. This state is called ketosis and has many health benefits. We will go into detail on this plan later in the R4L **ADVANCED-KETO NUTRITION** plan.

The only difference between Rejuv4LIFE **ACCELERATED** and **ADVANCED-KETO** plans is a lower carbohydrate consumption (usually around 50 or less grams) in the **ADVANCED-KETO** plan. They both will have higher amounts of healthy fats than you may be used to consuming but DO NOT FEAR FAT. It may be the secret ingredient to keeping your feeling full and not craving all the quick energy carbohydrates you have been dependent on for energy.

With all the plans, your protein amounts will stay constant. As you decrease the carbohydrate counts to increase fat burning, you can increase your healthy fat consumption to promote satiety and decrease food cravings.

Rejuv4LIFE is meant to be a way of life. It is not a diet. Use this as a guideline for both the clean eating and plant-based options until healthy eating becomes a

---

habit and a part of who you are every day. If you are hitting obstacles and plateauing with your weight loss or disease management goals, consider a ketogenic option, which we will explain next.

Rejuv4LIFE Keys to Success: For Any Nutrition Plan

TIMING IS LESS IMPORTANT THAN WE ONCE THOUGHT

Eat when you are hungry. If you wake up and are not hungry, do not eat. Your body will have a chance to use its fat stores for energy instead of using calories. Studies show that not eating or skipping meals does NOT slow down the metabolism. Studies on fasting up to three days will not affect metabolic rates. So, it is ok, in fact good, to skip meals or fast periodically.

Also, if you are not hungry before bed, do not eat. If you are hungry, avoid carbohydrates and eat a fat-protein combination like an egg or a few nuts. More on fasting in a bit.

MEAL BALANCE IS KEY

If one of your goals is weight loss, do not eat grains and legumes too often. If eating after 4:30 pm, eat mostly vegetables, small amounts of protein and or/fat. This will decrease the total calories and increase the fiber consumed later in the day and enhance the fat burning (ketosis state) in the evening and during sleep through avoiding an insulin spike. The extra fat can also keep you feeling full without the risk of any rebound cravings later.

PREPARE AHEAD OF TIME

It all starts in the grocery store. Have a list and know what to get and what to avoid in advance. Read labels and shop the periphery of the store - avoid the center isles (which is where the processed calorie-dense and nutrition-poor food is located).

Make sure you have healthy choices on hand at all times.

Pack healthy, balanced meals for work.

Cook in bulk and make use of portable storage containers.

PREPARE - OR PREPARE TO FAIL!

OTHER HEALTHY TIPS TO CONSIDER

Eat organic when you can, especially the "dirty dozen" (which you can see in a previously shown chart).

Some people benefit from allergy-free food living (i.e., grains, gluten, dairy, legumes, soy). For specific food sensitivities, consider getting tested.

Learn your caloric needs. Consider a metabolic test to see specific calorie needs.

Exercise around 30 minutes daily. It doesn't always have to be strenuous. Light prolonged movement is great and can be done daily. This would be like a brisk walk, leisurely bike ride, adventurous hike, playful tennis or a kayak ride. Increase to a more vigorous type of workout once or twice a week. This would be like an intense sprint/walk or intervals on a stationary bike. Too much long, repetitive cardio-type activity can actually do more harm than good.

Also, add weight and resistance training using large muscle group multi-joint movement around three times a week to increase metabolism and healing hormones. All forms of exercise - from a daily light walk to weight training and an occasional all-out sprint-type burst, will increase insulin sensitivity.

Get 7-9 hours a sleep at night. This is critical to health and longevity.

Take important supplements (i.e., Omega-3 Fish Oil, Vitamin D, Probiotics).

HYDRATION (refer to CHAPTER 6)

Drink water and green tea as your primary sources of hydration.

Drink of minimum of 64 ounces of water each day; you may need more depending on your body weight. Your goal is to consume half your IDEAL body weight in ounces a day.

Bring a water bottle with you wherever you go.

Drink before and during work outs as well as before and during meals.

AVOID:
- SUGAR and ALL sugar-containing processed food products.
- GLUTEN and GRAINS and ALL processed products.
- SUGAR SUBSTITUTES (i.e., Splenda, Aspartame, Saccharin, etc.).
- High SODIUM foods. Use Himalayan sea salts

instead. You may need an iodine supplement if you have no iodinated salt added to foods.

- HYDROGENATED oils, TRANS FATS and VEGETABLE oils.
- HIGH FRUCTOSE CORN SYRUP and maltodextrin.
- MSG. It is hidden in many processed and fast foods as flavor enhancer; it is a toxin.
- PROCESSED MEATS containing nitrates and sugar.

FIBER

Consume foods high in fiber to slow absorption rates and decrease insulin response (i.e., low glycemic index fruits and vegetables).

You can also add 15 grams of fiber (combination of soluble and insoluble) to your protein shakes if you are eating on the go and don't have access to REAL food.

Questions always arise as to what I can eat for my protein, carbohydrate and fat sources. Following, I break it down, so you can make healthy and informed choices.

PROTEIN:

ANIMAL-BASED	PLANT-BASED
Fish-Limit to 1-2 servings a week due to mercury toxicities.	Seitan -a wheat protein, resembles meat when cooked. Has 25 grams of protein per 100 grams.
Chicken or Turkey - A better choice for protein than beef.	Tofu, Tempeh and Edamame - from soybeans. Considered a complete protein with all essential amino acids.
Seafood (Shrimp, crab, scallops...)	Lentils - A powerhouse protein source with 18 grams of protein per cup. Also contain a lot of fiber and slowly digested carbohydrates for sustained energy. The fiber acts as a prebiotic promoting a healthy gut. Shown to decrease the risk of heart disease, excess body weight and some types of cancer. Also contain many antioxidants, folate, manganese and iron.

Wild Game - A lower fat and lower Omega-6 option.	**Nutritional Yeast** - it is a deactivated strain of yeast that is sold as a yellow powder or flake. It has a cheesy flavor that makes it a popular ingredient in mashed potatoes and scrambled tofu. You can also sprinkle it on top of pasta dishes or popcorn. It is a complete source of plant protein providing 14g of protein and 7g of fiber per ounce. It is a good source of zinc, magnesium, copper, manganese and all the B vitamins, including B12.
Dairy products (whey, milk, cottage cheese, yogurt) - Limit amounts for weight loss. Also possible link to cancer, obesity, heart disease and diabetes.[102,103,104,105, 106, 107]	**Spelt and Teff** - Spelt and teff belong to a category known as ancient grains. Spelt is a type of wheat and contains gluten. Teff originates from a grass and is gluten-free. They provide around 10g of protein per cup and are excellent sources for various nutrients including complex carbs, fiber, iron, magnesium, phosphorus and manganese.
Eggs - They are a complete protein with all essential amino acids.	**Hempseed** - it contains about 10g of complete and easily digestible protein per ounce which is 50% more than Chia seeds and flaxseed. It also contains a

	good amount of manganese, iron, calcium, zinc and selenium. It's also a good source of omega-3 fatty acids.
Limit all red meats (beef, pork, lamb) - High in saturated fats and a probable link to cancer and chronic diseases.	**Green Peas** - Green peas are often a side dish and contained 9g of protein per cooked cup. They're high in fiber as well as vitamin A, C, K, thymine, folate and manganese.
AVOID all processed meats (deli meats, sausage, salami, bacon, ham, jerky) - Definite link to cancer and chronic diseases.	**Spirulina** - 2 tablespoons provide you with 8g of complete protein as well as iron, thiamin, copper and magnesium.
	Amaranth and Quinoa - they provide around 9g of protein per cup and are a good source of complex carbs, fiber, iron, phosphorus and magnesium.
	Soy Milk - it is made from soybeans and fortified with vitamins. It contains 7g of protein per cup. It is also an excellent source of calcium, vitamin D and fortified B12.

	Oats and Oatmeal - a half cup of dry oats contains around 6g of protein and 4g of fiber.
	Chia seeds - they contain 6g of protein and 13g of fiber per 1.25 ounces. They also contain iron, calcium, selenium, magnesium and are high in omega-3 fatty acids, antioxidants and other beneficial plant compounds. They are very versatile and mature in water, forming a gel-like substance. They add easily to a variety of recipes including smoothies, baked goods and Chia puddings.
	Nuts, Nut Butters and Other seeds - one ounce contains between 5 to 7g of protein, depending on the nuts or seed variety. They are also great sources of fiber, healthy fats, phosphorus, vitamin EE and certain B vitamins. They also contain antioxidants and other beneficial plant compounds.

	Protein-rich vegetables - vegetables with the most protein content include broccoli, spinach, asparagus, artichokes, potatoes, sweet potatoes and brussels sprouts. They contain about 5g of protein per pre-cooked cup. Sweet corn, which is technically a grain, also contains about the same amount of protein. **Fresh fruits** generally have a lower protein content but those with the highest amount include guava, mulberries, blackberries, nectarines and bananas. They have about 2 to 4g of protein per cup.

Protein should be 20-30% of Daily Calorie Intake.

With the **FOUNDATIONAL NUTRITION** option, 1-2 servings of whole grain carbohydrates or additional fruits can be added back to your nutrition plan if you desire. The other 4-5 servings should be from vegetables. Go salads go! Carbohydrates should be less than 150 grams total a day for weight maintenance and lower if weight loss is a goal.

Carbohydrate intake should still be from whole food sources, predominately vegetables and some fruits. If your weight loss stalls, consider cutting out these extra carbohydrate sources as they are most likely increasing insulin and interfering with the utilization of fat stores for energy (ketosis). This is where decreasing your total carbohydrates to between 50 and 100 grams for **ACCELERATED NUTRITION,** or less than 50 grams a day for **ADVANCED NUTRITION,** would maximize fat burning as you most likely would be in a ketogenic state.

HEART-HEALTHY FATS: Focus on sources high in omega-3 fatty acids. You can also refer to our previous fat and oil discussion; here is a short list of heart-healthy fats.:

- Raw, unsalted nuts: Almonds, Walnuts, Cashews, Pistachios, Macadamias
- Avocados and Olives
- Natural nut butters (Almond) - avoid too much Peanut or Peanut butters as they are almost

completely omega-6 fatty acids and higher in antinutrients.

- Hummus (has omega-3 fats and a low glycemic index)
- Healthy Oils: Coconut, Olive, Grape Seed, Walnut Oil, Flax Seed or Flax Seed Oil

An important note with fats: If you are increasing fat consumption to help with the many health benefits, you MUST lower carbohydrate intake. If you continue a higher carb intake and add increased fats because of all the benefits we have discussed, you will end up with too many calories resulting in assured weight gain and disease risk. A higher fat diet ONLY works when you decrease the insulin response to the carbohydrates. If insulin is high with high fats, then the excess fat and carbs are both stored as fat. Subsequently, weight gain and chronic disease will be the outcome.

NON-KETOGENIC

Rejuv4LIFE-Plant Based A good plan for those with metabolic disease and cancer risk factors. A good plan to follow during detoxification or on a weekly intermittent basis to aid in increasing the protective antioxidants of phytonutrients. Can also be a way of life when practiced on a daily basis.

My sister, Jennifer, is an amazing person. She is passionate about health and sensitive to how our health decisions can affect those around us and the environment we live in. She challenged me to try and eat vegan and see how I felt. I, too, have always had a passion for health and was eating pretty clean. I was avoiding processed foods and excess simple sugars, but I really liked meat. I ate it most days - from buffalo and beef to chicken and fish. I liked veggies, but they definitely weren't filling my plate three-quarters full consistently.

My wonderful wife, Debbie, often told me often that I don't need so much meat, so we started doing about one or two vegetarian dinners a week. I enjoyed these flavorful meals and decided that I wanted to see what it was like to cut meat out entirely. I had read about the health benefits of a plant-based diet but thought "*There is no way I can give up meat.*" I was a true CARNIVORE. "*I was an athlete and I needed PROTEIN.*" I didn't want my fitness training to suffer, but I wanted to see how I felt and how my body would respond. I also always had a hard time getting those last 10 pounds off. After age 40… ugh… things didn't burn up as fast and maintaining my fitness was becoming more of a challenge. I thought, "*I will give it a try, I have nothing to lose… except a few unwanted pounds.*"

It was actually a pretty easy transition for me. The food tasted great and, after the first month, I had lost my "beef cravings". My fitness training and sports performance did not suffer, and I felt energized by the impact I was having on my health and the environment.

With the evidence showing that red meat consumption has been associated with the increased risk of chronic disease, a study in JAMA (Journal of American Medical Association) in 2016 looked at its relationship with mortality. They concluded that red meat consumption is associated with an increased risk of total, cerebrovascular disease (stroke) and cancer mortality. It also showed that substitution of other healthy protein sources for red meat is associated with a lower mortality risk.[88]

Another study in 2009, which was a prospective study of over half a million people, concluded that red and processed meat intake was associated with modest increases in total mortality, cancer mortality and cardiovascular disease mortality.[89]

A study in the British Journal of Nutrition in 2014 looked at the association between the total processed red and white meat consumption and all causes of cerebral-vascular disease and ischemic heart disease mortality. It was a meta-analysis of multiple studies. It showed that meat consumption increased the risk of mortality from any cause.[90] That is an incredible thought to think that meat consumption has an increased risk of death from any cause from cancer to heart disease.

One of the books that I read early on in my health journey had an impact on my choice to try a whole food plant-based nutrition plan. The book was *Proteinaholic*, by Garth Davis, M.D. He had many compelling literature references backing the health benefits of a whole foods plant-based approach to nutrition. I would recommend reading the book as it was fascinating and a real eye-opener about the benefits of a plant-based diet. That was until I was educated about the facts.

In *italics* below is a summary of some of the main points from the book which is good food for thought when we start to change our eating patterns. As a counter point, there is also good evidence on decreasing sugars and carbohydrates in the prevention of metabolic diseases and some of the research questions the no-meat notion. I have also tried a full-on healthy ketogenic-based plan and found good success with body composition and weight loss. I will present this research in the ketogenic lifestyle option.

In the end, you need to decide what works best for you, gives you healthy outcomes and what you can sustain as a lifestyle. It is good to try different options and then settle on the one that brings you the outcomes you desire. Let's look at what the NO MEAT camp is saying about meat consumption, then later we will look at the LOW CARB crew says about excessive carbohydrate consumption. Ultimately, both groups make compelling arguments and a blend of both approaches where you limit red meat, avoid processed meats and follow a low- carbohydrate lifestyle with the possible addition of intermittent fasting may be a lifestyle that OVERALL may help the most people.

I am currently in the middle camp that takes the evidence from both sides. I am eliminating all sugars and processed foods. I am increasing my intake of healthy fats to promote satiety and gain the benefits of burning my fat stores for fuel. I am making conscious decisions when eating meat products to limit red meats, avoid processed meats with chemicals like nitrates, and making sure the animal products I do consume are from humane grass-fed organic sources. As with the plant-based approach I did for over a year, I also like how I look and feel with this option. I feel like I am making evidence-based choices and my health is reflective of them. Let's first look at the NO MEAT camp.

REASONS TO THINK ABOUT DECREASING MEAT CONSUMPTION

Randomized controlled trials conclude that meat causes cancer through the formation of N-nitroso compounds. They found that cultures with high meat diets have higher rates of chronic disease. They also found that cultures with lower meat and higher vegetable diets have low rates of chronic diseases.

The BLUE ZONES of the world reflect this statistic. Blue Zones are areas of the world that have low disease rates and longer life expectancies. We can learn a lot about health and disease prevention from the lifestyle habits in these cultures.

Following is a summary of some of the studies on **plant-based nutrition**.

EPIC Study: Followed a thousand people for 12 years: The study concluded that those eating meat (especially processed) had higher Diabetes rates and that fruit and vegetable consumption was associated with a lower risk of Diabetes.

Loma Linda university studying the 7th Day Adventist population: Animal protein was associated with Diabetes.

Nurse's Health Study and Health Professionals Study at Harvard University: Showed an association between meat, processed meat and Diabetes.
Women's Health Initiative: This study followed 37,001 for eight years and concluded that there is a correlation between animal product consumption and Diabetes.

Many other studies show that a plant-based diet actually protects us from Diabetes. Aune et al. 2009 Chui, Huang, et al. 2014.

Here is a look at specific chronic diseases and the how a plant-based diet can have a positive influence on them.

DIABETES MELLITUS

- *It has been found that beef consumption raises insulin more than carbohydrates. The problem is not the insulin, but it is the body's inability to respond to the high insulin levels and* subsequently store the consumed carbohydrates. When the body cannot respond to and use the insulin released after a meal, this is called insulin resistance. Muscle is our body's greatest consumer of sugar/carbohydrates and, when sugar is consumed, insulin must most work to push the carbohydrate into the muscle cell for energy storage. When we eat meat, we are eating protein and mostly saturated fat. The protein raises insulin levels, while the fat blocks the cells' ability to metabolize and push the carbohydrate into the cell. This leads to high blood sugar levels because the sugar can't be stored in the muscle cells. The resulting high blood sugar is damaging to our organs and nerves. Insulin resistance is due to fat toxicity to the muscle cell. Another study in the Journal of Diabetes in 2015 showed that moderate to high intake of meat is associated with insulin resistance. Many studies are showing a correlation between meat and fat consumption and insulin resistance and diabetes.

- *People often choose chicken as the "healthy" white meat; however, 97% of chicken breasts contain hazardous bacteria. When we cook the chicken breast, it kills the bacteria, but they leave behind the endotoxin produced by the bacteria which is embedded in the muscle and fat of the animal. With consumption of the chicken meat, the saturated fat causes the endotoxin to be absorbed into our body and sets off a state of inflammation. Inflammation in our bodies leads to more chronic disease.*

- *High protein consumption causes increased inflammation in the body with an increase in the levels of cortisol. Protein is an independent risk factor for diabetes and heart disease. It also causes an increase in C-reactive protein (CRP) which is also an independent risk factor for diabetes. Once the fat gets inside the muscle cells, it interferes with that cell's ability to develop new insulin receptors. With fewer receptors, it becomes more difficult to get sugar into the cell for processing and causes the sugar to build up in the* blood. This is insulin resistance. The pancreas then has to increase insulin secretion to drive the sugar into the cell. Since insulin is a storage hormone, the very high insulin level will cause more fat to develop in the cells which creates a vicious cycle. Also, iron found in meat causes oxidation and affects the pancreas's ability to secrete insulin. Meat eaters have higher iron stores which are directly related with diabetes formation. The problem with diabetes is the fact that the fat and inflammation is destroying the body's ability to utilize sugar safely and efficiently.

The etiology of diabetes is complex. There is mixed evidence on whether meat consumption contributes to the risk of diabetes. Decreased consumption of sugar and refined carbohydrates is definitely needed for health. If your sugar levels are not decreasing, then a decrease in meat consumption could be tried.

HYPERTENSION

42 million men and 28 million women in the U.S. have hypertension - over one billion people are affected from hypertension worldwide. Hypertension is the direct cause of the two number one killers in our society - heart disease and stroke. A plant-based diet will actually decrease your risk of diabetes, cancer, heart disease and stroke. This refers to a plant-based diet, NOT a grain high-processed carbohydrate diet.

- *Many studies have looked at the link between blood pressure and animal protein. The Western Electric Study followed over a million employees for 18 years and examined the relationship between their diet and their health. They found that the more animal protein and fat people ate, the more at risk they were for developing hypertension. They also found the opposite for those consuming plant proteins - a higher plant consumption actually lowers blood pressure.*

- *This is also seen in the 2012 Seventh-Day Adventist Health Study which show that vegetarians and vegans had less hypertension than the meat eaters.*
- *One of the best regarded hypertension studies is known as the International Study of Macronutrients and Micronutrients and Blood Pressure. The in-depth analysis of over 4,000 people showed high animal protein had a significant effect on blood pressure. A blood pressure-lowering effect seen in plant eaters was most likely due to the high fiber in a vegetable diet. They also found higher glutamic acid levels in the plant eater's urine. It is from higher levels of glutathione, which is a very important antioxidant.*
- *Studies show that when people are put on a vegetarian diet, their blood pressure lowers. The blood pressure was found to elevate again after meat consumption was started again. Many studies conclude that high animal protein diets will likely lead to high blood pressure.*

The high blood pressure leads to the need for expensive medications with an array of side effects as well as an increased burden to the healthcare system. The best way to decrease healthcare costs is to prevent disease in the first place.

HEART DISEASE

The American Heart Association stated, in February of 2017, that cardiovascular disease will exceed $1 trillion by 2035. This latest study projects that, by 2035, there will be:

- 123.2 million Americans with high blood pressure.
- 24 million coronary heart disease patients.
- 11.2 million suffering from stroke.
- 7.2 million Americans with atrial fibrillation.

Some other key findings:

- *By age 45, your CVD (cardiovascular) risk is 50 percent; at 65, it jumps to 80 percent.*
- *Black Americans will have the highest rates of CVD by 2035, followed by Hispanics.*

- *Men will suffer from CVD at a greater rate than women between now and 2035.*
- *A 29-country study concluded that animal protein is correlated with the development of heart disease. Other studies show a plant-based diet protects against heart disease.*
- *The EPIC study in 2013 showed a statistically significant reduction in the risk of developing heart disease by eliminating animal protein from the diet. This is also seen in the Adventist Health Study which showed a clear correlation between animal protein consumption and the risk of heart disease after controlling for other factors.*
- *There are also two excellent meta-analysis studies of vegetarians versus omnivores as it relates to heart disease. The conclusion was a significant decreased risk of heart disease and stroke in about 29% of people consuming a plant-based diet compared to meat eaters.*
- *Another study was done following 29,000 post-menopausal women in Iowa for 15 years. They concluded if you substitute vegetable protein for*

animal protein, you can expect a 30% reduction in the risk of developing heart disease. The authors concluded that a long-term adherence to a high protein diet without discrimination of protein source may have adverse consequences. Other studies show that simply eating less animal protein is associated with less heart disease.

- *A recent Harvard review showed people who had a prior heart attack who consume a high-protein and low-carb diet are at a significantly higher risk of dying from heart disease than someone consuming a high-plant protein diet. Those who eat animal proteins have a higher C-reactive protein (CRP), which is an independent risk factor for heart disease and hypertension. The increase in CRP could be from inflammation from the acidosis and the endotoxemia (toxins from the bacteria) that occurs after eating animal meat.*

When you eat more fruits and vegetables, you're also increasing your ingestion of flavonoids and antioxidants that decrease inflammation and, thereby, decrease the risk of heart disease. The consumption of meat and fat interferes with a breakdown of the amino acid arginine. Without effects of arginine, we cannot release nitric oxide which is needed for vasodilation and essential blood flow to our vital organs.

- *An article in the New England Journal of Medicine looked at replacing animal protein with soy protein. Results showed that soy protein led to a reduction in LDL cholesterol and triglycerides, which are two risk factors for heart disease. Similar studies have shown that a plant-based diet is as effective as taking statins for high cholesterol without the negative side effects. Plants only have positive side effects on our bodies.*
- *Dr. Dean Ornish has published many studies showing you can actually reverse heart disease with lifestyle changes. He found that by eliminating animal proteins along with other lifestyle interventions, including exercise and*

stress management, the result was an 8% improvement in the stenosis of the vessels while the control group had a usual expected 20% worsening of their vessels.

- *Another study in 2014 showed similar results with an actual reversal of heart disease on a plant-based, no animal protein diet. The study did not include the exercise and stress management component, showing that reversal of heart disease can be accomplished with a low-fat plant-based diet alone.*

- *Another study in 2009 compared to the Atkins diet to the South Beach diet. They concluded that the South Beach diet caused less inflammation and better relaxation of blood vessels than the high meat-protein Atkins diet.*

It's also been studied that the vegetarian diets are very well-tolerated by those starting to embark on that lifestyle, and that on a plant-based diet, it is less important to count calories to be healthy and to maintain an ideal body weight. Again, remember that plant-based plans CANNOT include excessive amounts of breads, cereals, pastas or refined carbohydrates, or the excessive carbohydrate load and constant insulin spikes which could negate the benefits of all the extra great veggies and fiber.

CANCER

Cancer is the second leading cause of death after heart disease. Animal protein has been strongly correlated with the development of cancer.

HCAs (Heterocyclic amines) form during the cooking process from any animal protein cooked at high temperatures or over an open flame. A study in 2003 looked at 1,600 people and found that not only was meat consumption associated with cancer, but the strength of the association was related to the cooking method. The worst way of cooking meat was pan-fried and well-done. This is most likely due to the fact that HCA's form when you burn animal protein. It may be more the way meat is cooked than the fact that it is meat which contributes to the cancer risk.

- A large study of post-menopausal women showed grilled, barbecued, and smoked meat was associated with increased risk of breast cancer. Another study found that the total HCA intake and consumption of fried meat, beef and processed meat were all correlated to precancerous damage to breast tissue. Other studies show that fruits and vegetables can block the effects of these carcinogens.

- Our diet can have a direct effect on our bowel bacteria. It has been shown that a diet heavy in meat alters the good bacteria rapidly and allows colonization of certain bacteria which may cause inflammation in the bowels.

- A study analyzing 48,000 men showed an increase in all cancers in middle-aged American men who consumed meat. A study in 2009 looking at meat consumption showed a definite association between the development of colon, gastric and *pharyngeal cancer. Of further interest, the animals in this study were grass-fed and hormone-free.*

• *Phytonutrients have a protective role. Phytonutrients seem to have a protective effect against cancer. A review article in 1991 identified many potential cancer-fighting compounds in plants: indoles, isothiocyanates, flavonoids, phenols, protease inhibitors, plant sterols and limonene. More compounds have been identified in plants that may have a protective role against cancer. The Epic Study shows that increased flavonoid consumption led to a decrease in gastric cancer in women.*

CANCER-PROTEIN LINK

COLON CANCER:

• *The Epic Study in 2006 showed an increased gastric cancer risk with increased consumption of red meat and processed meat. The more fiber people ate, the less cancer they got. Other findings of the study showed that fruit helps decrease cancer and that* saturated fat found in animal products may be associated with increased breast-cancer.

- A meta-analysis in 2002 of several studies showed that red meat and processed meat were associated with an increased risk of colorectal cancer. It also showed the less fiber, the more cancer - independent of whether the person was eating meat or not.

- A meta-analysis in 2011 looking at ten different studies showed that red meat and processed meat definitely correlated with colorectal cancer.

BREAST CANCER:

- A 2002 meta-analysis of multiple studies showed that animal protein intake was associated with an increased risk for breast cancer. Saturated fat and meat specifically were identified as reasons for the increased cancer risk.

- The Health Professionals Follow-up Study and the Nurses' Health Study clearly show the more red meat and processed meat in the diet, the more cancer. It also showed the cancer death rate was *significantly lower in those who eat less meat overall.*

- *A 2012 meta-analysis that looked at cardiovascular disease mortality and cancer incidence in vegetarians compared to the general population showed that vegetarians get roughly 18% less cancer than meat eaters.*

- *In addition to breast and colon cancer, multiple studies show less cancer in other areas as well, including pancreatic cancer, other cancers of the GI track, renal cell cancer of the kidneys, bladder cancer, and lung cancer.*

- *In 2004, an article entitled Diet, Nutrition and Prevention of Cancer was published in the Journal of Public Health Nutrition. A summary from the article reads, "overweight and obesity convincingly increase the risk of several common cancers. After tobacco, overweight and obesity is the most important cause of cancer in populations. Among the non-smoking populations, avoidance of being overweight is the most important strategy for cancer prevention." A plant-based diet helps people lose weight and keep the weight off. This would be critically important in decreasing obesity rates as well as cancer - almost as important as smoking cessation.*

The World Cancer Research Fund, along with the American Society for Cancer Research, published a report with recommendations on cancer prevention. The report was created after three years of study and debate, in which the expert panel reviewed close to 1,000 papers. They concluded, "*none of the recommendations are based on could-be conclusions. All are based on judgment that the evidence was definite or probable.*"

The report went on to clarify two issues. First, the cancer rates have been increasing and this increase is not from better reporting or early detection. Second, only a small percentage of cancer is genetic. Most cases of cancer can be prevented by lifestyle and environmental improvements. Here is the list of their recommendations, which the American Cancer Society also endorses:

1. Be as light as possible, within the normal range of bodyweight. Aim for the lower end of normal body mass index (BMI).

2. Be physically active as part of everyday life.

3. Limit consumption of energy-dense food. Avoid sugary foods. Eat foods low in fat, high in fiber and high in water content.

4. Eat mostly food from plant origins. They recommended to have at least five servings of fruits and vegetables each day and include unprocessed grains with each meal. If weight loss is a goal, this recommendation may not help your waist line.

5. Limit intake of red meat and avoid processed meat. They recommended to consume less than 300g, or 2/3 of a pound, per week. Other studies show to be completely vegetarian does protect against cancer.

6. Limit alcoholic drinks.

7. Limit consumption of salt.

8. Aim to meet nutritional needs through diet alone.

The panel concluded that fruits and vegetables decrease the risk of cancer of the mouth, esophagus, lung, stomach and rectum. Eating more plants also reduces the risk of cancer of the pancreas, breast, bladder, liver, ovary, and prostate.

Cutting back on animal protein and increasing your consumption of fruits and vegetables can have a profound benefit on your health and decrease your risk of many chronic diseases including cancer, obesity, hypertension and diabetes.

IS EATING LESS MEAT BETTER FOR OVERALL HEALTH?

- *A study in 2013 followed 500,000 Europeans between 10 and 18 years and they found that fruit and vegetable consumption decreased mortality. They found that meat consumption, most specifically processed meat as well as unprocessed red meat, increased the risk of death by 29%.*

- *Fruits and vegetables are full of fiber, antioxidants and phytochemicals. They also buffer acid which also will improve overall health. The World Health Report estimates a low fruit and vegetable consumption is responsible for 14% of G.I. cancers, 11% of coronary artery disease, and 9% of strokes.*

It seems that, along with vitamins, antioxidants and phytochemicals, that fiber may be the most beneficial aspect of the increased consumption of fruits and vegetables. The 2012 Epic Study showed that fiber intake is correlated with lower mortality, especially from coronary artery disease, as well as digestive and inflammatory disease.

The bottom line is that plants in the form of vegetables and fruits do have many wonderful micronutrients and fiber that can be very healthy. It seems that more vegetables and less meats are a healthy dietary shift that may help in our health in many ways. If you are consuming meat, eggs or dairy, make sure that they are grass-fed and organically-raised which may help negate some of the negative findings in the research.

Dairy

Growing up, we have all heard the advertising slogan *"Milk, It Does a Body Good"* and that by drinking three glasses a day, we will have strong bones and teeth. While this is very effective marketing for the dairy industry, it is not fully grounded in facts. Does milk, in fact, protect our bones and make them strong? A prospective study that followed over 70,000 post-menopausal women showed neither milk consumption or calcium supplementation protected them from fractures. Vitamin D supplementation did, however, decrease their fracture risk by 37%. How about milk consumption for children? A literature review published in Pediatrics in 2005 concluded that *"Scant evidence supports nutrition guidelines focused specifically on increasing milk or other dairy product intake for promoting child and adolescent bone mineralization."*

There also seems to be a link between dairy products and cancer. Six of twelve case-control studies and five of eleven cohort studies found significant associations between milk or dairy product consumption and prostate cancer incidence and mortality. Particularly among cohort studies, those reporting significant associations were generally larger and more recent in terms of participants. Several lines of evidence indicate that consumption of dairy products is associated with increased risk of prostate cancer incidence and mortality. Avoidance of these products may offer a means of reducing risk of this common illness.[91,92,93,94,95,96,97,98,99]

Dairy also seems to increase the risk of breast cancer as well. In a large study including 1,893 women from the Life After Cancer Epidemiology Study who had been diagnosed with early-stage invasive breast cancer, higher amounts of high-fat dairy product consumption were associated with higher mortality rates. As little as 0.5 servings a day increased risk significantly. This is probably due to the fact that estrogenic hormones reside primarily in fat, making the concern most pronounced for consumption of high-fat dairy products.

The Iowa Women's Health Study found that women who consumed more than one glass of milk per day had a 73 percent greater chance of developing ovarian cancer than women who drank less than one glass per day.[100,101]

Other harmful chemicals are found in dairy products that can have a profound negative effect on our health. Pesticides, polychlorinated biphenyls (PCBs), and dioxins are all contaminants found in milk. Dairy products have been found to contribute to one-fourth to one-half of the dietary intake of total dioxins.[101]

These toxins cannot be eliminated from our body and, eventually, build to toxic levels that may negatively affect the immune, reproductive, and central nervous systems. Also, PCBs and dioxins are also linked to cancer in humans.[102] Dairy may not have all the benefits we once thought, and some studies are showing that it may actually have some negative effects.

In children, dairy has been associated with obesity, heart disease and diabetes.[103] The American Academy of Pediatrics observed up to a 30% reduction in the incidence of type I diabetes in infants who avoid exposure to cow's milk protein for at least the first three months of their lives. They do not recommend that infants below one year of age be given whole cow's milk.[104,105,106]

Lactose intolerance is much more common than you would think -95% of Asian- Americans, 74% of Native Americans, 70% of African-Americans, 53% of Mexican-Americans and 15% of Caucasians are lactose intolerant.[107] This population lacks the enzyme lactase, which is needed to digest the milk sugar lactose. Symptoms include abdominal discomfort, diarrhea and flatulence. It is important for this population to avoid dairy intake. Since dairy is high in saturated fat and calories, the general population should also avoid consumption when focusing on a healthy lifestyle.

Dairy can be a source of fat and protein, but it is not for everyone. Those trying to decrease their risk for cancer or those who are hitting a plateau with their weight loss goals may want to try dropping dairy to see if the plateau resolves.

My sister is practicing a mostly plant-based lifestyle and challenged me to read the research on the benefits of plants in our diet. I had my sister, Jen, contribute on transitioning to a more plant-based diet, as well as recommend some good recipes to help those who want to make the transition to less meat and more plant-based nutrition. Go to JoelBaumgartnerMD.com for delicious recipes.

We came up with a whole food plant-based plan as an option with **Rejuv4LIFE**. It is described next and is called **Rejuv4LIFE Plant-Based**.

More Than Meatless Mondays: Plant-Based Whole Foods

In this section, we will present meat and dairy-free dishes. A little more explanation is given as cooking plant-based (without meat or dairy) may not be familiar. You will still get enough protein - it will just be from plant sources, such as beans, lentils, tofu, nuts and seeds. Fruits and vegetables alone also have protein. Once you get used to cooking this way, it will be easy to substitute plant-based protein options in your favorite recipes. For example, if you love fajitas, skip the chicken, steak, sour cream and cheese and, instead, marinate and grill some juicy Portobello mushrooms, peppers and onions, then combine that with some black beans and salsa and you have a nutritious meal that is bursting with fiber, vitamins and minerals, not to mention delicious.

Most people know how to cook with meat and dairy to make things satisfying and tasty. When thinking about going meatless, they automatically think tasteless and unsatisfying. This couldn't be further from the truth as some of the most flavorful cuisines have many dishes without meat. Just a few examples include food from Thailand, China, India, and the Mediterranean. They are bursting with savory flavor. Expanding your palate to new flavors can be a culinary adventure you can make from the comfort of your own home. If exotic flavors are not your thing, fret not as you can still make flavorful and healthy meatless American classics such as burgers, "egg" salad and tacos.

Some people, when educated on the facts about meat consumption, decide to go all-in and take out all meat products at once, while others find it overwhelming and push back altogether thinking they cannot do it and it is too complex. Some find it easy to take one or two days a week and go meatless. Another option is to cut down daily on the consumption and slowly make habit changes.

Any shift to a diet with less meat and more plant variety will be a healthy decision. It also may be the type of meat consumed (wild or organic grass-fed vs. lot grain-fed, hormone, antibiotic given) as well as how cooked, or over-cooked, the meat is when consumed (due to HCAs, or heterocyclic amines, which are a chemical that results from cooking meat).

Rejuv4LIFE Plant-Based. This nutrition plan is a plant-based whole foods plan designed for optimal health and disease prevention. For those wanting to decrease cancer risks or who have a history of cancer, this is an option to consider. With the research on meat and dairy consumption, this version of PHASE 1 will focus on whole food plant-based options and does not include animal products. It will include a variety of delicious foods to keep you satisfied and fill you with energy throughout the day.

Top Ten Tips for Transitioning to Plant-Based Eating

1. **Stock up!** Stock your fridge and pantry with healthy plant-based foods that can come together for a satisfying meal.
2. **Don't be afraid to try something new.** Embrace cooking with ingredients that may not be familiar but may become your new favorites.
3. **Find your go-to dishes.** Find a few recipes that you really like and keep these in regular rotation.
4. **Plan ahead.** When going to a friend's house for dinner who does not cook plant-based, have a healthy snack before you go. Offer to bring a plant-based dish and share with others. When eating out, look at the menu ahead of time if possible to see if they have plant-based options.
5. **Get inspired.** Read a book about the benefits of plant-based eating to excite you about the benefits for your body and the planet.
6. **Plug in.** Find a plant-based blog or pod-cast and plug in to hear new ideas and find encouragement in the stories of others.
7. **Go global.** Many delicious dishes from around the world are plant-based. Thai, Vietnamese, Chinese and Indian cuisines are all loaded with flavor and great options for eating out or cooking at home and having plant-based options.
8. **Have a support system.** Connect with a friend or family member who is already plant-based to get ideas or better yet find someone to make the transition with you.
9. **Embrace the bounty of foods that you can eat instead of worrying about those that you cannot.**
10. **Adapt some of your favorite meals.** Can't imagine giving up burgers? Make a delicious homemade veggie burger and you will be fully satisfied.

Here is a list of some of the foods you can look forward to enjoying.

- A wide variety of colorful and delicious fruits and vegetables.
- Beans and legumes - they are filled with plant protein and fiber.
- Tempeh - fermented and pressed soybeans that is sometimes combined with grains and is high in protein.
- Tofu - bean curd that is a flavor-sponge full of calcium and high in protein.
- Nuts and seeds - consume raw to maintain maximize nutrition.
- Quinoa - technically a seed but cooks up like a grain and is loaded with protein, fiber and minerals. Again, if concerned about lectins, use a pressure cooker to get rid of the lectins.

Seitan - made from wheat protein and the highest in protein/calorie of all plant-based protein products.

Veggie burgers - they are best when made at home to avoid processed ingredients (combines beans, whole grains, and vegetables).

Meat substitute products - There are an array of products available that can be direct substitutes for animal products like beef and chicken. However, a lot of them are made with processed soy, preservatives and a lot of salt. Eating these products occasionally is ok but consuming them daily is not advised.

Initially, this list may not excite you but, when combined with the right flavors, meatless meals can be just as satisfying than those with meat. The outcomes and the health benefits can be the fuel to motivate your lifestyle changes.

To be successful with **ACCELERATED NUTRITION Plant-Based**, a little prep time is helpful. Try to set aside some time at the beginning of the week to gather and prep ingredients to ensure you are ready for the week. If you have to head out first thing in the morning, consider having breakfast already made and waiting for you in the fridge. The tofu dishes in the recipe section store well in the fridge for several days and you will hardly know you aren't eating eggs. Fruit smoothies are a nutrition-packed quick and tasty way to start the day as well but will have a higher carbohydrate content, thus slowing or limiting your weight loss and insulin sensitivity goals.

While we would all love to have a new recipe for each meal, that is not practical for most of us and our busy lifestyles. By adapting a few time-saving tricks, you can make these meat-free days a breeze. Making a big batch and storing extras in the fridge or freezer makes for a quick and nutritious meal.

Let's break it down by meals and then go on to give some recipes.

Breakfast

During **ACCELERATED NUTRITION Plant-Based**, you will focus on fruits and vegetables. You can make smoothies and add a plant-based protein or tofu to make a complete meal with the all nutrients needed to start the day. Also remember that guava, mulberries, blackberries, nectarines and bananas are fruits with a higher protein content.

If you are having a higher carbohydrate maintenance level with **FOUNDATIONAL NUTRITION Plant-Based,** you can add some of these delicious ideas (below) with power-packed whole grains as long as your activity level is high enough to burn off the excess carbohydrate energy as follows.

• **Steel cut oats**

These are a powerhouse of a plant-based breakfast as they are high in fiber and protein. Because they are a whole grain and are minimally processed, they do take longer to cook than rolled oats. For ease, cook them the day before and store them in the fridge. A quick re-heat and you have breakfast ready. Soaking overnight can also cut their cook time in half.

Another option is to make a double batch while cleaning up from dinner and store them for up to five days in the fridge. You can keep it simple and top with a few teaspoons of maple syrup or - even better - top with fruit, nuts and seeds. Just don't get too heavy-handed with the nuts because even though they are nutritious, they are calorically dense. Try a dairy-free milk to add for creaminess. These kinds of milks have come a long way and the stores are filled with tasty options such as almond milk, coconut milk and hemp milk to name just a few.

- **Toast**

Sounds simple enough, right? Toast can be as basic or exciting as you want to make it. The important thing is starting with a whole-grain base. Try a sprouted grain bread, such as Ezekiel bread, for a nutritious platform on which to build. From there, you can keep it simple and top with a nut butter and thin layer of jam. If you want to branch out, try topping it with some leftover refried beans, avocado and salsa. Other interesting and healthful ideas could be peanut butter and a mashed banana or hummus, jarred roasted red peppers and a few black olives. The options are endless.

- ## Pancakes and muffins

If you have the time to make these at home, there are many delicious plant-based recipes to choose from - the important part here is to make sure they aren't loaded with refined flours and sugars.

- ## Tofu

Yes, you read that right. Tofu for breakfast? That may not sound appealing initially, but tofu can be the base for many delicious scrambles and even a frittata. Leftover eggless tofu egg salad on a whole grain toast can also be quick and delicious option as well.

- ## Chia seed pudding

Sounds strange but, when you combine chia seeds with liquid, they gel and make a tasty and super simple "pudding". Chia seeds are high in Omega-3 fats, fiber and protein and a great way to start your day. Chia seed pudding can be eaten on its own, topped with fruit or added to oatmeal or a smoothie.

- **Smoothies**

These are easy to make plant-based by simply avoiding whey protein or milk.

Lunch

Most people don't have time to make an involved lunch. Try to purposely make more for dinner the night before so you have leftovers for lunch the next day. Another option is to make a few things ahead, such as a bean-based salad, soup or sandwich spread that you can pull out for a quick option. Having chopped vegetables in the fridge to throw together a salad or stir-fry is also helpful.

- **Salad**

This can be easy enough. Use whatever veggies you like and add 1/2 cup of beans in place of the animal protein you would normally add. Lentils, black beans and chickpeas all mix easily into a tasty salad. Try to avoid adding cheese or a dairy-based dressing.

• Sandwiches

Sandwiches are an American lunch staple, but often are loaded with processed meat, cheese and mayonnaise which makes them less than healthy. Plant-based options for sandwiches can include roasted vegetables, bean salads and tofu egg salad. Remember that whole grain bread as your base and consider an open-faced sandwich to keep it a bit lighter.

• Soup

Make a big batch of veggie or lentil soup and eat the leftovers throughout the week or freeze to eat at a later date. Storing leftovers in cup-sized jars makes for easy portion control and portability to grab on the go later.

- **Left-overs**

Store in pre-portioned glass containers or jars in the fridge if you need lunch to take with you to make it that much easier to have accessible healthy options.

Dinner

Ahhh, dinner... you made it through your busy day and now get to sit around the table and relax and enjoy a meal. Sounds lovely but, in reality, may be stressful for many people as they come home late from work or get home after shuttling the kids around to their various activities. Everyone is hungry and wants to eat now. A little prep time and planning can make this meal more enjoyable and a nutritional success.

- **Veggie Burgers**

Homemade veggie burgers are nothing like the cardboard frozen store-bought versions you may have passed in the freezer section of your grocery store. Homemade versions are filled with delicious ingredients such as beans, mushrooms, onions and other vegetables as well as a grain and a binder, such as ground flax seed. Make a double batch and have these waiting for you in the freezer for nights when you are short on time. Remember to also have some whole grain buns in the freezer too! Try to keep the bun size small or use a lettuce wrap if trying to lower your total carbohydrate intake.

• **Soup**

This is a meal that is easy to adapt to your favorite recipe. If you have a family favorite, such as Mexican tortilla soup, simply use vegetable stock instead of chicken broth, leave out the chicken and add black beans. Skip the cheese and sour cream on top and, instead, top with avocado and baked tortilla strips. Easy substitutions can be made to any recipe. Just remember to use vegetable broth and leave out the dairy and animal protein. Soups are a great vehicle to load with veggies and add your protein through beans or tofu. A few ideas will be given below but you can also adapt any of the recipes you find throughout this book.

- Salad

Load up those veggies and greens and top with a healthy dressing and nuts. Try to avoid using dressing loaded with vegetable oil or processed dressings with added preservatives and high in salt and sugar. A 1/2 cup of beans added to your salad will give you a boost of protein and fiber and can convert it into a main dish.

- Pasta

Whole wheat or bean-based pastas can be a part of a nutritious diet when consumed in moderation. Add roasted or sautéed vegetables to add flavor and bulk. Think more veggies than pasta. Spiralizers are a fun gadget that can make "noodles" out of veggies such as zucchini, carrots and even beets. You can skip the pasta all together or combine spaghetti noodles with the spiralized vegetables.

To make plant-based sauces, try adding lentils to a red sauce or a cashew-based béchamel.

- **Stir-fry**

Stir-fries are a great way to get a plate full of veggies. Instead of animal protein, add tofu or beans. Add a 1/2 cup side of a whole grain such as brown rice or quinoa and you are set.

Cauliflower "rice" is another option you could use during Phase I or continue to use as it is quite satisfying. To make it simple, roughly chop cauliflower and then pulse in the food processor into small bits or "rice". Sauté on the stove-top for a few minutes until tender. Many grocery stores now carry cauliflower rice in the refrigerated or freezer sections.

- **Bowls**

"Bowls" are a dish that simply combines vegetables, a whole grain and a plant based- protein and then topped with a flavorful sauce. There are many tasty combinations that can be adjusted according to your food preferences.

- Curry

Curry naturally lends itself to be meat-free as many curries, such as Indian or Thai curry, are already meat-free and often coconut milk based, which makes them dairy-free as well. Indian curries often contain cream or clarified butter so to make a true plant-based version, you may need to make it at home. Try the Thai Coconut Curry Shrimp or That Coconut recipe and substitute tofu for the animal protein.

- Beans

Beans are a wonderful source of protein and fiber and easy to incorporate into your meals. Tacos, soup, dips and salad are a great way to work beans into your diet.

- Tofu

Tofu is not only for Asian foods but can also be added to desserts to achieve a creamy texture and boost protein as well as to dishes such as "eggless" egg salad, frittatas and breakfast scrambles.

Now whether you go full vegan or vegetarian is up to you. It will naturally have a higher carbohydrate content and may be a bit more difficult to get under 150 grams of carbs a day. If you also cut out all grains, this should be easily attainable. You can utilize the recipes and new healthy food sources described to fill in your meal planning and add variety to your nutritional palate. Feel free to start adding days where you go meatless and just see how you feel.

KETOGENIC

Rejuv4LIFE – ADVANCED NUTRITION. This is a good plan to induce maximal weight loss and a good option for restoring insulin sensitivity with Diabetes Type 2 and metabolic syndrome. It may be more difficult to maintain long term due to dietary carbohydrate restrictions, but it can be used for a faster weight loss induction. Success is based on strict adherence to the plan. Carbohydrates can be increased or decreased based on your goals.

KETOGENIC

Let's look at some of the research and what we now know about a low-carb or ketogenic plan.

ADVANCED-KETOGENIC or LOW CARB NUTRITION PLAN:

Overview, the Evidence and How to Start

First of all, this plan follows all the same guidelines as the standard Rejuv4LIFE. Like the standard healthy Rejuv4LIFE plan, healthy protein sources from animals or plants, and healthy fats with no added sugar or processed carbohydrates is the foundation.

Avoiding grains is also helpful due to their high carbohydrate content. The important difference between the **FOUNDATIONAL, ACCELERATED** and **ADVANCED** options is when you get the total daily carbs under 50 grams, your body will start to burn its fat stores and utilize ketones as an energy source instead of carbohydrates. Increasing your "good" fats to help with satiety is important as you decrease your total carbohydrate intake.

In this section, we will detail how to get into a ketosis state if you want the benefits of this lifestyle. It is not a new or totally different diet or meal plan from our standard plan - it is just lowering the total carbs a bit more (mostly by limiting fruit and continuing to avoid grains and legumes) until you start to burn your fat stores. You can add whole grains and legumes back once you hit your body composition goal.

Your approach to nutrition should follow healthy guidelines, but you should approach it without stress or self-judgment. Your food should be enjoyed and, as your carbohydrate intakes increase due to social engagements or indulgence, enjoy them fully and then return to your healthy patterns. There is no failure or judgment. Enjoy the journey and enjoy your healthy delicious foods, knowing you are making choices that will impact your health in a positive way.

This plan is a low-carb, high-fat diet associated with many health benefits. Multiple studies show that this type of plan can assist in weight loss and improve your overall health[95]. Ketogenic plans may also have additional benefits against diabetes, cancer, epilepsy and Alzheimer's disease[96]. It can also be combined with intermittent fasting for optimal results in regard to weight loss and disease prevention and treatment.

What is a Ketogenic or Low Carb Diet?

Upfront, it seems straightforward. It is a nutrition plan that is low in carbohydrates, but there are many options and variables in this sort of lifestyle. What you decide to do and how you approach this on a daily basis will depend on what your goals, lifestyle, activity level, body composition, gender, age and nutritional needs are daily. How low in carbs you go and what your body takes to get the benefits of a low-carb lifestyle will be different for each person, but all types have been shown that this is the most effective way to lose weight, along with experiencing many other health benefits.

The ketogenic diet (often termed *keto*) is a very low-carb, high-fat diet that shares similarities to the Atkins and other low-carb diets. It involves reducing your carbohydrate intake and replacing it with fat. To be considered ketogenic, your total carb intake usually needs to be less than 50 grams a day. Lowering your refined sugars and processed carbs any amount is a step in the right direction.

At first, you may need to keep track of your total carb intake to make sure you are aware of what you are taking in daily. This also helps to problem-solve if you are not losing weight or achieving your health goals from sticking to the plan. I know it sounds a bit counter-intuitive to what you have been taught and heard for a healthy lifestyle but stick with me here and let's examine the evidence a bit more.

The decrease in carbohydrate (sugar) intake puts your body into a metabolic state called ketosis. When this happens, your body becomes amazingly efficient at burning fat for energy instead of the excessive carbohydrates it has been used to using. It also turns fat into ketones in the liver, which can supply energy for the brain and muscle[97]. The main reason for its overall success is that eating this way will cause massive reductions in blood sugar and insulin levels as well as an increase in insulin sensitivity in the body. This, along with the increased ketones, has many additional health benefits[97] which we will detail soon. High insulin with high blood sugar results in storing the extra carbohydrate energy as fat and contributes to the development of chronic disease.

The ketogenic diet (keto) is a low-carb, high-fat diet. It lowers blood sugar and insulin levels and shifts the body's metabolism away from carbs and towards fat and ketones. This shift in energy away from carbs will cause the body to burn fat stores for energy.

DIFFERENT TYPES OF KETOGENIC PLANS

There are several versions of the ketogenic diet, including:

Standard ketogenic diet (SKD): This is a very low-carb, moderate-protein and high-fat diet. It normally

---

includes 75% fat, 20% protein and only 5% carbs[96]. This is the simplest and easiest to follow. You will need to adjust your carbohydrate percentage/grams as it is an individualized amount that is tolerated to stay in a ketosis state.

Cyclical ketogenic diet (CKD): This diet has periods of higher carb re-feeds, such as five ketogenic days followed by two high-carb days. This approach is not as well studied but may be easier to stick with for some people. Others like to go all or nothing, and this can sometimes make it difficult to get back on the wagon. Once you have hit your weight loss goals, this plan works well for maintenance as it allows more opportunity for socializing and indulgence. Again, I would not use this plan is you are plateauing or if a more rapid weight loss is the goal.

Targeted ketogenic diet (TKD): This diet allows you to add carbs around workouts to increase high-intensity workout results and possibly gains. There is some evidence which shows strength training in ketosis can provide energy and strength gains as well.

High-protein ketogenic diet: This plan is similar to a standard ketogenic diet but includes more protein. The ratio is often 60% fat, 35% protein and 5% carbs. This is similar to the Atkins plan. Note that only the standard and high-protein ketogenic diets have been studied extensively. Cyclical or targeted ketogenic diets are more advanced methods, and primarily used by bodybuilders or athletes. What we discuss here applies more to the standard ketogenic diet (SKD). Many of the same principles also apply to the other versions as well.

What is a Carbohydrate?

We covered carbohydrates already, but let's review them and discuss how they need to be approached in a ketogenic plan. In its simplest terms, carbs are a form of energy. They are one of three macronutrients - protein, fat and carbohydrates. Out of the three, fat is the slowest-burning macronutrient (meaning it takes the longest to be broken down and utilized by the body), followed by protein and then carbs. Carbs are fast-burning fuel for the body. They naturally are found in foods like sugars, starches and fiber. Carbs are found in higher amounts in vegetables, fruits, grains and processed foods, such as breads, pastas and baked goods.

A very important fact is that not all carbohydrates are created equal and they all have different effects once ingested. Vegetables and high-fiber fruits are incredibly nutritious and are almost 100% carbohydrate. These are known as *complex carbohydrates*. Whole grains are also complex carbohydrates but offer less nutritional value than vegetables and fruits. *Simple carbohydrates* are refined carbs. This means that they have had their fiber, vitamins and minerals largely stripped through processing. Simple carbs have been shown to contribute to a variety of diseases such as Diabetes Type 2, obesity and heart disease.

Let's look at the different carbohydrate intake levels.

Simply lowering your refined carbohydrates and sugar will be a giant step in the right direction. It is difficult for some people to go from 300-400 grams a day to 30 grams a day without significant cravings, mental fog and irritability. This is the "keto flu" and is short-lived but can affect some people with the transition.

Start by simply cutting out sugars, then grains and see how you feel. Continue to decrease you refined carbohydrate intake until you are at a level you can sustain. If weight loss is part of your goal, it will be important to get to a level (usually around 30-50 grams or less) where you are in a state of fat-burning and are using ketones as an energy source to get all the health benefits of low-carb living. Also remember that low-carb is NOT no carb. You will be eating an abundance of healthy nuts, vegetables and some fruits that themselves have carbs and many health benefits.

- **>150 grams of carbs - This is the Standard American Diet (SAD).** The ironic thing is that major health authorities are still recommending a shocking 225-325 grams a day, which is around 45 to 60% of all our calories consumed. No one, except an elite athlete working out hours a day, would be able to not gain weight with this carb consumption. This is why the average American is gaining around 1.5 pounds a year. Over 10 years, you have that 15-pound weight gain. With this many carbs, your body is in a constant state of insulin chasing the carbohydrate boluses.

The constant elevation of blood sugar causes two basic problems. First, the sugar spikes will cause immediate micro-damage and glycosylation of the tissues which can be accumulative with repetitive spikes. This leads to heart, brain, kidney and neurologic disease over time.
Next, the elevation of sugars will increase triglycerides and also be stored as fat by the constantly high insulin. This is NOT a

recommended option for disease prevention or weight loss. It may be ok for athletes who are putting in hours of training a day. Even in that case, healthy fruit and vegetables sources would be the fuel of choice.

- **100-150 grams of carbs - PHASE 2 Rejuv4LIFE.** This is certainly the most moderate way of adopting the low-carb diet and could be a good place to start. Simply excluding refined grains and sugar will largely get you to this point and will go a long way in supporting overall health and helping you to maintain your current weight, and maybe lose a bit. This is about cutting out sugar, candy, breads and pastas, and soda. If you are a very active person, this may be an option, but it will not result in very rapid weight loss as the body still may not dive into its fat stores for energy. With this option, you can still eat as many vegetables as you'd like, moderate amounts of fruit (about two pieces per day), and some starchy vegetables, such as sweet potatoes and winter squash.

Overall, it is a good idea to avoid all grains if optimal health and any weight loss is desirable. For most healthy active individuals, this is a good balance where you are often in a "dual fuel" mode. During times of increased exercise, less carbohydrate intake or short fasting intervals, you may burn some fat stores and utilize ketones for energy.

- **50-100 grams of carbs - PHASE 1 Rejuv4LIFE.** This option is more restrictive but will allow you to lose weight more easily, rapidly averaging about 1-2 pounds per week. It still allows for some carbohydrates (especially at the top end of the range), such as most vegetables and 1-2 pieces of high-fiber fruits per day, but you will have to limit starchy carbohydrates and refrain from grains and processed carbohydrates if you want to continue to lose body fat.

- **Under 30-50 grams of carbs - Rejuv4Life KETO-Accelerated weight loss plan.** This level of carbohydrate intake is what is truly considered a ketogenic diet. It is a good option for those needing to lose significant amounts of weight and also for those with diabetes and other metabolic diseases who want to reset their insulin metabolism to become more sensitive. To get into ketosis, your diet must cross a sustained threshold of high fat (around 70% of your calories), moderate protein (25%), and low amounts of carbohydrates (5%). Some people can tolerate a higher percentage of carbs. Everyone is different and sometimes we need to test for the presence of ketones to assure we are truly in ketosis. Eating under 30 grams (and some health authorities would say under 50) is where the most impressive benefits of the low-carb lifestyle start to show up. If you are overweight or obese, and want to lose weight safely and quickly, this is a good option for you.

Remember that you can slowly lower your carbohydrate intake over a few weeks to get to this point. Consuming under 30-50 grams of carbs a day will put your body into a state of ketosis. This is a state where your body will switch the brain and muscles' source of energy from glucose (carbs) to ketones (from fat stores). Using fat for energy and having ketones in the blood will naturally lower your appetite, leading to weight loss.

You can eat protein from meats, vegetables and dairy, healthy fats, low-carbohydrate vegetables, smaller amounts of low-carb fruits and some also trace carbohydrates found in foods like nuts, seeds and avocados. Starchy vegetables like corn, parsnips, green peas, potatoes, pumpkins, winter squash and yams all fall into this category and should be avoided due to their higher carbohydrate content.

A good health benefit of this plan is that you will end up eating a lot of non-starchy veggies, which have great health benefits in more ways than just weight loss. Once you have met your goals, you can maintain your weight while continuing to fuel your body with healthy whole foods by increasing your healthy carbohydrates. This way you will be using the "dual fuel" method of some carbs for energy for the muscles and brain as well as well as occasionally tapping into the fat stores and utilizing ketones. It is ok to have flexibility - try not to be so restrictive that you lose the enjoyment of food and social interaction.

This type of lifestyle is restrictive only on decreasing your total carb intake. It is not a carb elimination. The challenge is our eating patterns, social habits and tastes have become so accustomed to a high carbohydrate-based diet. Our bodies do not need carbs to function. In fact, too many carbs - which all become sugar in our body - can be damaging.

It is about retraining our palates to enjoy and, yes, even crave other types of food. You will have to make conscious decisions to change your patterns. Just like becoming a vegetarian or vegan can be as "restrictive", if you are currently a meat and dairy eater, this plan will take an adjustment.

Many find that, once they get accustomed to less carbs, they feel better physically and mentally, and it no longer becomes a restriction. It actually turns into a liberation. You are liberated in that you are now able to lose weight, gain energy and become healthy. You are free from the constant battle of always dieting and feeling guilty when all the weight comes back.

Many people have no problem cutting out meat, dairy, or gluten because it's socially acceptable, but eating more fat and fewer carbs is not a norm, although it is gaining much more popularity and acceptance over the last few years. For those who do not feel they can cut out carbs because they "*do not have the will power*", I challenge you to truly try a higher-fat diet and decrease carbs. It comes naturally over time. I'm not saying it is easy or without challenges but, over time, those cravings get less and less and - sometimes - go away altogether once your body is fueled and fulfilled. It is not a willpower problem but that sugar / carb cravings can also be triggered by stress, lack of sleep, mindless eating, or other nutritional or hormonal deficiencies or imbalances that need to be addressed.

A ketogenic, or high-fat low-carb way of eating can be just as varied and tasteful as any other nutrition plan. In fact, you can eat many whole, rich, healthy foods that you once avoided because of the fat content. Remember, we are finding that fat doesn't make you fat. It is the insulin response to a high carbohydrate / sugar load that stimulates your body to store all that extra energy as fat for future use.

Also, keep in mind that this is not a free-for-all diet plan where you can have more fats, thinking you will lose weight. If you do not decrease your insulin through decreasing total carbohydrate consumption, the fat you eat will indeed make you fat. You can NOT have high-fat and high-carb, or the carbs will tell your body to spike insulin and store it ALL as fat.

You need to relearn how to cook, as discussed in the plant-based section. What is cool is that a keto diet can also be plant-based. In fact, all nutrition plans should have a healthy plant base to them. Green leafy vegetables and cruciferous vegetable should always fill the bulk of your plate. Those foods are packed with water, phytonutrients and fiber and low in calories and carbohydrates for the room they take up on your plate. It is more difficult to be strict vegan, but it can still be a plant-focused approach with sensible meat and dairy consumption. Skipping meat a few days a week is easy as is making sure that the meats you do consume are **high-quality, pasture grass-fed and organic to negate any negative effects from the high grain-fed, hormone- and antibiotic-pumped mass-produced animal protein sources.** This is a point to emphasize - that it is not a free-for-all meat extravaganza. You need to be able to control what the animals you consume are eating. What they eat will affect your health as well.

A large part of changing your way of life and diet is re-learning to cook, which takes time and getting back in the kitchen and grocery store as a family, but you and your family are worth it. There are quick and easy meals to make just as with other plans. I can make many tasty, nutritious low-carb meals that the entire family is excited about in under 30 minutes, especially with some meal prep and planning.

How to Choose Your Plan

The option above that is best for you is the one you can stick to and gain health benefits. The lower amount of refined carbohydrates and sugar you can get to, the more health benefits and the easier it will be to obtain your ideal body composition. It will take some adjustment (mentally and physically), so give it some time before deciding that it's not right for you, or that you need to up your carb intake. Start with a higher carb count and slowly decrease as you get used to it and your taste buds have less sugar cravings.

Are All Carbs "BAD"?

The answer is a definite "no." With a low-carb diet, you will naturally eliminate the "bad" carbs, such as refined flour in the form of bread, pasta and baked goods and all refined sugar. You will also likely eat far more "good" carbs, such as dark, leafy greens and other non-starchy vegetables, and the starchy foods you do eat will come from nutrient-dense sources such as sweet potatoes, winter squashes and fruits.

What Are the Benefits of a Low-Carb Lifestyle?

The secret to success with such a lifestyle change starts with the motivation to achieve a state of health and well-being that enables you to enjoy the benefits of a healthy body and mind. Once your mind is committed, the body will follow and, after you feel the changes in your energy, mind and body, it will fuel you to continue your journey to health and well-being.

Will a Ketogenic Lifestyle Can Help Me Lose Weight?

A ketogenic diet is an effective way to lose weight and, more specifically, body fat. It also lowers risk factors for many other chronic diseases[98]. Research reveals that the ketogenic diet is far superior to the often-recommended low-fat diet[99].

An added benefit is that it is more filling, so you can lose weight without counting calories or tracking your food. This is due to the fact that you feel full longer and have fewer cravings[100]. One study found that people on a ketogenic diet lost 2.2 times more weight than those on a calorie-restricted low-fat diet. Triglyceride and HDL cholesterol levels also improved. Another study found that participants on the ketogenic diet lost three times more weight than those on the Diabetes U.K.'s recommended diet[101].

There are several reasons why a ketogenic diet is proving superior to a low-fat diet. One is the increased fat intake, which provides numerous benefits. The increased ketones, lowered blood sugar levels and improved insulin sensitivity may also contribute to the success rates and superior outcomes[102].

A ketogenic diet can help you lose much more weight than the standard low-fat or calorie-restricted diet. This often happens without hunger as fat can make us feel full longer. Carbohydrates tend to have a hunger-rebound effect secondary to insulin and blood sugar spikes and troughs. More detailed information to come.

HEALTH BENEFITS WITH A KETOGENIC PLAN

Few things are as well-established in nutrition science as the immense health benefits of low-carb and ketogenic diets. Following are some of the health benefits that may help motivate you to make lifestyle changes.

1. Diabetes, Prediabetes and Metabolic Syndrome. Diabetes is defined by changes in metabolism, high blood sugar and impaired insulin function (elevated insulin levels and decreased insulin sensitivity). The ketogenic diet can help you lose excess body fat and especially abdominal fat, which is closely linked to Diabetes Type 2, prediabetes and metabolic syndrome as well as cardiovascular disease. [103] One study found that the ketogenic diet improved insulin sensitivity by a massive 75%[104]. Medications are often prescribed for diabetes in an attempt to improve insulin sensitivity.

Another study in patients with Diabetes Type 2 discovered that seven of the 21 participants were able to stop all diabetes medications because of the effectiveness of this type of lifestyle[103]. Imagine the healthcare savings with less medications, strokes, heart attacks, hospital admissions and medical office visits. In yet another study, the ketogenic group lost 24.4 lbs (11.1 kg), compared to 15.2 lbs (6.9 kg) in the higher-carb group. This is an important benefit when considering the relationship between weight/body fat and Diabetes Type 2. Furthermore, 95.2% of the ketogenic group was also able to stop or reduce diabetes medication, compared to 62% in the higher-carb group. Those are great stats in favor of a ketogenic plan for diabetes, metabolic syndrome and insulin sensitivity.

2. **Appetite** (in a good way). When people cut carbs, their appetite tends to go down and they often end up eating much fewer calories without trying.

3. **Weight Loss**. Almost without exception, low-carb diets lead to more weight loss than the diets they are compared to, especially in the first six months. A large percentage of the fat lost on low-carb diets tends to come from the harmful fat in the abdominal cavity that is known to cause serious metabolic problems.

4. **Triglycerides Tend to Go Way Down.** Low-carb diets are very effective at lowering blood triglycerides, which are fat molecules in the blood and a well-known risk factor for heart disease. Triglycerides correlate with body insulin and blood sugar levels. So as these

levels drop, it is a good sign that your insulin is also decreasing. We addressed all the problems with chronically high insulin and blood sugar levels earlier.

5. Increased Levels of HDL (the "Good") Cholesterol. Low-carb diets tend to be high in fat, which leads to an impressive increase in blood levels of HDL, often referred to as the "good" cholesterol. A note on LDL cholesterol with a ketogenic plan: at first, the LDL level looks to increase temporarily on a low-carb, high-fat nutrition plan but, when analyzed further, the LDL that increases is the large "fluffy" LDL which do not correlate with heart disease. The very small LDL that can wedge into arterial walls and start the cascade leading to heart disease and heart attack actually go down with a sustained low-carb, higher-fat lifestyle.

This analysis takes more than the standard lipid panel done in most doctors' offices. If adopting a low-carb/higher-fat lifestyle, we recommend getting a more in-depth panel done to evaluate this. Also, you can take a standard panel and look at your triglyceride to HDL ratio (TG:HDL). This ratio has been studied and does correlate directly with heart disease risk. Your goal is to get your TG down and your HDL up. A ratio of 2:1 is ideal and, if getting over 5:1, your risk of heart disease is defiantly going up - this is a good indicator for you to dial in your lifestyle with a less-carb, higher-fat approach to abate that looming heart attack or stroke that is directly related to your lifestyle. Cholesterol medications are not the answer, but changing your lifestyle is!

6. Blood Pressure Tends to Go Down. Studies show that reducing carbs leads to a significant reduction in blood pressure, which should lead to a reduced risk of many common diseases.

7. Metabolic Syndrome. Metabolic syndrome is a medical condition that is highly associated with the risk of diabetes and heart disease. It is actually a collection of symptoms:

- Abdominal obesity
- Elevated blood pressure

- Elevated fasting blood sugar levels
- High triglycerides
- Low HDL levels

Low-carb diets effectively reverse all five of these key symptoms of metabolic syndrome, a serious condition known to predispose people to heart disease and Diabetes Type 2.

8. LDL Cholesterol. When you eat a low-carb diet, your LDL particles change from small (bad) LDL to large LDL - which is benign. Cutting carbs may also reduce the number of LDL particles floating around in the bloodstream.

9. Several Brain Disorders. In many cases, this diet can cure children of **epilepsy**. In one study, over half of children on a ketogenic diet had a greater than 50% reduction in seizures. 16% of the children became seizure free[105]. Very low-carb/ketogenic diets are now being studied for other brain disorders as well, including **Alzheimer's** disease and **Parkinson's** disease.

10. Polycystic ovary syndrome: The ketogenic diet can help reduce insulin levels, which may play a key role in polycystic ovary syndrome[103].

11. Cancer: The diet is currently being used to treat several types of cancer and slow tumor growth[106].

12. Brain injuries: One animal study found that the diet can reduce concussions and aid recovery after brain injury[107]. More research needs to be done to confirm benefit in the human population.

13. Other benefits: Better sleep, mood, skin and mental clarity.

Changing your eating habits can be difficult at first. Some people do well slowly transitioning to this lifestyle while others like to make the shift quickly. There is no perfect way to transition so do whatever feels easiest for you. You will be surprised once you make the mental shift how well you will feel once you are adapted in burning fat for energy. Following are lists of **FOODS TO AVOID** and **FOODS TO ENJOY**.

FOODS TO AVOID

In short, any food that is high in carbs and, especially, a high glycemic index should be limited. No foods with added sugar, syrups, molasses, etc. Here is a list of foods that need to be reduced or eliminated on a ketogenic diet:

- **Sugary foods:** Soda, fruit juice, smoothies, cake, ice cream, candy, etc.
- **Grains or starches:** Wheat-based products, rice, pasta, cereal, etc.
- **Fruit:** Avoid high glycemic index fruits. Will show specific fruits later.
- **Beans or legumes:** Peas, kidney beans, lentils, chickpeas, etc.
- **Root vegetables and tubers:** Potatoes, sweet potatoes, carrots, parsnips, etc.

- **Low-fat or diet products:** These are highly processed and often high in carbs.
- **Some condiments or sauces:** These often contain sugar and unhealthy fat.
- **Unhealthy fat:** Limit your intake of processed vegetable oils, mayonnaise, etc.
- **Alcohol:** Due to its carb content, many alcoholic beverages can throw you out of ketosis.
- **Sugar-free diet foods:** These are often high in sugar alcohols, which can affect ketone levels in some cases. These foods also tend to be highly processed.

In general, avoid carb-based foods like grains, sugars, legumes, rice, potatoes, candy, juice and even most fruits.

FOODS TO ENJOY

You should base the majority of your meals around these foods. Much more detail will be given on the food choices later in the chapter. An overview is presented here.

Low-carb veggies: Most green veggies, including:
- Broccoli
- Cauliflower
- Tomatoes
- Onion
- Brussels sprouts
- Kale and swiss chard
- Cabbage
- Cucumber
- Eggplant
- Bell peppers
- Asparagus
- Mushrooms
- Green beans
- Celery
- Spinach

Low-carb Fruits: (These are high in fiber and have almost no effect on Insulin.)
- Grapefruit
- Lemons
- Oranges
- Strawberries
- Raspberries
- Apricots
- Kiwi

Meat: Meat should be a side dish or garnish but should not always be your main course. Remember that too much protein will cause an insulin spike and impair fat-burning and ketosis. Enough evidence points to the over-consumption of meat products having negative outcomes on our health. With meat and health outcomes, it could be the source of the meat (grass-fed vs. grain-fed), how the meat is cooked (over-cooked with AGEs) and / or whether hormones and antibiotics were added to their diet. Chicken, turkey and fish/seafood is preferred over larger animals. Red meat (which includes pork, beef and lamb) and processed meats (which include salami, bacon, and other meats like sausages and hot dogs) should be consumed less frequently due to associations with cancer.

The International Agency for Research on Cancer (IAFC) is a group of international experts who reviewed over 800 studies. They concluded that processed meat has been classified as a 'definite' cause of cancer and red meat is a 'probable' cause.

Some of the speculated reasons is the conversion in the gut of the red pigment from blood in the meat to N-nitroso compounds. These compounds have been found to damage the cells that line the bowel and increase the risk of cell proliferation and cancer in the bowel.

Also compounding the risk is that processed red meats contain nitrate preservatives that increase N-nitroso compounds in the gut. Furthermore, cooking the meat at high temperatures (browning) generates chemicals from the cooking process that increase the risk of cancer. The evidence so far suggests that it's probably the processing of the meat, or chemicals naturally present within it, along with the cooking process that increases cancer risk.

For all meats, focus on free-range, chemical- and nitrate-free and organic when possible. This will decrease the cancer risks associated with it. Also, do not overcook and dark-brown the meat during the cooking process.

For seafood/fish, focus on wild vs. farm-raised. These decisions will increase your omega-3 fats. Non-grass/range animals and farm fish are fed mostly high omega-6 fatty acid corn and grains. You may consider limiting processed meat that carries a risk for colon cancer. If you are used to consuming a lot of red meat, a good place to start is having red meat twice a week and decreasing your consumption from there as you see able.

Here is what the National Institute for Health and the National Cancer Institute have to say about how meat is cooked and its relationship to cancer.

What are heterocyclic amines and polycyclic aromatic hydrocarbons, and how are they formed in cooked meats?

Heterocyclic amines (HCAs) and polycyclic aromatic hydrocarbons (PAHs) are chemicals formed when muscle meat, including beef, pork, fish, or poultry, is cooked using high-temperature methods, such as pan frying or grilling directly over an open flame[1]. In laboratory experiments, HCAs and PAHs have been found to be mutagenic—that is, they cause changes in DNA that may increase the risk of cancer.

HCAs are formed when amino acids (the building blocks of proteins), sugars, and creatinine (substances found in muscle) react at high temperatures. PAHs are formed when fat and juices from meat grilled directly over a heated surface or open fire drip onto the surface or fire, causing flames and smoke. The smoke contains PAHs that then adhere to the surface of the meat. PAHs can also be formed during other food preparation processes, such as smoking of meats[1].

HCAs are not found in significant amounts in foods other than meat cooked at high temperatures. PAHs can be found in other smoked foods, as well as in cigarette smoke and car exhaust fumes.

What factors influence the formation of HCA and PAH in cooked meats?

The formation of HCAs and PAHs varies by meat type, cooking method, and "doneness" level (rare, medium, or well-done). Whatever the type of meat, however, meats cooked at high temperatures, especially above 300 °F (as in grilling or pan frying), or that are cooked for a long time tend to form more HCAs. For example, well-done, grilled, or barbecued chicken and steak all have high concentrations of HCAs. Cooking methods that expose meat to smoke contribute to PAH formation [2].

HCAs and PAHs become capable of damaging DNA only after they are metabolized by specific enzymes in the body, a process called "bioactivation." Studies have found that the activity of these enzymes, which can differ among people, may be relevant to the cancer risks associated with exposure to these compounds [3-9].

What evidence is there that HCAs and PAHs in cooked meats may increase cancer risk?

Studies have shown that exposure to HCAs and PAHs can cause cancer in animal models [10]. In many experiments, rodents fed a diet supplemented with HCAs developed tumors of the breast, colon, liver, skin, lung, prostate, and other organs [11-16]. Rodents fed PAHs also developed cancers, including leukemia and tumors of the gastrointestinal tract and lungs [17]. However, the doses of HCAs and PAHs used in these studies were very high—equivalent to thousands of times the doses that a person would consume in a normal diet.

Population studies have not established a definitive link between HCA and PAH exposure from cooked meats and cancer in humans. One difficulty with conducting such studies is that it can be difficult to determine the exact level of HCA and/or PAH exposure a person gets from cooked meats. Although dietary questionnaires can provide good estimates, they may not capture all the detail about cooking techniques that is necessary to determine HCA and PAH exposure levels.

In addition, individual variation in the activity of enzymes that metabolize HCAs and PAHs may result in exposure differences, even among people who ingest (take in) the same amount of these compounds. Also, people may have been exposed to PAHs from other environmental sources, not just food.

Numerous epidemiologic studies have used detailed questionnaires to examine participants' meat consumption and cooking methods[18]. Researchers found that high consumption of well-done, fried, or barbecued meats was associated with increased risks of colorectal[19-21], pancreatic[21-23], and prostate [24-25] cancer. However, other studies have found no association with risks of colorectal [26] or prostate[27] cancer.

In 2015, an independent panel of experts convened by the International Agency for Research on Cancer (IARC) determined consumption of red meat to be "probably carcinogenic to humans" (Group 2A), based largely on data from the epidemiologic studies and on the strong evidence from mechanistic studies. However, IARC did not conclude that HCAs and PAHs were associated with cancer incidence.

Are there ways to reduce HCA and PAH formation in cooked meats?

Even though no specific guidelines for HCA/PAH consumption exist, concerned individuals can reduce their exposure by using several cooking methods:

- *Avoiding direct exposure of meat to an open flame or a hot metal surface and avoiding prolonged cooking times (especially at high temperatures) can help reduce HCA and PAH formation[29].*
- *Using a microwave oven to cook meat prior to exposure to high temperatures can also substantially reduce HCA formation by reducing the time that meat must be in contact with high heat to finish cooking [29].*
- *Continuously turning meat over on a high heat source can substantially reduce HCA formation compared with just leaving the meat on the heat source without flipping it often[29].*

- *Removing charred portions of meat and refraining from using gravy made from meat drippings can also reduce HCA and PAH exposure[29].*

It is good to be informed on the current research so you can make educated decisions on the amount of meat, the type of meat you choose and how you cook your meat. Remember from the plant-based section that there are plenty of good non-meat protein and fat sources with which to supplement your diet. A meat-free day may be good for you and the environment.

Fatty fish: Such as salmon, trout, tuna and mackerel. (*Wild-caught preferable*).

Eggs: Look for pastured or omega-3 whole eggs (*organic free range is ideal containing more omega-3 and less omega-6*).

Butter and cream: Look for grass-fed when possible (*Ghee is an Indian butter - a great option and tastes amazing*).

Cheese: Unprocessed cheese (cheddar, goat, cream, blue or mozzarella).

Vegan and Vegetarian Options: See special section below.

Nuts and seeds: Almonds, walnuts, flaxseeds, pumpkin seeds, chia seeds, etc. (*Nut butters are a good option as well as long as no sugar is added for flavor*)

Healthy oils: Primarily extra virgin olive oil, coconut oil and avocado oil. Refer to our discussion on healthy fats for more information on what oils and fats to be consuming. We will go into more detail in a bit as well.

Remember to avoid vegetable oils as well as trans fats and hydrogenation oils. MCT (medium-chain triglyceride) oils are great as they are easily digested and aid in getting into ketosis. You can get MCTs from whole foods - here's a list of MCTs in foods, as a percentage of total fats:

- Coconut oil: 15%
- Palm kernel oil: 7.9%
- Cheese (if you tolerate dairy): 7.3%
- Butter: 6.8%
- Milk: 6.9%
- Yogurt: 6.6%

Avocados (Actually a fruit) Whole avocados or freshly made guacamole. High in good fat.

Olives: (Actually a fruit)

Condiments: You can use salt, pepper and various healthy herbs and spices. (Tabasco and other hot sauces are great if no sugar on the label.)

It is best to base your diet mostly on whole, single ingredient foods. A complete list of foods, spices and condiments will be detailed below. Again, the majority of your diet should be from whole foods such as healthy meat choices, fish, eggs, butter, nuts, healthy vegetarian protein and fat choices, healthy oils, avocados and plenty of low-carb veggies. More detailed food information below.

If you have decided that this is something you would like to try to see if you can enjoy all the benefits of a fit body, sharp mind and decrease or eliminate chronic disease, then dive in and start your journey.

GETTING STARTED

First, you'll want to make sure you're prepared before your low-carb lifestyle overhaul. This includes stocking your kitchen with the right foods and donating those that do not fit this plan and may throw you off your health train. You also need to set the stage mentally to overcome the initial challenges that can occur during any type of transition.

- **Physical Challenges**

As with any dietary change, switching to a low-carb model of eating can take a few days to get used to on

---

a number of levels. Physically, you may experience symptoms such as a foggy brain, fatigue, increased hunger, cravings and irritability. You may be a bit "hangry". Be aware this may happen and plan for it - let those around you know what you are doing so they can understand. You could even ask them to join you on the journey.

This is completely normal and is simply your body adjusting to switching its fuel source from carbs to fat. Some health experts even refer to this as the "low carb flu," but the good news is it will soon pass, and abundant energy is around the corner. During the "induction" period while you are decreasing your carb intake and letting your body switch to burning fat, take it easy. Rest and plan some fun, relaxing down time. You might cut down your workout intensity and, instead, try some soothing yoga, walking or meditation. Remember, if this transition period is tough on you, ease into your low-carb lifestyle with several days of the **FOUNDATIONAL NUTRITION** approach by consuming 100-150 carbs, and then work your way down.

- **Mental, Emotional and Social Challenges**

Regrettably, most eating today is high-carb, high-sugar from the office breakroom to the birthday party or even the "let's meet for coffee" outing with friends. This approach is a totally different way to eat and consume your nutrients so, in public, you might feel a bit mentally, emotionally and socially snubbed at first. Share with your friends and family why you are taking on this dietary change, and all the benefits. They might even want a change in their health as well and decide to join you. But be prepared for funny looks and some interesting conversations with those around you. Most importantly, remember you are making a decision to become healthy and have life a zest-filled life and THAT is something to be proud of with your goals always in mind. Also, see below for how to eat out on the low-carb diet, as that can make eating out much less stressful.

Get the Kitchen Ready

It is important to get your kitchen ready to help ensure success with the transition from a carb-dominant lifestyle. First, it is helpful to have the right tools. A vegetable spiralizer is great to have as you can make "pasta" from zucchini and other vegetables. A small food processor or blender enables you to make cauliflower rice to be consumed as a substitute for pastas and rice. Also, a short shopping list can be helpful to get started with some keto staples. Here is a basic start list:

- Beef, Pork or Lamb (if you decide to include red meat - organic and free-range)
- Chicken
- Seafood-Fish or Shrimp
- Eggs (free-range organic)
- Butter and/or ghee (Free-range grass-fed)
- Virgin coconut oil
- Extra-virgin olive oil
- Cheese (white cheeses)

- Plain Greek yogurt (no sugar)
- Berries (strawberries are especially low-carb)
- Olives
- Nuts
- Fresh and frozen vegetables
- Salsa
- Himalayan Pink or Celtic Sea Salt
- Pepper
- Mustards
- Garlic
- Vinegar

Clear the kitchen of foods that will tempt you or throw you off track. See **FOODS TO AVOID**.

Now that you are on your way and committed to make this lifestyle change, there are a few more things to know about and be prepared for as follows.

Assessing Your Progress

On your journey, there are a few things you can do to track your progress. Your weight will drop on the scale as you dial in your nutrition plan, but pounds are not the only number to monitor. Your initial poundage lost is usually water weight over the first week or two.

As you persist with your changes and continue to decrease your carb consumption, you will begin to tap into your fat stores. That is when it gets fun. Your lean muscle mass should stay while the fat melts away. During this time, you and others should notice a change in body composition. This is an excellent marker of headway, and the easiest way to gauge this is by observing how your clothes fit. Your pants should become looser as you lose fat from the abdominal area and from around your internal organs.

Body measurements like your waist and hip circumference using a tape measure can also be tracked. This can also be done with a personal trainer or other healthcare professional who may have the ability to track your actual body fat percentage. Get a before picture and take pictures as you go to show the progress you are making. You will hear from friends and those around you about the difference they are noticing as you lose the unwanted fat.

When tracking your body weight, weigh yourself at the same time each day (the morning is the best and most consistent time); try to do this once a week. Getting some blood internal markers like fasting cholesterol, blood sugar and insulin levels can be helpful to monitor your progress. Get some basic lab work done before you start so you can see where you are at and then monitor your progress as you move forward with your low-carb lifestyle.

At Rejuv, we do a BioSCORE at the beginning your journey and use it to monitor your progress. It consists of both external measurements and internal blood parameters that will show, in detail, the healthy changes occurring in your body.

Am I in Ketosis? Are my carbohydrates low enough to tap into my fat stores?

To gain all the benefits of this lifestyle, you need to be in ketosis. Ketosis is a change in your metabolism where you no longer are burning carbs as your main fuel source, but you are instead utilizing your fat stores. If you are looking to get the ultimate benefits from your low-carb plan, being in ketosis and burning fat as your energy fuel will be important. Again, this will usually occur when you eat less than 50 (and definitely less than 30) carbs total per day. Between 50 and 100 grams a day, you will most likely be burning fat and ketones intermittently but will not see as rapid a decrease in weight loss as a more carb restricted approach. This diet will be high in healthy fats, moderate in protein and very low in carbohydrates.

After sustaining this for a few days to weeks, your body will begin the convert your fat stores into ketone bodies that will then give energy to your brain and muscles. The body becomes adapted to utilize ketones as an energy source and you are no longer dependent on carbohydrates or sugars as your primary fuel source. This state is call being **KETO-ADAPTED**.

Some professionals recommend checking ketone levels to confirm you are in ketosis and burning your fat stores, and some just say to go on how you feel. Also, the longer you are in ketosis, and become keto-adapted, you may notice continued improvements and be better able to tell when you are not utilizing ketones. Knowing if you are utilizing ketones or not is helpful in determining the amount of carbohydrates you can consume and still be utilizing your fat stores for energy.

Once you are keto-adapted, which may take between three weeks to three months, you can start to introduce different carbs (a few berries, sweet potatoes, but still no grains, gluten, refined carbs, or sugar) and see how you feel and how your body responds. The longer you are in ketosis, the more flexibility you will have in tolerating variations in your diet like more carbohydrates or proteins. This is where you can individualize your plan. Many factors play a role; some people can still be in ketosis with having 60% fat, so more carbs and protein, while others may need to stay in the 70-80% fat range.

So how do you know if you are in ketosis? There is urine, blood, and breathalyzer ketone testing that will let you know if you are burning your fat stores for energy. Urine strips are the cheapest and many people will start with these, but they lack accuracy and do not tell us if your body is actually utilizing the ketones for energy. It just tells us that you are excreting a ketone bi-product acetoacetate (AcAc). Urine strips only check acetoacetate (AcAc).

Oversimplifying a complicated process, ketones are made of beta-hydroxybutyrate (BOHB) and AcAc with BOHB being the predominant form, usually in a 4:1 ratio. Testing with urine strips have not been closely correlated with blood tests. Some theorize as you become more fat-adapted, your body is able to better utilize ketones, so you have less "extra" that is being lost in urine through the kidneys. This means you can be in ketosis, but the urine strips will be negative. Some people who have a lot of extra fat storage will continue to test positive for a while, but you will not know unless you confirm with another test like a blood test.

A fingerstick blood test is the best test for now. Breathalyzers are being analyzed and are showing good promise. You can buy a ketometer with ketone strips and lancets online. This is similar to a diabetic checking their blood sugars but is a different test strip specific for ketones. There are some meters that will do both blood sugar and ketones. I think it is worthwhile checking the first few weeks to few months to make sure you are actually in ketosis as many times we are not as good with our food intake as we think. It will help you dial in your nutrition and get you to your goals faster.

Also, many foods have hidden carbs in them that we may not be aware we are consuming. Artificial sweeteners and sugar alcohols may throw some people out of ketosis, so it can be worthwhile checking. If you are not getting the results you want or are expecting, you need to know if you are truly in ketosis. Most experts feel that a range of 0.5-3 millimolar seems to be optimal. Having ketones in this level is safe.

Nutritional ketosis is very different from diabetic ketoacidosis. Nutritional ketosis is having low level ketones in your blood with normal a blood ph at rest, normal blood glucose, and low insulin levels. Keto-acidosis is very high ketone levels (more than 10x than with nutritional ketosis), high blood sugars, and minimal insulin present to lower your blood sugar levels. If you are not diabetic, it is essentially impossible to get into a dangerous level of ketoacidosis. Remember the morning time is when your ketones are at their lowest and tend to spike after workouts or fasting.

If you are feeling good and are losing weight, monitoring is not that important, but if you are just starting out and not sure if you dialed in enough with your carbohydrate lowering, monitoring can be very helpful to give you feedback on whether you are truly starting to tap into your fat stores. Most people, once they are in a state of using ketones for energy, just track their progress with their body composition and how well they feel.

At the beginning of this conversion, you may feel a little sluggish and have some carb and sugar cravings. The good news is that studies once your body is keto-adapted, you will have less cravings and a decrease in hunger as your body is adapted to burning its fat stores for energy. It will not always be easy, and you should be prepared to work through the difficulties that will arise any time you make a lifestyle change. Stay persistent and be prepared for road blocks.

Road Blocks

Barriers and road blocks will develop but, if you are mentally and physically primed for them, they will less likely throw you off track. Once again, the "keto flu" occurs early in the process and includes nausea, sleep difficulties, carb and sugar cravings, fatigue and digestive issues. The ketogenic process cuts out many processed sources of carbohydrates that also once gave you many electrolytes as well. The flu-like symptoms are usually the lack of electrolytes like sodium, potassium and magnesium. This is one element that you will want to supplement with this plan.

Taking a simple electrolyte supplement can help (essentially, a powder that can be added to your water and tastes great). Also, take it easy and give your body the rest it needs during the transition. Decrease your stressors, including maybe even the intensity of your workouts for a few days, and rest assured that is only temporary. Don't let it derail you. This stage doesn't seem happen to everyone and a slower transition to a lower carb intake may decrease it. Sleep is critical. Poor sleep, even just one night, will increase your hunger hormone ghrelin and make you crave more food in the morning. You will be more prone to eat junk food and processed carbs and sugar with inadequate sleep.

Have your plan ready with the number of carbs you will shoot for and have your shopping list ready - review different recipes and food prep options ahead of jumping on the keto train. Know your **FOODS TO AVOID** and **FOODS TO ENJOY** lists well so you can stock up on the delicious foods you will consume as you make the change. Get your low-carb, higher-fat staples, such as meat, fish, eggs, raw cheese, nuts and seeds, avocado, olive and coconut oil, grass-fed butter and/or ghee. Supplements can be helpful as well; we will expand on this later.

Remember, while you are preparing for this, low-carb does not mean low or no vegetables. Actually, you'll need to enjoy a lot of low-starch veggies to fill up and gain the many health and antioxidant benefits of this lifestyle. Still try to shoot for at least half of your plate being filled with vegetables. Sit back, turn on some good relaxing music and enjoy your meal times to the fullest. Use this transition time to overhaul other areas in your life that will contribute to your health and longevity. Sleep, stress reduction, consistent exercise, prayer and meditation can all be utilized to optimize your transition to vitality and zest.

Being Consistent Leads to Success. Keep On Chugging...

To fully achieve your goals of weight loss and health, you will need to be consistent with your chosen low-carb intake. The more you "cheat" with occasional carb fixes, the more the process of training your body to burn its fat for fuel will not occur or will be more difficult to sustain. Your cravings and hunger may return as your body becomes confused on what energy source to utilize (glucose/carbs vs. fat).

Challenge yourself to be dialed in for a 21-day timeframe. It takes time for behavior change to become a habit and it also takes time for the body to become adapted to using your fat stores. During this transformation time, you also may need more salt, as ketogenesis changes your fluid mineral balance. It is sometimes important to supplement with electrolytes or magnesium.

Remember that Fat is Your Friend

Low-carb diets are much higher in fat than the way you are used to eating. It will be a change in habit fueled by innovation and research plus your desire to be the healthiest version of you possible. Research and let your taste buds confirm that you do not need to fear fats. They can actually be your friend during your health journey as opposed to what we have been taught in the past. Know that trying to do a low-carb and low-fat diet concurrently is not a good idea. You will find yourself very hungry, and the benefits of the lifestyle will not be achieved. Most people who restrict to this level cannot maintain and fail as the weight returns rapidly once they stop the extremely restrictive pattern.

Multiple studies have revealed that HEALTHY FATS are NOT the cause of heart disease and other diseases of the standard American diet. With your low-carb lifestyle, you will be gaining the many health benefits of monounsaturated, saturated, and omega-3 fats and you will be eliminating the unhealthy fats, such as rancid vegetable oils and trans fats. Your fat consumption will be at least 50% of your food intake; this creates a healthy change in your body composition and disease risk profile.

Benefits of Healthy Fats

- Fat is an essential ingredient for your brain to function optimally. It helps to make the myelin sheath that protects and insulates the neurons in your brain. Omega-3 fatty acids are a precursor to hormones and chemicals produced in the brain that affect our mood and behavior.

- Fat protects your organs.
- Fat helps to regulate your body temperature.
- Fats are needed for optimal hormonal balance, in both men and women. In fact, deficient dietary fat can contribute of infertility.
- Omega-3 fatty acids are fundamental for decreasing inflammation.
- Without enough fat, we experience increased cravings for sugar and carbohydrates. Fat provides us with a feeling of satiety... a sense of fullness. We don't have the sugar highs and lows.
- Fats are critical to absorbing fat-soluble vitamins A, E, K and D, along with other essential nutrients.

KETOGENIC PLAN-FOODS IN MORE DETAIL:
Let's talk a bit about the macronutrients need for a healthy lifestyle. FATS- PROTEINS-CARBS.

Healthy fats are the foundation of a ketogenic or lower-carb lifestyle. To keep your body in a state of ketosis (breaking down fat instead of carbs or protein for fuel), you need to eat a lot of fat. The goal is about 60-70% of your calories should be from healthy fat sources. This can be a great benefit of the lifestyle as fat make you feel full and it tastes great which means eating can be for pleasure as well as a source of sustaining energy. It is important to eat the right kinds of fats.

There are four categories of fat allowed on the Keto diet: Saturated fats, Monounsaturated fats (MUFAS), Polyunsaturated fats (PUFAS) and Naturally-occurring trans fats.

You also need to make sure you are getting your omegas, which are essential fatty acids you must get from your food. You want a balance of omega-3s and omega-6s to support overall health, including proper nerve and brain function, and reduce the risk for heart disease, Alzheimer's disease and Diabetes Type 2. Although omega-6 is essential, too much of it compared to the omega-3s is inflammatory to the body. Be aware of your intake of sources higher in omega-6, such as peanuts and plant oils like corn oil or sunflower oil as well as non-grass-fed animals and non-free-range eggs (both higher in omega-6s). Focus mostly on omega-3s from fish, like trout, salmon, tuna and mackerel, or take a high-quality fish oil supplement.

Finally, be aware that some nuts and seeds contain carbs as well, especially cashews, pistachios and almonds (see following chart).

Food	Serving Size	Calories	Protein	Fat	Total Carb	Fiber	Net Carb
Butter or ghee	1 tblsp (14.2g)	102	0.12g	11.5g	0g	0g	0g
Lard/ Dripping	1 tblsp (12.8g)	115	0g	12.8g	0g	0g	0g
Mayonnaise	1 tblsp (13.8g)	94	0.13g	10.33g	0.08g	0g	0.08g
Coconut Oil	1 tblsp (13.6g)	121	0g	13.47g	0g	0g	0g
Coconut butter	1 tblsp (16g)	105	1g	10.5g	4g	2.5g	1.5g
Flaxseed oil	1 tblsp (13.6g)	120	0.01g	13.6g	0g	0g	0g
Olive oil	1 tblsp (13.5g)	119	0g	13.5g	0g	0g	0g
Sesame seed oil	1 tblsp (13.6g)	120	0g	13.6g	0g	0g	0g
MCT oil	1 tblsp /15 mL	130	0g	14g	0g	0g	0g
MCT powder	1 scoop (10g)	70	0.5g	7g	1g	1g	0g
Walnut oil	1 tblsp (13.6g)	120	0g	13.6	0g	0g	0g

NUTS AND SEEDS

Food	Serving Size	Calories	Protein	Fat	Total Carb	Fiber	Net Carb
Almonds	23 nuts (28g)	164	6g	14g	6g	3.5g	2.5
Almond butter (w/o salt)	1 tblsp (16g)	98	3.5g	9g	3g	1.5	1.5
Almond meal/flour	1/4 cup (25g)	150	6g	11g	6g	3g	3g
Brazil nuts	5 nuts (25g)	165	3.5g	17g	3g	2g	1g
Cashews	1/4 cup (28g)	150	4g	12g	10g	1g	9g
Cashew butter (w/o salt)	1 tblsp (16g)	94	3g	8g	4.5g	0.5g	4g
Coconut (shredded unsweetened)	1/4 cup (20g)	71	1g	7g	3g	2g	1g
Macadamias	6 kernels (14g)	102	1g	11g	2g	.2g	0.8g
Macadamia butter	1 tblsp (14g)	97	2g	10g	2g	1g	1g
Hazelnuts	12 nuts (17g)	106	2.5g	10g	3g	1.5g	1.5g
Peanuts	1/4cup (36.5g)	207	9.5g	18g	6g	3.5g	3g
Peanut butter (chunky salted)	1 tblsp (16g)	94	4g	8g	3.5g	1.5g	2g
Peanut butter (smooth salted)	1 tblsp (16g)	96	3.5g	8g	4g	1g	3g
Pecans	10 halves (14g)	98	1.3g	10g	2g	1.5g	0.5g
Pili nuts	1/4 cup (30g)	210	3g	24g	1g	1g	0g
Pine nuts	2 tblsp (20g)	148	2.7g	14g	2g	1.3g	0.7g
Pistachios	25 nuts (17.5g)	98	3.5g	8g	5g	2g	3g
Pumpkin seeds (hulled)	1/4 cup (30g)	180	9g	14g	4g	3g	1g
Sesame seeds	2 tblsp (18g)	103	3.2g	9g	4g	2g	2g
Sunflower seeds (hulled)	1/4 cup (30g)	160	6g	15g	6g	3g	3g
Sunflower seed butter	1 tblsp (16g)	99	2.8g	9g	4g	1g	3g
Tahini (sesame paste)	1 tblsp (15g)	89	2.6g	8g	3g	1g	2g
Walnuts	7 halves (14g)	93	2g	9g	2g	1g	1g

DAIRY

Most dairy falls into both the "fat" and "protein" category. Most dairy products are ok when enjoying a ketogenic lifestyle. Eat the full-fat version and preferably organic and raw, when possible.

Remember, fat is fuel, and the reason we would eat dairy is for the high-quality fat. Some dairy, like yogurts, can have a lot of added sugars, so beware and always read labels.

Also, for some, dairy may inhibit weight loss and some people have food sensitivities to lactose or casein. If you don't feel good, have bowel issues, are not losing weight or not experiencing the health benefits of the lifestyle, try dropping dairy and observe any differences in your success.

Food	Serving Size	Calories	Protein	Fat	Total Carb	Fiber	Net Carb
Blue cheese	1 oz. (28g)	100	6g	8g	0.7g	0g	0.7g
Brie	1 oz. (28g)	95	6g	8g	0.1g	0g	0.1g
Cheddar or Colby	1 oz. (28g)	115	6.5g	9.5g	1g	0g	1g
Cream cheese	2 tblsp (29g)	100	2g	10g	1.6g	0g	0.6g
Feta	1 oz. (28g)	75	4g	6g	1g	0g	1g
Goat cheese (soft)	1 oz. (28g)	75	5g	6g	0g	0g	0g
Gouda	1 oz. (28g)	100	7g	8g	0.6g	0g	0.6g
Mozzarella (whole milk)	1 oz. (28g)	85	6.3g	6.3g	0.6g	0g	0.6g
Parmesan	1 oz. (28g)	111	10g	7.3g	1g	0g	1g
Swiss	1 oz. (28g)	111	7.6g	9g	0.4g	0g	0.4g
Cottage cheese (2% fat)	1/2 cup (113g)	92	12g	2.5g	5g	0g	5g
Cottage cheese (creamed)	1/2 cup (105g)	103	11.7g	4.5g	3.5g	0g	3.5g
Ricotta (whole milk)	1/2 cup (124g)	216	14g	16g	4g	0g	4g
Sour cream	1 tblsp (12g)	24	0.3g	2.3g	0.6g	0g	0.6g
Yogurt (plain unsweetened/whole milk)	4 oz. (113g)	69	4g	3.7g	5.3	0g	5.3
Heavy whipping cream or double cream (fluid)	1 tblsp (15g)	51	0.4g	5.4g	0.4g	0g	0.4g
Heavy whipping cream or double cream (whipped)	1/2 cup (60g)	204	1.7g	22g	1.6g	0g	1.6g

PROTEINS

Protein is very important part of any complete nutritional plan. Protein contains the essential amino acids that our organs and muscles utilize for optimal function and repair. We don't need as much protein in our diets as we once thought and often with this lifestyle it is easy to consume too much protein. This can increase insulin (like carbs do) and not allow you to get into ketosis and burn the fat stores.

Gluconeogenesis is where the body breaks down amino acids from the ingested protein and converts it into glucose that is then used as energy. As said previously, this increases your insulin release and decreases the level of ketones in your blood. This is the reason that moderate protein is needed to stay in ketosis.

To prevent gluconeogenesis while maintaining muscle mass, around 30% of your total calories should be from protein. Like we described with fats, make sure these calories come from healthy protein sources. We discussed previously some research on red and processed meats and that should be considered when choosing your protein sources. If consuming meat, obtain the highest-quality meat and eggs you can find and focus on grass-fed, organic, and pasture-raised options whenever possible. Don't overcook meat and make sure any processed meats are nitrate- and chemical-free. Remember there are many tasty vegetarian 'meat substitutes' that are high in healthy fats and good proteins. Read the label with these sources to be aware of the carb/sugar contents.

Another important point to consider is that we do not need as much protein as we once thought. The ideal amount of protein for the average adult seems to be around 56 grams for men and 46 grams for women. Remember that there is an increased need for protein and amino acids with exercise and weight loss to avoid lean muscle loss. Studies also show when dealing with injuries and when the body is trying to repair itself, you may require a slightly higher protein intake. Research shows that infants and the elderly also have a higher protein percentage of diet need, as do athletes and active weekend warriors who have more lean muscle breakdown.

Here are some acceptable protein sources you can consider for your plan.

- **Poultry,** including chicken, quail, duck, turkey and wild game
- **Pork,** including pork loin, tenderloin, chops, ham, and ground pork
- **Fish,** including mackerel, tuna, salmon, trout, halibut, cod, catfish and mahi-mahi
- **Shellfish,** including oysters, clams, crab, mussels and lobster
- **Organ meats,** including heart, liver, tongue, kidney and offal
- **Beef,** grass-fed and organic
- **Eggs,** including deviled, fried, scrambled and boiled. Use the whole egg as the fat is a good fat.

Should consume free-range and organic for a higher omega-3 content.

- **Lamb** meat
- **Goat** meat
- **Vegetarian, (Tofu, Tempeh and Edamame)** from soybeans. It is considered a complete protein with all essential amino acids.
- **Cheese** is both a fat and protein source. Also, remember that if you are having difficulty achieving your goals, you may want to cut back or eliminate cheese and dairy for a while and see the outcome to make informed decisions about your plan.

Beware of processed and cured meats that can contain additives, chemicals, and added sugars. Avoid breaded meats, like fried chicken and read the labels to know what ingredients are in the product as well as the macronutrient content. Both processed and breaded meats can drastically increase your carb and sugar intake for the day.

Finally, be sensitive to research showing the consumption of processed meats, like sausages, bologna, deli meats, hot dogs and bratwurst, have an increased risk of certain cancers and should be limited or avoided.

CARBOHYDRATES

When following a ketogenic diet, it is best to get most of your carbohydrates from vegetables like leafy greens, asparagus, broccoli, cauliflower and most other vegetables that grow ABOVE the ground. Avoid starchy vegetables like potatoes, corn and parsnips. The remainder of your carbohydrate intake should come from the carbs in nuts and seeds, the small amount in dairy and, on occasion, from fruits like berries. See below the carbohydrate content of different fruits and vegetables and focus on those with less carbs and higher fiber. The net carb is a good number to refer to as it is the total carb minus the fiber. This shows the actual impact the carb will have on insulin and metabolism. The more fiber, the less the net carb!

Remember, avoid all wheat (bread, pasta, cereal, etc.) and rice. Quinoa, barley, beans and legumes have more fiber and can be consumed occasionally but will have the potential to decrease your weight loss and ability to stay in ketosis if that is important to you. This is due to the higher carbohydrate load. AVOID - at all costs - any sweets, candies and any processed foods containing sugar or a lot of artificial sweeteners (as they also increase insulin and can decrease weight loss and ketosis).

Raw Vegetables:

Food	Serving Size	Calories	Protein	Fat	Total Carb	Fiber	Net Carb
Alfalfa sprouts	1/2 cup (43g)	15	1.5g	0g	2g	1g	1g
Artichoke hearts, marinated	4 pieces (64g)	60	0g	6g	4g	2g	2g
Artichoke hearts, canned	1 heart (16g)	15	0g	1.5g	1g	0.5g	0.5g
Arugula	1 cup (20g)	5	0.5g	0g	0.5g	0g	0.5g
Beans, green, snap, string, wax	1/2 cup (50g)	16	1g	0g	3.5g	1.5g	2g
Bok choy (pak choi)	1 cup (70g)	9	1g	0g	1.5g	1g	0.5g
Boston/bibb lettuce	1 cup (55g)	7	1g	0g	1g	1g	0g
Broccoli florets	1/2 cup (36g)	10	1g	0g	2g	1g	1g
Cabbage, green, red, savoy	1/2 cup (60g	8	0.4	0g	2g	.9g	1.1g
Cauliflower florets	1/2 cup (54g)	13	1g	0g	3g	1g	2g
Celery	1 stalk (40g)	6	0g	0g	1g	0.5g	0.5g
Chicory greens	1/2	3	0g	0g	1g	0.5g	0.5g
Chinese cabbage (pak-choi)	1/2 cup, shredded (35g)	5	0.5g	0g	1g	0.5g	0.5g
Chives	1 tblsp (3g)	1	0.1g	0g	0.1g	0.1g	0g
Cucumber (with peel)	1/2 cup, sliced (52g)	8	0.3g	0g	2g	0.3g	1.7g
Daikon radish	1/2 cup (58g)	9	0.4g	0g	2g	1g	1g
Endive	1/2 cup (25g)	4	0.3g	0g	1g	1g	0g
Escarole	1/2 cup (75g)	14	1g	0g	2.3g	2g	0.3g

Food	Serving						
Fennel, bulb	1/2 cup (44g)	13	0.5g	0g	3g	1g	2g
Greens, mixed	1 cup (36g)	5	0.5g	0g	1g	0.5g	0.5g
Iceberg lettuce	1 cup (72g)	10	0.7g	0g	2g	1g	1g
Jicama	1/2 cup (60g)	23	0.5g	0g	5g	3g	2g
Loose-leaf lettuce	1 cup (57g)	8	0.5g	0g	3g	1g	2g
Mung bean sprouts	1/2 cup (52g)	16	1.5g	0g	3g	1g	2g
Mushrooms, button, fresh	1/2 cup (35g)	8	1g	0g	1g	0.3g	0.7g
Olives, black	5 (19g)	30	0g	3g	1g	0g	1g
Olives, green	5 (14g)	20	0g	2g	0.5g	0.4g	0.1g
Onion	2 tblsp, chopped (20g)	8	0.2g	0g	2g	0.5g	1.5g
Parsley	1 tablespoon (4g)	1	0.1g	0g	0.2g	0.1g	0.1g
Peppers, green bell	1/2 cup (75g)	15	1g	0g	3.5g	1.5g	2g
Peppers, red bell	1/2 cup (75g)	23	1g	0g	4.5g	1.5g	3g
Radicchio	1/2 cup (20g)	5	0.3g	0g	1g	0.2g	0.8g
Radishes	6 (12g)	2	0g	0g	0.4g	0.2g	0.2g
Romaine lettuce	1 cup (47g)	8	0.5g	0g	1.5g	1g	0.5g
Scallion/green onion	1/4 cup (25g)	8	0.5g	0g	2g	1g	1g
Spinach	1 cup (30g)	7	1g	0g	1g	0.7g	0.3g
Tomato	1 small (90g)	16	1g	0g	3.5g	1g	2.5g
Tomato	1 medium (123g)	22	1g	0.25g	5g	1.5g	3.5g
Tomato, cherry	5 (85g)	15	1g	0.2g	3.3g	1g	2.3g
Watercress	1/2 cup (17g)	2	0.4g	0g	0.2g	0.1g	0.1g

Cooked Vegetables:

Food	Serving Size	Calories	Protein	Fat	Total Carb	Fiber	Net Carb
Artichoke	1/2 medium (60g)	32	1.7g	0g	7g	3.5g	3.5g
Asparagus	6 spears (90g)	20	2g	0g	4g	2g	2g
Bamboo shoots, canned, sliced	1/2 cup (66g)	12	1g	0g	2g	1g	1g
Beans, green, wax, string, snap	1/2 cup (63g)	22	1g	0g	5g	2g	3g
Beet greens	1/2 cup (72g)	19	2g	0g	4g	2g	2g
Bok choy (pak choi)	1/2 cup (85g)	10	1.3g	0g	1.5g	1g	0.5g
Broccoflower	1/2 cup (34g)	10	1g	0g	2g	1g	1g
Broccoli	1/2 cup (78g)	27	2g	0g	5.5g	2.5g	3g
Broccoli rabe	1/2 cup (85g)	28	3.3g	0.5g	2.7g	2.4g	0.3g
Brussels sprouts	1/4 cup (40g)	14	1g	0g	3g	1g	2g
Cabbage, green	1/2 cup (75g)	17	1g	0g	4g	1.5g	2.5g
Cabbage, red	1/2 cup (75g)	22	1g	0g	5g	2g	3g
Cabbage, savoy	1/2 cup (73g)	17	1.3g	0g	4g	2g	2g
Cardoon	1/2 cup (80g)	18	0.5g	0g	4g	1.5g	2.5g
Cauliflower	1/2 cup (62g)	14	1g	0.3g	2.5g	1.5g	1g
Celery	1/2 cup (75g)	14	0.5g	0g	3g	1.2g	1.8g
Chard, swiss	1/2 cup (88g)	18	2g	0g	3.5g	2g	1.5g

Chayote	1/2 cup (80g)	19	0.5g	0.4g	4g	2g	2g
Collard greens	1/2 cup (95g)	31	2.5g	1g	5.5g	4g	1.5g
Dandelion greens	1/2 cup (53g)	17	1g	0.3g	3.5g	1.5g	2g
Eggplant	1/2 cup (50g)	17	1g	0g	4g	1g	3g
Escarole	1/2 cup (75g)	14	1g	0g	2.3g	2.1g	0.1g
Fennel, bulb	1/2 cup (44g)	13	0.5g	0g	3g	1.5g	1.5g
Hearts of palm	1 heart (33g)	9	1g	0.2g	1.5g	1g	0.5g
Kale	1/2 cup (65g)	18	1g	0g	4g	1.5g	2.5g
Kohlrabi	1/4 cup (41g)	12	1g	0g	3g	0.5g	2.5g
Leeks	1/2 cup (52g)	16	0.5g	0g	4g	0.5g	3.5g
Mushrooms, button	1/4 cup (39g)	11	1g	0g	2g	1g	1g
Mushrooms, shiitake	1/4 cup (36g)	20	0.5g	0g	5g	1g	4g
Mustard greens	1/2 cup (70g)	18	2g	0.3g	3g	1.5g	1.5g
Nopales (cactus pads)	1/2 cup (75g)	11	1g	0g	2.5g	1.5g	1g
Okra	1/2 cup (80g)	18	1.5g	0g	3.5g	2g	1.5g
Onion, yellow; sauteed	1/4 cup (22g)	29	0g	2.5g	2g	0.5g	1.5g
Peppers, green bell; chopped	1/4 cup (29g)	37	0g	3.5g	1g	0.5g	0.5g
Peppers, red bell; chopped	1/4 cup (27g)	35	0.3g	3.5g	2g	0.5g	1.5g

Pumpkin	1/4 cup (61g)	12	0.5g	0g	3g	1g	2g
Sauerkraut	1/2 cup; drained (71g)	13	0.7g	0g	3g	2g	1g
Shallots	2 tblsp (20g)	14	0.5g	0g	3.5g	0.5g	3g
Spaghetti squash	1/2 cup (78g)	21	0.5g	0g	5g	1g	4g
Spinach	1/2 cup (90g)	21	3g	0g	3g	2g	1g
Summer squash	1/2 cup (90g)	21	1g	0.4g	3.5g	1g	2.5g
Tomato	1/4 cup (60g)	11	0.5g	0g	2.5g	0.5g	2g
Turnips (white), mashed	1/2 cup (115g)	25	1g	0g	6g	2.5g	3.5g
Zucchini	1/2 cup (90g)	14	1g	0.3g	2.5g	1g	1.5g

Fruit

To stay in ketosis, most fruits should be limited and eaten in *very* small amounts, as they have a high sugar content. One problem with most varieties of apples, plums and other large tree fruits is that, over the last hundred years, they have been modified to produce large, high-sugar (especially fructose) fruits. Just150 years ago, the natural fruit trees of the prairies grew small, bitter fruits with much less sugar and could not be consumed in large amounts due to taste. It is NOT the same apple of the pioneer days. Avocados, which are actually a fruit, have a great healthy fat profile and can be eaten and enjoyed frequently. Go Guacamole!

When you do eat delicious fruits, choose lower-sugar and lower glycemic index options like the following.

Food	Serving Size	Calories	Protein	Fat	Total Carb	Fiber	Net Carb
Avocado, Hass (Florida)	1/2 fruit (152g)	182	3.5g	15g	12g	8.5g	3.5g
Blackberries, fresh	1/4 cup (36g)	15	0.5g	0.2g	3.5g	2g	4g
Blackberries, frozen	1/4 cup (38g)	24	0.5g	0.2g	6g	2g	4g
Blueberries, frozen	1/4 cup (39g)	20	0.2g	0.3g	5g	1g	4g
Cherries, sour, fresh, w/o pit	1/4 cup (39g)	19	0.4g	0.1g	5g	1g	4g
Cherries, sweet, fresh, w/o pit	1/4 cup (39g)	24	0.4g	0.1g	6g	1g	5g
Cranberries, raw, chopped	1/4 cup (28g)	13	0.1g	0g	3g	1g	2g
Currants, fresh, red and white	1/4 cup (28g)	16	0.4g	0.1g	4g	1g	3g
Gooseberries, raw	1/4 cup (38g)	16	0.3g	0.2g	4g	1.5g	2.5g
Loganberries, frozen	1/4 cup (37g)	20	0.6g	0.1g	5g	2g	3g
Melon, cantaloupe, balls	1/4 cup (44g)	15	0.4g	0.1g	3.5g	0.5g	3g

Melon, honeydew, balls	1/4 cup (44g)	16	0.2g	0.1g	4g	0.5g	3.5g
Melon, balls, frozen	1/4 cup (43g)	14	0.4g	0.1g	3.5g	0.5g	3g
Raspberries, fresh	1/4 cup (31g)	16	0.4g	0.2g	4g	0.5g	3.5g
Raspberries, frozen	1/4 cup (35g)	18	0.4g	0.2g	4g	2g	2g
Strawberries, fresh, sliced	1/4 cup (42g)	13	0.3g	0.2g	3g	1g	2g
Strawberries, frozen	1/4 cup (37g)	13	0.2g	0g	3.5g	1g	2.5g
Strawberry, fresh	1 large (18g)	6	0.1g	0.1g	1.5g	0.5g	1g

For fruits and vegetables, fresh or frozen is fine, and organic is best but not essential. Make sure the frozen fruit does not have added sugar as many of them do to enhance the flavor. Smoothies can be make combining coconut milk (full fat), avocados, spinach and a few berries. Can you say delicious out loud!

VEGAN OPTIONS

Many people question whether or not it is possible to follow a ketogenic diet while being a vegan or vegetarian. Vegans avoid all meat, dairy, eggs and anything that uses or contains animal products. Although difficult, it's not impossible to become a keto vegan. The list below includes keto options that can be enjoyed by vegans, vegetarians and all others following a healthy ketogenic diet. Be aware that the carbohydrate content may be slightly higher in these types of foods and drinks, so make sure you factor that into your daily carb limit.

Vegan Keto Options:

Food	Serving Size	Calories	Protein	Fat	Total Carb	Fiber	Net Carb
Almond milk, unsweetened	1 cup (240 mL)	29	1g	3g	2g	1g	1g
Hemp milk, unsweetened	1 cup (236 mL)	50	2g	4g	1g	0g	1g
Natto	1/4 cup (44g)	92	8.5g	5g	5.5g	2.5g	3g
Shirataki noodles	4 oz. (113g)	20	1g	0.5g	2g	2g	0g
Soy milk, plain, unsweetened	1 cup (240 mL)	79	7g	4g	4g	1g	3g
Tempeh	1/2 cup (83g)	159	17g	9g	6g	0g	6g
Tofu, firm	4 oz. (113g)	70	8g	3g	3g	0g	3g
Tofu silken, soft	4 oz. (113g)	62	5.5g	3g	3.3g	0g	3.3g
Tofu bacon	2 strips (20g)	40	4g	2g	0.53g	0.3g	0.23g

Tofu Canadian bacon	3 slices (57g)	70	14g	0.5g	2.g	0.5g	1.5g
Tofu bulk sausage	2 oz. (57g)	60	7g	0g	7g	3g	4g
Tofu link sausage	2 links (64g)	130	9g	4g	15g	3g	12g
Vegan cheese (no casein)	1 slice (19g)	35	1g	2g	5g	0g	5g
Vegan cheese (no casein)	1 oz. (28g)	70	1g	7g	2g	1g	1g
Veggie burger	1 burger (70g)	124	11g	4.4g	10g	3.5g	6.5g
Veggie crumbles	3/4 cup (55g)	80	8g	1;5g	9g	1g	8g

Drinks and Alcohol

There are many other drink options other just water, coffee and tea that you can enjoy on a ketogenic diet. You can even enjoy some alcoholic beverages that are low to no carbs. Just make sure you don't overdo it and remember your goals. Also, monitor your progress and drop alcohol if hitting any barriers. With cocktails, it is not always the alcohol that is the problem - it is the juices and sugars added for flavor.

Acceptable Keto Drinks:

Food	Serving Size	Calories	Protein	Fat	Total Carb	Fiber	Net Carb
Broth/bouillon (not low sodium; no added sugar)	1 cup (235g)	27	6.25	0g	0.79	0g	0.79
Club soda	1 can (474g)	0	0g	0g	0g	0g	0g
Caffeinated or decaffeinated coffee	1 cup (237g)	2	0.54g	0.05g	0g	0g	0g
Caffeinated or decaffeinated tea	1 cup (245g)	2	0.54g	0g	0g	0g	0g
Kombucha (plain)- *read label*	6 ounces	10	0g	0g	3g	0g	3g
Lemon juice (2.5g) and lime juice (2.9g)	1 lemon or lime (48g)	11	0.17g	0.12g	3.31g	0.1g	3;21g
Unsweetened almond milk	1 cup (262g)	39	1.55g	2.88g	1.52g	0g	0g
Unsweetened hemp milk	1 cup (236g)	50	2g	4g	1g	0g	1g

ALCOHOL

Food	Serving Size	Calories	Protein	Fat	Total Carb	Fiber	Net Carb
Beer (light)	12 oz. (336g)	96	0g	0g	3g	0g	3g
Bourbon	1 oz. (28g)	70	0g	0g	0.03g	0g	0.03g
Champagne	3.5oz. (100g)	87	0.07g	0g	2.9g	0g	2.8g
Gin	1 oz. (28g)	73	0g	0g	0g	0g	0g
Rum	1 oz. (28g)	64	0g	0g	0g	0g	0g
Scotch	1 oz. (28g)	70	0g	0g	0g	0g	0g
Sherry (dry)	2 oz. (57g)	69	0g	0g	0g	0g	0g
Vodka	1 oz. (28g)	64	0g	0g	0g	0g	0g

Wine (red)	5 oz. (140g)	125	0.1g	0g	3.84g	0g	3.84g
Wine (white)	5 oz. (140g)	121	0.1g	0g	3.82g	0g	3.82g

EXTRAS (Condiments, Spices, Sweeteners)

When it comes to topping foods on the keto diet, homemade is always best. When possible, it's best to make your own versions of sauces and other condiments to keep at home. That being said, we know life is busy, so following are some pre-made condiments that are safe to use in sticking with your plan.

CONDIMENTS AND SAUCES

Food	Serving Size	Calories	Protein	Fat	Total Carb	Fiber	Net Carb
Ancho chili pepper	1 pepper (17g)	48	2g	1.4g	9g	4g	5g
Anchovy paste	1 tblsp (15g)	25	3g	1.5g	0g	0g	0g
Capers	1 tblsp (8.6g)	2	0.2g	0.07g	0.42g	0.3g	0.1g
Chipotle en adobo	2 peppers (30g)	20	0g	1g	3g	1g	2g
Clam juice	1 cup (237mL)	78	15.8g	0g	0g	0g	0g
Coconut aminos	1 teaspoon (5mL)	5	0g	0g	1g	0g	1g

Food	Serving						
Coconut milk (canned and unsweetened)	1/2 cup (113g)	212	2.3g	24g	3g	0g	3g
Cocoa powder, unsweetened	1 tblsp (5.4g)	12	1g	0;74g	3g	0g	3g
Enchilada sauce	1/4 cup (60g)	24	1g	0g	5g	1g	4g
Fish sauce	1 teaspoon (5mL)	3	0.66g	0g	0g	0g	0g
Horseradish sauce	1 teaspoon (5.6g)	28	0.6g	2.85g	0.56g	0.1g	0.4g
Jalapeno chili pepper	1/2 cup; sliced (75g)	30	1.4g	0.33g	6.6g	1.1g	5.5g
Miso paste	1 tblsp (18g)	30	2g	1g	4g	1g	3g
Mustard (Dijon)	1 teaspoon (5g)	10	0g	0g	1g	0g	1g
Mustard (yellow)	1 teaspoon (5g)	3	0g	0g	0g	0g	0g
Pasilla chili pepper	1 pepper (7g)	24	0.86g	1.11g	3.58g	1.9g	1.68g
Pesto sauce	1 tblsp (15g)	58	0.7g	5.8g	1.2g	0.2g	1g
Pickapeppa sauce	1 teaspoon (5mL)	5	0g	0g	1g	0g	1g
Pickle (dill or kosher)	1/2 pickle (32.5g)	4	0.11g	0.07g	0.73g	0.4g	0.3g
Pimento or roasted red pepper	1 oz. (28g)	6	0.3g	0.08g	1;41g	0.5g	0.9g
Salsa, green (no added sugar)	1 tblsp (10g)	0	0g	0g	0.6g	0g	0.6
Salsa, red (no added sugar)	1 tblsp (14g)	3	0g	0g	1g	0g	1g

Food	Serving	Calories					
Serrano chili pepper	1/2 cup (52.5g)	17	0.9	0.23g	3.5g	1.9g	1.6g
Soy sauce	1 tblsp (18g)	11	1.9g	0g	1g	0.1g	0.9g
Sriracha	1 teaspoon (6.5g)	6	1.13g	0.06g	1.25g	0.1g	1.15g
Tabasco or other hot sauce	1 teaspoon (4.7g)	1	0.06g	0.04g	0.04g	0g	0.04g
Taco sauce	1 tblsp (16g)	8	0g	0g	2g	0g	2g
Tahini (sesame paste)	2 tblsp (30g)	178	5.2g	16g	6.5g	1.5g	5g
Vinegar, balsamic	1 tblsp (16g)	14	0.08g	0g	2.7g	0g	2.7g
Vinegar, cider	1 tblsp (15g)	3	0g	0g	0.14g	0g	0.14g
Vinegar, red wine	1 tblsp (15g)	3	0.01g	0g	0.04g	0g	0.04g
Vinegar, sherry	1 tblsp (15g)	5	0g	0g	2g	0g	2g
Vinegar, white wine	1 tblsp (15g)	4	0.01g	0g	0.12g	0g	0.12g
Wasabi paste	1 teaspoon (5g)	10	0g	0g	2g	0g	2g
Worcestershire sauce	1 tblsp (17g)	13	0g	0g	3.3g	0g	3.3g

DRESSINGS

We discussed in the section on fats that vegetable oils are not part of a healthy lifestyle. The problem with most sauces and dressings is that many of them contain vegetable oils (canola, soybean, vegetable, etc.). You must read the labels and choose brands without these oils in them. Those that use olive or avocado oil as the oil base are the options to choose. There are great recipes on how to make your own dressings and mayonnaise using avocado oil. When you make your own, you are in charge of how healthy and also how delicious it can be to really suit your tastes and cravings.

Food	Serving Size	Calories	Protein	Fat	Total Carb	Fiber	Net Carb
Blue cheese dressing	2 tblsp (30g)	140	1g	14g	1g	0g	1g
Caesar salad dressing	2 tblsp (30g)	140	1g	16g	1g	0g	0.5g
Italian dressing	2 tblsp (30g)	71	0.12g	6.2g	3.6g	0g	3.6g
Lemon juice	2 tblsp (30g)	7	0.11g	0.07g	2.1g	0.1g	2g
Lime juice	2 tblsp (30g)	8	0.13g	0.02g	2.6g	0.1g	2.4g
Oil and vinegar	2 tblsp (32g)	144	0g	16g	0.8g	0g	0.8g
Ranch dressing	2 tblsp (30g)	129	0.4g	13.4g	1.7g	0g	1.7g

HERBS AND SPICES

A lot of the traditional seasonings and sauces are NOT ketogenic lifestyle-friendly because they contain added sugars and carbs. On the other hand, herbs and spices are great because they add some flavorful variety without additional carbs. As with anything additive to foods, just make sure they don't contain any sugars and are just the herb or spice alone. Examples include:

- Basil
- Rosemary
- Salt
- Cinnamon
- Cayenne Pepper

- Oregano
- Thyme
- Chili powder
- Nutmeg
- Pepper

- Parsley
- Cilantro
- Cumin
- Lemon juice
- Lime juice

SWEETENERS

Sweeteners can be a bit complicated, so choose them with caution if you do use them. The best option is to avoid sweet foods as much as possible because all

---

artificial sweeteners will spike the insulin response. The more you go without excessive sweetness in foods or drinks, the less you crave and want them in your foods. When or if you do use sweeteners, here are some guidelines to help you make better informed choices.

- Only use low glycemic index sweeteners, as they won't affect your blood sugar levels or contribute to your carb intake. They may still increase insulin levels if insulin resistance is a problem.

- Try to stay away from sweeteners that use the sugar alcohol maltitol (which is high glycemic) or other filler ingredients, like dextrose or maltodextrin. This also applies to low- or no-calorie and low- no-sugar sweeteners.

- Keep in mind that **ALL** sweeteners will have an effect on spiking insulin, which will have an effect on causing a carb craving response and studies show will impair weight loss. Some artificial sweeteners like aspartame have been linked to cancers as well.

Here are some, low-glycemic sweetener options (nutrition facts may differ based on the brand you choose) you can try while sticking with your plan.

Food	Serving Size	Calories	Protein	Fat	Total Carb	Fiber	Net Carb
Stevia (liquid)	4 drops (0.13mL)	0	0g	0g	0g	0g	0g
Erythritol	1 teaspoon (4g)	0	0g	0g	4g	0g	1g
Monk fruit (Luo Han Guo)	1 teaspoon (0.5g)	0	0g	0g	1g	0g	1g
Xylitol	1 teaspoon (4g)	10	0g	0g	4g	0g	1g

For granulated sweeteners, count every teaspoon as 1g net carbs because these products can have other bulking compounds which may promote an insulin reaction.

A SAMPLE KETOGENIC MEAL PLAN FOR 1 WEEK
To help get you started, here is a sample ketogenic diet meal plan for one week.

Monday
Breakfast: Scrambled eggs with spinach avocado and tomatoes.

Lunch: Chicken salad with olive oil and feta cheese.

Dinner: Salmon with asparagus cooked in butter.

Tuesday

Breakfast: Egg, tomato, basil and goat cheese omelet.

Lunch: Almond milk, peanut butter, cocoa powder and stevia milkshake.

Dinner: Meatballs, cheddar cheese and vegetables.

Wednesday

Breakfast: Coconut milk-based smoothie with spinach and some berries.

Lunch: Shrimp salad with olive oil and avocado.

Dinner: Pork chops with Parmesan cheese, broccoli and salad.

Thursday

Breakfast: Omelet with avocado, salsa, peppers, onion and spices.

Lunch: A handful of nuts and celery sticks with guacamole and salsa.

Dinner: Chicken stuffed with pesto and cream cheese, along with vegetables.

Friday

Breakfast: Sugar-free yogurt with peanut butter, cocoa powder and stevia.

Lunch: Beef stir-fry cooked in coconut oil with vegetables.

Dinner: Bun-less burger with bacon, egg and cheese.

Saturday

Breakfast: Ham and cheese omelet with vegetables.

Lunch: Ham and cheese slices with nuts.

Dinner: White fish, egg and spinach cooked in coconut oil.

Sunday

Breakfast: Fried eggs with bacon and mushrooms.

Lunch: Burger with salsa, cheese and guacamole.

Dinner: Steak and eggs with a side salad.

Always try to rotate the vegetables and meat over the long term, as each provides different nutrients and health benefits. You can eat a wide variety of tasty and nutritious meals on a ketogenic diet. Make healthy choices with the types of foods you consume. Make sure you are getting healthy low glycemic fruit and vegetables with your fats and proteins.

Healthy Ketogenic Snacks

Usually, you will not crave or need many snacks with this lifestyle but, in case you get hungry between meals, here are some healthy, keto-approved snacks.

- Fatty meat or fish.
- Cheese.
- A handful of nuts or seeds.
- Cheese with olives.
- 1–2 hard-boiled eggs.
- 90% dark chocolate.
- A low-carb blended shake with almond milk, cocoa powder and nut butter.

- Full-fat yogurt mixed with nut butter and cocoa powder.
- Strawberries and cream.
- Celery with salsa and guacamole.
- Smaller portions of leftover meals.

Great snacks for a keto diet include pieces of meat, cheese, olives, boiled eggs, nuts and dark chocolate. Vegan options are also available.

> ### *KETOGENIC*
>
> **Rejuv4LIFE-INTERMITTENT FASTING** Intermittent fasting can be an addition to any healthy nutrition plan for those wanting to optimize stem cell production, healing, hormone optimization and weight loss. It is also a good additional strategy for restoring insulin sensitivity with Diabetes Type 2 and metabolic syndrome. It can be used to induce weight loss, maintain weight loss or break a weight loss plateau.

INTERMITTENT FASTING

Intermittent Fasting (IF) is a great tool that can be added to any nutrition plan to optimize results, break a plateau and just start the body's regenerative processes. I am currently combining IF with my whole foods ketogenic lifestyle and having good energy, good outcomes with my fitness and increased mental focus. Once you read and realize the body and mind benefits, you may want to try it as well.

Intermittent fasting is one of the world's most popular health and fitness trends, yet it has been part of our cultures, health and nutrition practices for centuries. The warriors in ancient Rome would eat one large meal a day, and they had great strength and stamina to fight and survive. Native cultures from around the world fasted regularly as food wasn't always available and then would eat when times allowed. Their cultures had none of the metabolic diseases they are seeing today. Many major religions, including Islam, Christianity, Judaism and Buddhism, use fasting as part of their culture and have shown no increase in disease or mortality from those practices. People are using it to lose weight, improve health and simplify their healthy lifestyle.

Many studies show that IF can have powerful effects on your body and brain and may even help you live longer[108].

Intermittent fasting is a term for an eating pattern that cycles between periods of fasting and periods of eating. It does not dictate what foods to eat during your eating time but rather *when* you should eat. We will talk more about what to eat to break the fast as well. It is not a "diet" in the conventional sense but is more accurately described as an "eating pattern." It can become a way of life or just a strategy to jumpstart health and weight loss to help achieve a certain health goal. It has become very popular in the health and fitness community and much research is being dedicated to its application to various medical conditions as well as athletic performance.

Common intermittent fasting methods involve daily 16-hour fasts, or fasting for 24 hours, twice per week. There are other patterns of eating that we will describe later.

How to Do Intermittent Fasting

IF has been growing in popularity due to its clinical success and the growing amount of research supporting it. I first heard about it at a conference about 10 years ago and found it fascinating but did not think I would be able to incorporate it into my lifestyle. Now it actually has simplified things and I really like the ease of it.

There are a few different protocols that can be used. They all involve splitting the day or week into "eating periods" and "fasting periods." During the fasting periods, you eat either very little or not at all. Water, tea or coffee is always consumed throughout the fasting period. The most popular methods are as follows.

- **The 16/8 Method:** It is also called the Lean Gains Protocol and involves skipping breakfast and restricting your daily eating period to 8 hours - for example, from 1 pm to 9 pm. Then you "fast" for 16 hours in between. This works well as a daily lifestyle with prolonged fasting periods added intermittently if needed. This is the method I use, and I find it very simple and easy to start. It actually simplifies my day.

- **Eat-Stop-Eat:** This method involves fasting for 24 hours, once or twice a week. An example would be not eating from dinner one day until dinner the next day.

- **The 5:2 Diet:** On two non-consecutive days of the week, only eat 500-600 calories. Eat normally the other five days.

By making you eat fewer calories daily, all these methods should make you lose weight as long as you don't compensate by over-eating after you break your fast. It is also important to eat heathy using one of the other Rejuv protocols described previously after your fasting period. The 16/8 method is the simplest, most sustainable and easiest to stick to for most people.

How Intermittent Fasting Affects Your Cells and Hormones

When you fast, several good things happen in your body on the cellular and molecular level. For example, your body changes hormone levels, like decreasing insulin, to make stored body fat more accessible as a source of energy. Your cells also initiate important repair processes, recycle old cellular proteins and change the expression of genes. Following are some changes that occur in your body when you fast.

- **Human Growth Hormone (HGH):** We all want more of this youth-preserving hormone. The levels of growth hormone go up substantially with fasting, increasing up to five times normal levels. This equates to more fat loss and muscle gained[109].

- **Insulin:** Insulin sensitivity improves, and levels of insulin drop substantially. Lower insulin levels make stored body fat more accessible and is one of the most important effects of IF[110].

- **Cellular repair:** During fasting, your cells start a cellular repair process. This is called autophagy, where cells digest and remove old and dysfunctional proteins that build up inside cells and recycle those proteins in order to create new healthy cells[111]. It also has a positive effect on your stem cells, making them more viable and able to assist in repairing your body. Based on the research on stem cells, we always recommend IF for our Stem Cell patients to OPTIMIZE their outcomes with any regenerative procedure or after an injury.

- **Gene expression:** During times of fasting, there are changes in the function of genes related to longevity and protection against disease[112]. This is called epigenetics and it means we can influence what genes are expressed so we can prevent chronic diseases regardless of our genetics.

During a fast, human growth hormone levels rise and insulin levels decrease. Your body's cells also change the expression of genes and initiate important cellular repair processes that lead to repair and regeneration of old and damaged tissues. Again, we see the body can **REGENERATE!**

Intermittent Fasting Is a Very Powerful Weight Loss Tool

Weight loss has been a mystery for many people for years. So many different diets and fads have left us frustrated and without weight loss, or we gain the weight back quickly after stopping the fad. Weight loss is the most common reason that people try intermittent fasting. By making you eat fewer meals, you will naturally decrease total calories consumption in day.

Additionally, intermittent fasting changes hormone levels (described previously) that are key to successful and sustained weight loss. In addition to lower insulin and increased growth hormone levels, it increases release of the fat-burning hormone norepinephrine (noradrenaline). This also gives you more focus and energy to attack the responsibilities of the day.

One of the criticisms of IF was the concern that it may decrease the metabolism but, due the changes in hormones, short-term fasting actually increases your metabolic rate by 3.6-14% [113]. Through eating less (fewer calories in) and burning more (more calories out), intermittent fasting causes weight loss by improving both sides of the calorie equation.

Also important is that IF has been shown to be not only a great weight loss tool, but also has been shown to keep the weight off as well. In a review study from 2014, it was shown to cause weight loss of 3-8% over periods of 3-24 weeks [108]. Compared to most studies on weight loss programs, that is a good outcome. According to this study, people lost 4-7% of their waist circumference [108]. This shows that they lost much of the weight from harmful belly fat stores that builds up around the organs and are associated with disease risk. Another study shows that IF causes less muscle loss than the more standard method of continuous calorie restriction[114]. You want to retain as much lean muscle as possible with any weight loss that occurs. Again, remember if you binge and eat massive amounts during the eating periods, then you may not lose any weight at all as it will cancel out the calorie deficit that occurs with IF.

BENEFITS OF INTERMITTENT FASTING

This is what it is all about - getting healthier and decreasing disease risks. There has been a lot of research on intermittent fasting in both animals and humans. These studies have revealed that it can have great benefits for weight control and the health of your body and brain. Some studies show IF could actually help us live longer and healthier lives with less disease.

Following are the main health benefits of intermittent fasting.

- **Weight loss:** As mentioned earlier, intermittent fasting can help you lose weight and especially belly fat, without having to consciously restrict your calories [108].

- **Insulin resistance:** Intermittent fasting can reduce insulin resistance and is shown to lower blood sugar by 3-6% and fasting insulin levels by 20-31% [108]. This will protect you from Diabetes Type 2 and other metabolic diseases related to elevated insulin and blood sugar levels. It is very complimentary to a low-carb and ketosis lifestyle.

- **Inflammation:** Some studies show reductions in the blood indicators of inflammation. We know that inflammation drives many of the chronic diseases processes[115].

- **Heart health:** Intermittent fasting may reduce LDL cholesterol, blood triglycerides, inflammatory markers, blood sugar and insulin resistance. These are all considered risk factors for heart disease[116].

- **Cancer:** Animal studies have suggested that intermittent fasting may help prevent cancer[117].

- **Brain health:** Intermittent fasting increases a brain hormone called BDNF and may aid the growth of new nerve cells[118]. It may also protect against Alzheimer's disease, which is the most common memory disease of aging[119].

- **Anti-aging:** Intermittent fasting can extend the lifespan in rats. Studies showed that fasted rats live as much as 36-83% longer[120]. Many of the studies were small, short in duration, or conducted in animals so there are still questions to be answered in higher-quality human studies.

Intermittent Fasting Makes Your Life Simpler

This is what I like best about fasting. Eating healthy is simple, but it can be incredibly hard to stick to in the long haul. With IF, you eat less frequently which means less meal prep time, eating time and clean up time. You save hours a day and simplify your daily nutrition.

Intermittent Fasting Is Powerful, But It May Not Be for Everyone

If you are underweight, or have a history of eating disorders, then IF may not be a great option for you. For women of child-bearing age, start slowly and if you stop having a menstrual cycle, then discontinue fasting and increase your calorie and protein intake. If you have issues with fertility and are trying to conceive, then you may not want to fast as it may affect a normal menstrual cycle. If you are pregnant or breastfeeding, do not consider IF.

Safety and Side Effects

Hunger is the main issue with intermittent fasting that makes it difficult at first. You may also feel less energy and experience some brain fog in the beginning. This may only be temporary, as your body adapts to the new meal timing. Also, if you have a medical condition, you should consult with your doctor before trying intermittent fasting. These conditions would include:

- Diabetes or problems with blood sugar regulation
- Have low blood pressure
- Take medications
- Are underweight
- Have a history of eating disorders
- Are a female who is trying to conceive
- Are a female with a history of amenorrhea
- Are pregnant or breastfeeding

Intermittent fasting does have a great safety profile and there is nothing "dangerous" about not eating for a period of time if you are healthy otherwise. The most common side effect of intermittent fasting is feeling hungry.

Frequently Asked Questions About Intermittent Fasting

- *Can I drink liquids during the fast?* Yes, and it is encouraged for cell health. Water, coffee, tea and other non-caloric beverages are great. Avoid adding sugar to your coffee. Small amounts cream may be okay but black coffee is best. Coffee can be particularly helpful during a fast as it can decrease hunger and still gives you something to look forward psychologically. I also like to add electrolytes to my morning water bottle. They add some flavor and needed electrolytes that can sometimes be low with fasting or ketosis.

- *Isn't it unhealthy to skip breakfast?* No. Of course, skipping breakfast for a cigarette and a diet Coke is not healthy. You also need to make sure when you break your fast that you break it with a healthy meal.

- *Can I take supplements while fasting?* Yes. Remember that some supplements (like fat-soluble vitamins A, D, E and K) will be absorbed better with the fat of a meal. Or take them with your omega-3 supplement.

- *Can I work out while fasting?* Yes, fasted workouts are ok and will increase your ketosis and also fat burn. Some people who are concerned about muscle gains with resistance take branched-chain amino acids (BCAAs) before a fasted workout and then break the fast fully after the workout with a healthy post-workout meal. I add BCCAs to my workout water and drink it throughout my workout.

- *Will fasting cause muscle loss?* Know that all weight loss plans can cause muscle loss. That is why it is key to lift weights and keep protein intake high enough while fasting. Consume around 60-100 grams of protein a day if you are exercising. The good news is that one study shows that intermittent fasting causes less muscle loss than a regular calorie restricted diet[114].

- *Will fasting slow down my metabolism?* No. Studies show that short-term fasts actually increase metabolism though an increase in adrenalin [121]. Studies also show that longer fasts of more than three days can suppress the metabolism[122]. Longer fasts may have other benefits for certain disease conditions but should be done under the guidance of a health practitioner with experience with fasting plans.

- *Should children fast?* With all the growth and hormone changes of youth, fasting is not a good plan. Overweight children need to adopt a healthy nutrition plan by cutting out sugar and processed foods and find an activity they enjoy for movement and exercise.

HOW TO START WITH INTERMITTENT FASTING

Most likely, you have already done some "intermittent fasts" in your life. Skipping breakfast after sleeping in is a fast. Many people actually naturally eat this way on their own. They wake up and are not hungry first thing in the morning. If you are wondering which way to start, I started with the 16/8 method and find if very easy and simple.

If that goes well, and you feel energetic during your fast, then you can try a more advanced fast, like 24-hour fasts 1-2 times per week (Eat-Stop-Eat) or only eating 500-600 calories 1-2 days per week (the 5:2 diet).

Another way to approach fasting is to just fast whenever it is convenient. For example, skip meals from time to time when you're not hungry or don't have time to cook or when you have a plane flight. Another good time is when you don't have access to healthy foods, simply skip the convenience store and wait until you can get your mouth on some healthy foods. You do not need to follow an organized intermittent fasting plan to gain at least some benefits. Try different approaches out and see what works for you and your lifestyle.

Again, intermittent fasting is not needed for everyone, but it can improve your health, increase healing, break weight loss plateaus, improve inflammation and simplify your life. It is important no matter what plan you choose to eat real food, exercise regularly and focus on good sleep hygiene. With nutrition, you need to find a plan that works for you and that you can maintain for the long haul. Results come from consistency to a program.

When fasting, if you feel energetic, mentally sharp and are getting the outcomes you desire, then continue utilizing it as a tool for health and weight loss. Also, it is NOT a rule that you have to do every day. You can do it on weekdays and eat on a normal three meals a day pattern on weekends if you want. You can also mix up the different methods below. The biggest thing to learn from this is that you no longer need to feel like you should be eating every two hours. Skipping meals, not eating before bedtime and going for longer periods of time without eating is healthy and can have many positive benefits to your health.

Let's expand on each of the METHODS so you can make a decision on what will work best for you.

1. The 16/8 Method: Fast for 14-16 hours each day and enjoy an 8-hour eating window. During the eating period, you can consume 1, 2, 3 or more meals. This method is also known as the Lean Gains Protocol. A popular example of this method is to not eat anything after dinner and skipping breakfast the next day. Break your fast around 12 or 1 pm the next day. I generally will exercise at noon and then break my fast after the workout.

It is generally recommended that women only fast 14-15 hours as they seem to do better with slightly shorter fasting periods. You can even get some of the benefits doing a 12-hour fasting to 12-hour eating window, knowing that the longer the fasting period, the more powerful the results. Twelve hours is a good rule for most days and you can always extend the fasting period longer if you are not hungry and it is convenient for you. You can drink water, coffee and other non-caloric beverages during the fast, which will aid in reducing your hunger and cravings. Staying mentally or physically busy during your fast can help as well.

Once you break your fast, it is important to eat healthy foods during the eating period. If you fill the eating window with binges and low-quality junk foods, fasting will fail for you. In reality, this method is very easy way to start. Once it becomes a habit, it is simple to sustain. If you combined any fasting method with a low-carb or even ketogenic lifestyle eating plenty of "good" fats, your appetite will be decreased from the fats and you may not feel hungry until around 1 pm in the afternoon. Eat your last meal of the day around 6-

9 pm and you will end up fasting for 16-19 hours. This is enough time for you to start to dive into your fat stores for energy and gain some of the other benefits seen with fasting.

2. The 5:2 Diet: Fast for two days per week. This method involves eating normally five days of the week, while decreasing calories to 500-600 on any two days of the week. This diet is also called the Fast Diet.

On the fasting days, it is recommended that women eat 500 calories, and men 600 calories. You could eat normally on all days except Mondays and Thursdays. That is where you would eat two small meals (250 calories per meal for women, and 300 for men). No studies have been done testing the 5:2 diet specifically, but there are many studies on the benefits of intermittent fasting in general.

3. Eat-Stop-Eat: This method involves a 24-hour fast, once or twice a week. If you fast from dinner one day to dinner the next day, this will be a 24-hour fast. You can also fast from breakfast to breakfast, or lunch to lunch. They all will give you a 24-hour fast. Water, coffee and other non-caloric beverages are allowed during the fasting period, but no solid foods. If your goal with fasting is to lose weight, then it is important with this method that you eat normally during the eating periods.

The drawback of this plan is that a full 24-hour fast can be a bit difficult for some people. It may be an option if you start with the 16:8 method and work up to longer extended fasting time periods as you get used to it.

4. Alternate-Day Fasting: With this method, you simply fast every other day. There are several different varieties of this fasting method. Some of them allow about 500 calories during the fasting days. Many of the research studies showing health benefits of intermittent fasting have used this version of the fasting method. A full fast every other day is rather difficult, and this is not a good method for those just getting into fasting.

5. The Warrior Diet: Here you fast during the day and then eat a large meal at night. You can eat small amounts of raw fruits and vegetables during the day, then eating one large meal at night within a 4-hour eating window. This diet also emphasizes food choices that are quite similar to a paleo-style diet which would include whole, unprocessed foods that resemble what they look like in nature.

6. Spontaneous Meal Skipping: With this plan, you simply skip meals when it is convenient. You don't need to follow a schedule or structured plan to receive some of the benefits of fasting. You can just skip a meal every once in a while, if you are busy or not hungry. Do not feel like you always have to be eating. Feel free to not eat. You will not lose muscle or slow down your metabolism. This works well if you are traveling or just very busy. You just need to make sure to eat healthy foods with your other meals.

So, as you can see, there are a few things to consider as you make healthy transitions with your nutrition planning. Know that any change is a good step in the right direction. For example, cutting out soda or juice, eliminating fast food, substituting vegetable oils for olive and coconut oils, decreasing your total refined carbohydrate intake - you will see benefits from them all.

To gain the most benefits, actually diving in deep and sticking to a plan will be the best option. If you experience plateaus or feel you can't sustain a certain plan, try another. A few general rules to stick with no matter what plan you are on would be the following.

- Decrease sugar and refined carb intake.
- Substitute healthier fats for vegetable oils and trans fats.
- Do not feel you have to eat every 3-4 hours.
- Do not eat if you are not hungry and feel free to skip meals.

- Increase your consumption of green and cruciferous vegetables.
- Increase your water intake.

When you are motivated to make healthy nutritional decisions, this is also a great time to work on other core habits important for long-term health and healing. The **Rejuv4LIFE Core Elements** should all be started during the time you are making your nutrition changes. Let's look at the **8 Rejuv4LIFE Core Elements** in more detail now. They will also be explained in detail in the following chapters as well.

1. SELF CHANGE

During first few weeks of making your personal nutritional choices, it is critical that you psychologically set yourself up for success. It's important to set personal goals for health to increase your success. You should have daily, weekly, monthly as well as annual goals for yourself and create a plan that is written and accessible for you to see daily. A good place to post these goals is on your bathroom mirror so you can see them daily to help reinforce your decisions.

You also need to claim your why - your need to figure out what your deep core reason is for wanting to change. Is it for yourself? Is it to avoid the same health issues a family member may have gone through? Is it to set a good example for your children? Answering this question is essential as it will be the fuel to motivate your success. More detail in goal setting to come.

2. SLEEP

It is critical to your long-term health and healing to make sure you are getting good quality sleep. Eight hours of sleep is recommended for optimal healing, restoration and disease prevention. Hormones are released at night that are needed for fat loss and lean muscle growth. Your memories are consolidated during sleep. It is important to practice good sleep hygiene to make sure you are able to fall asleep and maintain a deep restorative slumber.

3. NUTRITION

Start with the healthy changes just mentioned. From there, dive into a plan that makes sense for you and that motivates you to continue with it. As stated before, if you hit a plateau, try another plan and get advice from a trained professional who can guide you on what plan may be best, and problem solve with you when you hit an obstacle.

4. EXERCISE

If you have a love-hate association with exercise, hopefully you can turn it into a more affectionate relationship! Exercise should be engaged in most days of the week. It should be a combination of resistance training, cardiovascular training, balance, proprioception (understanding your own movement) and stretching.

Weight training is essential to help increase lean muscle mass, which then increases your metabolism and fat-burning. It also increases the anabolic release of hormones, like growth hormone and testosterone.

Exercise is also important as it sensitizes your body to insulin. You can integrate your cardiovascular training with your resistance training by adding some cardio between resistance-based training sets. Finally, it's important to get balance and stretching into the mix. This is usually done at the end of a workout.

A good framework to follow to decrease your risk of injury and increase the outcomes of your workout is to start with a dynamic warm-up, followed by your core workout and ending with a focused cool-down.

The dynamic warm-up is a process with the goal of warming up the muscles, increasing your core temperature to boost metabolism while putting the joints, muscle and fascia through their entire ranges of motion.

The warm-up can include movements like walking, lunges, yoga poses, light jogging or rowing. Your warm-up should take 5 - 10 minutes. During the core workout, you will be doing your resistance training, cardiovascular training or a combination of both.

There are multiple variations of weights and cardio training that can be entertained to keep your workouts interesting and also to continue to shock and confuse your muscles for optimal fitness gains. It's important to keep your workouts fun and choose exercises and activities that keep you engaged and interested. It's also helpful to mix up your exercises over time so that you do not plateau in your weight loss.

High-intensity interval training can boost calorie burns and aid in weight loss. We use a process called the **LEVELS OF FITNESS** to progress our patients and clients from a white belt level up to a black belt level. The progression follows a specific advancement, starting in the white belt level with basic movement exercises, then progressing to yellow, red, blue and then black belt where the exercises are much more athletic and advanced. This progression keeps the workouts safe and fun, optimizes outcomes, and helps with goal setting.

We like to start all new clients and patients with a functional movement assessment, which will help identify any vulnerabilities that need to be corrected during their workouts to decrease risk of injury. In time, exercising will become a habit. Did you know exercise releases similar endorphins that are similar to opioids? That's why people who exercise get a stimulating 'runners high'. Hopefully you too can get a good buzz from your fitness plan.

Losing weight - especially the deep "visceral" fat from your liver and belly - will decrease insulin resistance. Fasting and a ketosis lifestyle are great ways to tap into these hard-to-mobilize fat stores.

5. WATER

The next core element is simply water. Water is an essential element when it comes to health, fitness and weight loss. Our body is composed mostly of water and, when dehydrated, our systems don't optimally perform. Water should be sipped throughout the day with the goal of consuming one-half your body weight in ounces of water per day. Aim for 2.5-6 L /day for men depending upon activity level and climate and 1.5-5 L per day for women depending on activity level, climate and if pregnant or lactating.

Water consumption should occur before and during each meal to help decrease the intake of unneeded calories and make you feel fuller. Also sip water before and throughout your workouts.

Make sure the water you consume has been filtered to take out any impurities, toxins or micro-organisms.

6. HORMONE OPTIMIZATION

Our endocrine systems and hormones need to be balanced to achieve optimal health. These systems are complex and interact with each other like a symphony. They all need to be tuned up for a synchronized performance. If one section is out of tune, the entire symphony sounds off and will not perform well. The same happens with our endocrine system. If one area is not functioning optimally, it will affect the performance of the others.

Hormone optimization should be done only after lab analysis with a practitioner who specializes in functional medicine and can interpret the labs and optimize their levels. Hormones like estrogen, progesterone, testosterone, thyroid hormone, DHEA and cortisol are examples. If they are out of balance, it will make it difficult to achieve the optimal body composition and heal our bodies. We will discuss hormone optimization in more detail later.

7. STRESS MANAGEMENT

We all deal with stressors daily. Stress can come from **environmental** stresses, like toxins in the water we drink, chemicals in our food and pollution in the air we breathe. It can also be in the form of **emotional** stresses, like the demands at work, our responsibilities at home and our chosen relationships.

Finally, stress comes in **physical** forms, like trauma and aging, occupational work stresses, physical activity and sports as well as the physical demands of daily life.

It is important that we plan into our schedule good stress management strategies to counteract the emotional, physical and environmental stresses we encounter daily. Activities like yoga, meditation, reading, light work, downtime and deep breathing are very important. These activities should be planned and engaged in most days of the week. Studies show that those who engage in these activities have decreases in weight gain and less elevation of inflammatory hormones.

8. GUT HEALTH

The gut microbiome (good vs bad bacteria) has an effect on obesity and insulin sensitivity. Insulin resistance is the central theme in the development of obesity. Research shows that overweight and obesity are strongly associated by changes in the gut microbiota. Health benefits of the gut microbiome related to obesity are mediated through favorable modulation of insulin sensitivity[92].

Remember to **PREPARE** the gut by stopping negative influences like chlorinated water, sugar and emulsifiers. **PLANT** the good bacteria with *probiotics* and fermented foods (Kombucha, pickles and sour kraut) and **PROMOTE** good growth with *prebiotics.* They are found in indigestible fibers found in onions, garlic, asparagus, leeks, artichokes, flaxseeds and seaweed.

9. STOP SMOKING

Tobacco smoking has been shown to cause insulin resistance. Quitting will improve it[43].

The next element that is important is supplements. This area can be confusing with so many supplements touting claims to health. We will review a few simple but very important supplements with good research that maybe helpful to reach your weight loss and fitness goals.

The main emphasis of your healthy lifestyle should be eating real whole foods that are *unprocessed and as natural as possible, so you get most of your micronutrients from food. Sometimes when you are trying to achieve a certain outcome, supplements in doses higher than we can get out of food can be beneficial.*

With weight loss and the low-carb lifestyle, it is all about **DECREASING INSULIN** and **INCREASING THE BODY'S SENSITIVITY TO INSULIN** when it is present. The nutrition plans outlined previously aim to achieve this healthy goal.

First let's look at some supplements that can be used to increase insulin sensitivity and result in improved weight loss and health.

INSULIN SENSITIZERS:

- **L-Arginine** 500mg a day

Increases insulin sensitivity through increased Nitric Oxide (NO) production and an increase in adiponectin concentration[86]. Also great for circulation and healthy hormones.

- **Berberine** 500mg twice a day

Acts to increase insulin sensitivity by inhibiting fat store and adjusting adipokine profile in human fat cells and overweight and metabolic syndrome patients[87].

- **Fiber** 15g up to twice a day in addition to the fiber from natural foods.

- Studies show that a total intake of fiber >25 g/d in women and >38 g/d in men increases insulin sensitivity and aids in weight loss and maintenance [88].

- Slows carbohydrate absorption and decreases cholesterol.

- Anti-inflammatory and helps in recovery.

- Helps balance hormones.

- Helps the body detoxify and eliminate toxins via the stool.

• **Chromium Picolinate** 200mcg a day.
Increases insulin sensitivity. Supplements containing 200-1,000mcg chromium as chromium picolinate a day have been found to improve blood glucose control. Chromium picolinate is the most efficacious form of chromium supplementation. Numerous animal studies and human clinical trials have demonstrated that chromium picolinate supplements are safe[89].

• **Cinnamon** 1-6 grams a day
You can add it to coffee or use it to flavor any food. Also comes in a supplement form.
- Cinnamon has been shown to improve insulin sensitivity. Cinnamon reduces mean fasting serum glucose (18-29%), TAG (23-30%), total cholesterol (12-26%) and LDL-cholesterol (7-27%) in subjects with Diabetes Type 2 after 40 days of daily consumption of 1-6g Cinnamon. Subjects with the metabolic

syndrome who consume an aqueous extract of cinnamon have been shown to have improved fasting blood glucose, lower systolic blood pressure, less percentage of body fat and increased lean body mass compared with the placebo group[90].

- **Apple Cider Vinegar** 1 teaspoon to 2 tablespoons per day is a common dosage.

It is used in cooking, salad dressings or simply mixed in a glass of water. I mix mine in water with my morning electrolytes when I am fasting. It only has three calories a teaspoon and will not affect blood sugar or insulin levels.

- Organic, unfiltered apple cider vinegar (like <u>Bragg's</u> brand) also contains "mother," strands of proteins, enzymes and friendly bacteria (probiotics) that give the product a murky appearance. It is high in Acetic Acid and has powerful biological effects.

- Vinegar has been shown to have *numerous* benefits for blood sugar and insulin levels: it improves insulin sensitivity during a high-carb meal by 19–34% and significantly lowers blood sugar and insulin responses[6]. It reduces blood sugar by 34% after eating 50 grams of white bread[7]. Two tablespoons of apple cider vinegar before bedtime can reduce fasting blood sugar in the morning by 4%[8]. Numerous other studies in humans show that vinegar can improve insulin function and lower blood sugar levels after meals[9-10]. It seems like apple cider vinegar is useful as a weight loss aid, mainly by promoting satiety and lowering blood sugar and insulin levels. But know that it won't be amazing on its own and needs lifestyle changes through nutrition, fasting, stress management, sleep and exercise to maximize your health!

Other positive health effects of Apple Cider Vinegar:
- It can kill harmful bacteria. It can be used as a disinfectant and natural preservative.
- Studies show that vinegar increases feelings of fullness and help people eat fewer calories a day, which can lead to weight loss.
- Several animal studies have shown that vinegar can reduce blood triglycerides, cholesterol and blood

pressure. This could lead to a reduced risk of developing heart disease.

- Some studies in rats have shown that vinegar can slow the growth of tumors.

- **Omega-3 Fatty Acids 1,000-2,000mg a day**

Eating omega-3 fatty acids can reduce insulin resistance. They can also lower blood triglycerides, which are often high in insulin-resistant people[44-45]. They have also been studied in polycystic ovarian syndrome to help with the insulin resistance associated with that disease pathology.

Other positive effects of omega-3 fatty acids include the following.

DEPRESSION: Depression is one of the most common mental disorders worldwide. Omega-3 supplements may help prevent and treat depression and anxiety. EPA, an omega-3 fatty acid, seems to be the most effective at treating depression. One study actually showed EPA to be as effective with treating depression as Prozac, a commonly prescribed antidepressant drug[10].

- **EYE**: DHA, an omega-3 fatty acid, is a major structural component of the retina of the eye. It may help prevent macular degeneration, which can cause vision impairment and blindness.

- **PREGNANCY**: Getting enough omega-3s during pregnancy and early life is crucial for the development of the child. Deficiency is linked to low intelligence, poor eyesight and an increased risk of several health problems.

- **HEART DISEASE**: Omega-3s have been found to improve a number of heart disease risk factors. However, omega-3 supplements do not reduce the risk of heart attacks or strokes.

- **Triglycerides:** Omega-3s can cause a large reduction in triglycerides, usually in the range of 15–30%[25-27].

- **Blood pressure:** Omega-3s can reduce blood pressure levels in people with high blood pressure[25,28].

- **HDL-Cholesterol:** Omega-3s can raise HDL (the "good") cholesterol levels[29-31].

- **Blood clots:** Omega-3s can help prevent blood platelets from sticking together. This helps prevent the formation of dangerous blood clots[32,33].

- **Plaque:** Omega-3s help prevent the plaque that can restrict and harden the arteries[34,35].

- **Inflammation:** Omega-3s reduce the many harmful substances released during the inflammatory response[36-38].

- **LDL-Cholesterol:** Omega-3s can also lower LDL (the "bad") cholesterol. Note that the evidence is mixed and some studies show increases in LDL levels[39,40]. Interestingly, despite all these beneficial effects on heart disease risk factors, there is no convincing evidence that omega-3 supplements can prevent heart attacks or strokes. Many studies find no benefit[41,42]. More studies are needed.

- **ADHD:** Omega-3 supplements can decrease ADHD in children. They also improve attention and reduce hyperactivity, impulsiveness and aggression.

- **CHRONIC INFLAMMATION:** Omega-3s can reduce chronic inflammation which has been shown to contribute to heart disease, cancer and other chronic diseases[55-57].

- AUTOIMMUNE DISEASE: Studies show that getting enough omega-3s during your first year of life is linked to a reduced risk of many autoimmune diseases. These include Diabetes Type 1, autoimmune diabetes in adults and multiple sclerosis[62-64]. Omega-3s have also been shown to help treat lupus, rheumatoid arthritis, ulcerative colitis, Crohn's disease and psoriasis[65-68].

- MENTAL DECLINE AND ALZHEIMER'S DISEASE: Several studies have shown that higher omega-3 intake is associated to decrease age-related mental decline and a reduced risk of Alzheimer's disease[73-75]. Also, one study found that people who eat fatty fish tend to have increased healthy gray matter in the brain. This is the area that processes information, memories and emotions[76].

- CANCER: Interestingly, studies have shown that people who consume the most omega-3s have up to a 55% lower risk of colon cancer[77,78]. Additionally, omega-3 consumption has been linked to a reduced risk of prostate cancer in men and breast cancer in women. Note: not all studies show the same findings [79-81].

- **ASTHMA**: Many studies have associated omega-3 consumption to a lower risk of asthma in children and young adults[83,84].

- **ARTHRITIS and OSTEOPOROSIS**: Studies reveal that omega-3s can improve bone strength through increasing the calcium density in bones. This should lead to a reduced risk of osteoporosis[87,88]. Studies show that omega-3s may also help with the pains of joint arthritis. Patients taking omega-3 supplements have reported reduced joint pain and increased grip strength[89,90].

- **MENSTRUAL PAIN**: Studies have shown that women who consume the most omega-3s have milder menstrual pain and cramping[91,92]. One study even found that an omega-3 supplement was more effective than ibuprofen in treating severe pain during menstruation[93] without all the negative NSAID side effects.

- **SLEEP**: Studies show that sleep deprivation is associated with many chronic diseases, including obesity, diabetes and depression[94-97]. Low levels of omega-3 fatty acids are associated with sleep problems in children and obstructive sleep apnea in adults[98,99]. Low levels of DHA have also been linked to lower levels of the hormone melatonin, which helps induce healthy sleep[100]. Studies in children and adults have shown that omega-3 intake increases the length and quality of sleep[98,100].

- **SKIN**: DHA is a vital structural component of the skin. It is responsible for the health of cell membranes, which make up a large part of skin. A healthy cell membrane equates to soft, moist, supple and less wrinkled skin. EPA also benefits the skin in several ways, including[101,102]:

- Managing oil production in skin.
- Managing hydration of the skin.
- Preventing hyperkeratinization of hair follicles (the little red bumps often seen on upper arms). In fact, these bumps on the outer surface of the upper arm

can be a sign of low omega-3 levels and another reason to supplement it.

- Preventing premature aging of the skin.
- Preventing acne.
- Omega-3s also protect your skin from sun damage. EPA helps block the release of substances that eat away at the collagen in your skin after prolonged sun exposure[101].

- **Probiotics and Prebiotics** - are needed for a healthy gut and immune system.

Now let's look at some other supplements that can be helpful with maintaining a ketogenic or low sugar and processed carbohydrate lifestyle

The first two, exogenous ketones and MCT oil, can be used for multiple purposes. They are a great way to help get the benefits of ketones, such as energy, at times when you need a boost.

Exogenous Ketones and MCT Oil

The purpose of exogenous ketone supplements is to provide the body with extra ketones (energy). Ketone supplements can be a big help when transitioning into a state of ketosis or extending a fasted state like in the morning during intermittent fasting. **Exogenous ketones help you get back into ketosis instantly,** instead of having to wait for at least a couple days of avoiding higher carb intake. They can be taken in between meals to provide a quick burst of ketones or before a workout for additional energy.

There are three different types of "ketones" that your body can use as energy: Acetoacetate, beta-hydroxybutyrate, and acetone. Beta-hydroxybutyrate is the active form that can most easily be used by your body. Therefore, that is the one comprising most exogenous ketone supplements.

- **Ketone Esters.** Ketone esters are the raw ketone (beta-hydroxybutyrate) and are not attached to any other compound, so it can be easily utilized by the body. Most people think the taste is not great and it can also be associated with some gastric side effects.

- **Ketone Salts**. This exogenous ketone supplement is bound to a salt such as sodium, calcium, magnesium or potassium. These ketone salts do not raise ketone levels as fast as ketone esters but, on the flip side, they have a better taste with less gastric issues. This supplement may be better tolerated due improved flavor and less gastric issues. I have been using *InstaKetones* and their Ester and Salt options both taste pretty good and give me good energy for extending a fast or before a workout.

- **MCT Oils** Dosages vary, but generally between 1-3 tablespoons per day.
- o MCT, or medium chain triglycerides, can also help boost your body's ketone production, but the effect is much slower then exogenous ketones as they don't cause an immediate rise in blood ketone

levels. Beta-hydroxybutryate from ketone salts or esters can provide instant energy while MCTs have to be converted into ketones that, over a few hours, can be used as energy.

MCTs are found in certain foods, such as coconut oil, and are metabolized differently than the long chain triglycerides.

Using MCTs as a supplement has been associated with many health benefits. It helps to increase your satiety (fullness) during the day as well as improve your ability to burn your body's fat stores and subsequently produce ketones. It may allow you to consume a few more carbohydrates while still staying in ketosis. A small amount may help with weight loss, but since it is a calorie-dense oil, too much may interfere with weight loss. It can be added to your coffee for sustained energy. Coconut oil has a high percentage of MCT oils and can be used in cooking and coffee as well.

Benefits of MCT Supplementation:

- **Weight Loss:** MCTs are easily digested and have a thermogenic (energy-creating) effect which has been shown to increase the metabolism. MCT oil powder can provide a creaminess that is incredible in coffee, tea, and any creative smoothie you can think of enjoying on your plan.

o **Energy:** MCTs are a sustaining source of energy since, as we described, they break down into ketones which can then be used as fuel by your brain and body.

o **Gut health:** MCTs support our gut microbiome by fighting harmful bacteria and parasites.

o **Overall Health:** MCTs contain antioxidants which reduce inflammation and improve function of your heart, brain and nervous system.

Caffeine up to 400mg a day is safe.

Caffeine (in moderation) can be a good supplement to help your low-carb diet. A recent study in the Journal of American Clinical Nutrition showed caffeine consumption can increase our metabolic rate around to 11%. That is good for weight loss, ketosis and intermittent fasting. Also, coffee increases adrenaline and has been shown to boost exercise and sports performance in athletes and weekend warriors like myself. Too much can be an added stressor for those that are already "amped up". So, the takeaway is to take it in moderation.

The good news with coffee is that it has many other health benefits as well:

- Reduces the risk of kidney stones.
- Treats asthma and headaches.
- Reduces the risk of liver disease.
- Decreases Parkinson's risk.
- Reduces work out pain and increases workout performance.
- Boosts your memory and is helpful with Alzheimer's disease.
- Protects the heart.
- Protects from Diabetes Type 2.
- Decreases depression risk.
- Decreases cancer risk.

Collagen Protein Supplements - CollaRegen Take one serving a day.

After a workout is a good time to consume collagen protein supplements if you are exercising. It can be mixed with your noon meal or when you break your fast. It does have calories so, if fasting, should be consumed after your fast.

Collagen is a type of protein. **It is the most abundant protein in your body, accounting for 25-35% of all your protein.** It is like the glue that holds your body together. A recent study on this product shows it is very healthy and helps to regenerate cartilage. It is a great supplement for anyone wanting to prevent joint degeneration and also for those whose goal is to regenerate.

Micronutrient GREENS - take one serving daily

One of the toughest parts of keto is that it cuts out lots of starchy fruits and vegetables that are high in carbohydrates. However, they are also packed with antioxidants and nutrients. Supplemental powdered greens are a solution to getting enough nutrition from produce, while eating a low-carb ketogenic diet.

Greens contain multiple servings of different fruits and vegetables to increase your anti-oxidant protection during a ketogenic plan since the intake of healthy fruits is limited with this lifestyle. They also have calories and should be consumed after breaking your fast if you are fasting.

Liver Support and Digestive Enzymes Take one before larger meals.
Without this, you would waste a lot of the benefit and micronutrients of the different products. It helps to digest and break down food for optimal absorption.

Pre-workout powders like *Rejuv PREformance Pure* and *Rejuv PREformance Pure PLUS* (has creatine added for strength gains if also working out).

These powders are for people who are on a ketogenic or otherwise low-carb diet and want a healthy, ketogenic pre-workout energy drink without all the crap in other pre-workout drink mixes. They can be used any time of day for a quick, clean and healthy energy boost for physical and cognitive performance.

Rejuv CarbCurb Take 4 capsules before breakfast (or in the morning to help control your fasting state) and 4 capsules before 3 pm.

This is a blend of natural supplements including; Phenylalanine, L-Tyrosine, L-Glutamate, and 5-HTP plus some additional vitamins. They synergistically work to curve addictive behavior from eating to smoking. It calms down the brain and helps us with self-control. This can be used to give you more restraint over carb cravings during transitioning into a healthy lifestyle and cutting the unhealthy addictive sugars and processed foods.

Rejuv hCG Support Mix 1 to 2 scoops (3 grams per scoop) with water before any larger meal.

This is a dietary fiber and can be used with intermittent fasting or ketogenic plans to enhance fullness through decreasing gastric emptying, decreases leptin levels (the hormone that makes us feel hungry), increases bowel motility and has been shown in studies to enhance weight loss.

Minerals and Salt Take one serving in the morning if fasting and again during the day if doing a ketogenic meal plan. It can be mixed it into your water for a tasty flavor.

Due to changes in mineral and water balance when beginning a low carb diet (especially a ketogenic diet), you might want to add a mineral supplement. You should always be eating a wide variety of brightly colored vegetables (and lots of dark, green, leafy veggies), but adding into a multi-mineral can also be helpful. Don't be afraid to liberally salt your foods with Himalayan or Celtic sea salt, as you are cutting out all sodium from processed and packaged foods. Also, they can be used when in fasting times.

BRANCHED CHAIN AMINO ACIDS (BCAAs)- Rejuv GAINZ 5,000mg a day

Can be used after workouts to enhance muscle recovery and minimize muscle loss if in a calorie-deficient state or when looking to optimize lean muscle.

CLA 3-4,000mg a day

It has been shown to increase abdominal fat loss and increase insulin sensitivity.

L-Carnitine 3-4,000mg a day

It has been shown to help mobilize fat to be used as energy, decreases cholesterol and increases memory.

Multivitamin One per day

May be needed to supplement micronutrients and minerals with weight loss as calories may be restricted and micronutrients deficient.

B12 1000mcg a day
Recommended for anyone on a mostly vegetable-based nutrition plan.

There you have it - an overview of the core elements needed to optimize your healing environment, body composition and health status. As you embark on this journey to optimize your health, these are the areas to focus on with the goal of creating habit changes, so they become a part of your daily life.

When you first start out, you will have to schedule these into your day until they become part of who you are consistently. You have the power to make a change! You have the ability to make decisions every day that will have long-lasting impact on not only your health, but the health of your family and those around you. Every journey starts with that first step. Before that first step there is contemplation and then comes the decision. It is time to move from "*I have thought about that*" to "*I am doing it!*"

Let's dive a bit deeper into some strategies that can help you get your mindset ready for the commitment and motivation needed for successful change.

TIME FOR A CHANGE: Establish your WHY, Set your GOAL and Develop your PLAN

If you have decided that you're ready to make a positive change in your health starting with nutrition, let's give you the tools to make that first step! We are all creatures of habit and so change happens to be very difficult. We all want to be healthy. We all want to enjoy life to its fullest. We want to be able to run, to play, and to experience all the adventures that having a healthy body can lead to every day. We don't want to live in pain, fatigue, apathetic and without zest. We want to thrive! Desire is a good thing. But change can only happen if we have the correct mindset to do so.

The first step to change starts in our brain. We have to make the mental commitment and have an organized plan for success. It is critical in this beginning step to rid yourself of any negative thoughts or labels that may hinder your success. The first step - and one most important - in making change is to establish your why, or your reason to make that change. This will be the fuel that gives you the energy to sustain the effort it will take during this transition time. This is your deep-rooted reason of why you want to make this change in your life. It has to be a very personal to you to be effective and compelling enough to pull you through the journey. You'll use this as a daily reminder to inspire you to continue with your health journey.

Next, set your goal. This is essential to your long-term success when trying to change behavioral patterns. You need to set both short- and long-term goals and get your mindset focused on the target. You should create long-term health, professional and personal goals. We will focus on your health goals here, but they could easily augment and overlap with your other goals.

Your short-term (weekly and monthly) goals should keep you focused on your long-term goals but give you consistent positive feedback and celebration as you obtain these steps of achievement. More on goal setting in CHAPTER 14. Go through the written steps in that chapter to guide you through the process of making a mental change and setting your goals after establishing your WHY!

Once you have your goals set and you have made the needed changes in your mindset, you are ready to start on the exciting journey of creating healthy change in your body. This will lead to an increased vitality and passion.

You need to first clear out the mental garbage you have of how you perceive yourself. Start with a clean slate without any judgement or bias. Wipe away any negative labels you have of yourself and replace them with new images and thoughts of who you truly are at your core. You are NOT "lazy", "unhealthy", "fat", "carnivorous", "unfit", "unattractive", "unloved". You are simply YOU... created to be amazing, loved, loving, beautiful, healthy, vibrant, smart, appealing and unique. That is who you are.

Close your eyes and erase the lies you once believed. There is only ONE TRUTH. You have the ability to change who you are in a second. Not many things can be changed this fast and have such a powerful effect on your destiny. Identify with the real you.

Once you have wiped your slate clean and replaced it with the truth, you can now reinforce that truth to help you obtain your goals. Take a few minutes, close your eyes, meditate on the words that define who you are as your essential self. Here is a list to help you get started, but you should create your own list that you relate to and gives you the power to change!

I am strong.
I am beautiful.
I am loved.
I am wanted.

I am healthy.

I am unique.

I am needed.

I am smart.

I am creative.

I have influence.

I have ability.

I have power.

I have purpose.

Make your own list, then start and end your day in meditation and prayer. Be thankful for all the "good" in your life. The amazing thing is that, once you love yourself, that love will spill over and you will become a powerful influence on those around you. More on this in CHAPTER 14. It is only once you BELIEVE you can that you TRULY CAN!

With the reality of who you were created to be, let's start with nutrition as it is your foundation for health and, in reality, can be a difficult pattern to change. How we eat and what we eat is often a very personal issue. We don't want to give up our learned behaviors, our cultural and ethnic customs and the way we have learned to consume foods. Food is our comfort, our entertainment and our celebration. It still can be, but it also can be your driving force to obtaining your health and fitness goals.

I can relate to how hard it is to change this pattern. The great thing is you CAN learn new habits, form new patterns, and create healthy family customs that reflect and reinforce your new identity and goals. This will not only change your life, but that of your family and generations to come. Think of what a powerful effect this will have - you are part of a movement and - together - we are redefining healthcare!

Use this time during your healthy nutrition transition to start implementing the **8 Rejuv4LIFE Core Elements** keys to success listed here.

1. Self-Change
2. Sleep
3. Nutrition

4. Exercise

5. Water

6. Supplements

7. Hormone Optimization

8. Stress Management

CHECKLIST

It is time to put your knowledge into action. It all starts with a plan. This checklist will help you organize your approach to starting a lifestyle that promotes long-term health and healing. The checklist is a summary of all you have learned. It is your basic guide to get you started, but also a great tool to use weekly if you are potentially off-track or not getting the results you desire. Refer to the checklist and make sure you are following the guidelines in each one. Ready. Set. Let's GO!

- **MINDSET**: It all starts here. Your ability to create lasting change in your health habits starts in your head. You need to make your decision to become healthy based on a deep-rooted reason that is special and personal to you. "I want to be healthy for my children and family, so I can be a role model for them as they develop healthy lifestyles of their own." "I want to run and play with my grandchildren and live an active, fit retirement." "I want to change my genetic tendencies and avoid the chronic diseases of my family." Write your WHY and refer to it daily.

- **NUTRITION GOALS**: Your first goal with your nutrition habits is to decrease your carb intake. This will decrease the negative effects of insulin and elevated blood sugar and also enable you to tap into fat stores via shifting metabolism to utilize ketones and burn fat for energy. This leads to a change in body composition to a leaner healthy physique.

As you progressively decrease your carbohydrate level, you will progressively train your body to utilize fat as a fuel source during times when your carbohydrate intake is low or during fasting states. Once you are utilizing your fat stores and burning ketones for energy in the muscles and brain, you are considered Keto- or Fat-adapted. Here your body can burn either carbohydrates or fat for fuel. This gives you the flexibility to eat less.

If your goal is fat weight loss, then a lower carb intake is needed to promote fat burning and ketosis. You are able to choose how fast you want the fat to burn by how much you restrict your carbohydrate intake. Next is increasing the good fats and eliminating harmful vegetable oils and products containing them as well as avoiding the trans and hydrogenated fats. Finally, getting adequate, but not excessive, protein is important.

• **CARBS**. Lowering your carbohydrate intake and eliminating certain sources of nutrient-deficient sources of carbs will be the most important step you take towards your new healthy lifestyle. Start the first week by eliminating all extra sugars in the form of sweets, snacks, processed foods, juices and soda. They all cause leptin hormone resistance. (Leptin is a hormone released by fat cells to tell the brain to shut down hunger. If the body is resistant to it, it will not suppress hunger and cravings for more food will continue).

Next, eliminate all grains and legumes. Both contain lectin which is thought to also cause leptin resistance. Avoid all grain products as well, including pasta, breads, tortillas, crackers, cereals, etc. This leaves you with vegetables and a limited amount of fruits. You may need to limit your intake of tubers, like sweet potatoes (yes - very healthy, but also high in carbohydrates) if you are doing PHASE 1 or KETO.

- **R4L-Foundational Nutrition**: 100-150 grams - around 1 pound a week
- **R4L-Accelerated Nutrition**: 50-100 gram - 1-2 pounds a week
- **R4L-Advanced Nutrition-KETO**: Less than 30-50 grams - accelerated weight loss.

To become keto/fat-adapted and maintain metabolic flexibility, for the inactive individual, most need to get their total carb intake to less than 20 grams a day. For the active individual with a physical job or exercising consistently, they may tolerate up to 50 grams total carbs a day. If you are not getting results, a lower amount may be needed to get the benefits of becoming adapted to using fat as an energy source.

Fat 60-75%. Protein 15-25%. Carbs 5-10%

- **FAT**. Getting the right types and enough of healthy fats is the next critical aspect of getting your healthy lifestyle dialed in so that you can effortlessly start to transform your body and health. Healthy fats have anti-inflammatory properties and can aid in making us feel full and satiated. This is where your new lifestyle will deviate from your past diet crashes and failures.

Fat is needed in the correct amount to give you ample energy plus it has anti-inflammatory effects. The right sources of fats are also packed with other nutrients your body needs for maximum performance.

Also, the wrong types of fats, or any fats combined with a high-carbohydrate diet, will not be healthy and will cause weight gain and chronic disease. You MUST lower your carbs when increasing your fat intake to enable you to increase your fat intake and transition your body to a fat-burning machine. If you consume high carbs, it will spike insulin and result in storing your high-fat intake as more body fat.

-As you lower carbs, increase fat to aid in satiety

-60-75% % total calorie intake if following R4L-KETO

- **PROTEIN.** You don't need as much protein as we once thought. Too much protein will tax the kidneys and also spike your insulin levels which will act as a storage hormone with any excess carbs or even fat consumed. Also focus on healthy organic, grass-fed animal sources (seafood, meat, dairy-cheese, butter, cream (avoid milk), and eggs, or choose low-carb vegetarian options.

Vegetarian proteins may have a higher carbohydrate content and may put you in to more of a PHASE 2 carb level, which will slow weight loss, but that is ok as long as you are aware. Vegetarians just need to track the carb intake to make sure they are not going over the limit needed to still tap into fat stores for weight loss.

Protein amount needed: .5-1 gram per pound of LEAN body weight

- Lower end if sedentary
- Higher end for athletes, pregnant or breastfeeding women, elderly people, those who had regenerative procedure or injury
- No matter what R4L carb level you choose, your protein needs will stay the same. You will just adjust your carbohydrate and fat amounts.

- **EXERCISE GOALS.** Exercise is an important part of your plan, but don't let it stress you out because your weight loss and health overhaul starts with your nutrition. You will not be successful if you don't reign in those high-carb intakes first. Studies show that those who exercise to lose weight fail due to the increased hunger after workouts and the more freedom they take from feeling they have "earned" the sugary treat because of their workout.

Exercise is important for increasing metabolism and will also increase good anabolic repair hormones, but it needs to be in the correct intensity and amount. Over-exercising can also create increased stress and oxidation to our systems, which may counteract attempts to create health and longevity. Super high-intensity workouts should be done only a few times a week with lower-intensity workouts on other days. Lower-intensity fun, even relaxing activities - like light sports, walking and hiking - can be done anytime and every day.

We are meant to move! Our jobs and lifestyles have taken out our need to move, so it is important to plan them into our schedule intentionally. Take a brisk walk after lunch. Park in the furthest away spot in any parking lot. Take the stairs whenever possible.

The more movement you add to your day, the better it will be for sensitizing your body to insulin and helping you hit your healthy goals. The guideline below is a great plan but remember that any increase from your current activity level is a "step" in the right direction.

- Low-Intensity Cardio (aerobic): Walk or low-intensity activity/play daily
  - HR= 180-age max rate. You want to keep your heart rate in the fat-burning zone and not get too high-intense with it.

- High-Intensity Cardio (anaerobic): This high-intensity should not be done every day. If your body is well-adapted, you can do a few high-intensity workouts a week but, if high fitness is not your goal, then doing a high-intensity workout once every week to 10 days is fine. Your body will need the time to repair and get ready for the next one anyway. These workouts do have a positive effect on metabolism and healthy hormones at the right frequency. If done too frequently, they can do the opposite and break you down.

- Sprint 8(8 min), Tabata (4 min)
- Sprinting, Cycling sets
  - 5 sets of 15-20 seconds all out
  - 1-2 min recovery
  - 10 min. max total time

• Higher-Intensity Resistance Training: This type of exercise is like weight training. It is very important to maintain strong and healthy bones and muscle. These exercises can be done a few times a week and should focus on large muscle full-body movements. They increase good hormone production, increase metabolism and calorie-burning after the workout as well as protect your joint and spine from degeneration.

- 2-3 times a week
- Full-body multi-joint exercises
- Push, Pull, Squat, Core
- 20-30 min.

- Low- Intensity Core/Stretching: This type of movement can be done every day or in between your higher-intensity days. They can help with your flexibility and decrease joint and spine stress and strain. They are also good for the mind and a way to unwind and relax.
  - Pilates, Yoga, Foam rolling, Stretching

- **SLEEP**

Your goal is 8 hours of uninterrupted sleep. Set the ideal sleep environment and refer to our recommended sleep hygiene tips

- Bedroom is for sleep only. No cell phones, computers or TV while in bed.
- Avoid blue light as sunset approaches (enhance melatonin release for deep sleep)
  - Wear light-blocking eye mask for sleep or have room as dark as possible. Any light will decrease melatonin release and impair sleep.
  - Limit screen time 1-2 hours before bedtime. Screens have high amounts of blue light waves that turn off melatonin.

- Wear blue light-locking glasses during evening hours.
- Set screens to night mode (low blue, higher red/yellow hues).
- Dim lighting in the evening hours (after sunset). This will start the release of melatonin and get you ready for a great night's sleep.

• Ear plugs or ambient sound (i.e., fan, rain sounds) for sleep.

• Warm shower before bed.

• Meditation or prayer with deep breathing to relax before or in bed.

• **RELAXATION**

• Stress Redox. Reduce stress with light exercise, short walks, playing a game or sport, talking to a good friend, sipping tea or coffee, meditation, taking a bath, yoga and listening to soothing music.

• Relaxation time should be scheduled into your day as Part of your new healthy routine. That is why it is on the daily checklist. You should do something relaxing every day. Look forward to it. Make it a ritual.

A TALE OF TWO HORMONES

A final note on the two hormones that regulate our appetites and can powerfully influence weight loss vs. weight gain as well as keeping the weight off after we have lost body fat. The two opposing players are leptin and ghrelin.

While ghrelin is an appetite-stimulating peptide, leptin is an appetite-suppressing one. Ghrelin, secreted from the stomach, particularly influences the metabolism of fat tissue by promoting its storage during hard times. Leptin and ghrelin function interdependently in healthy humans. The world leptin means "full" in Greek. Leptin is produced in the fat cells and released in the brain. Leptin gives us a feeling of satisfaction. While ghrelin enhances appetite, leptin acts as a satiety signal to diminish it.

Other tricks to **INCREASE LEPTIN** (secreted from fat cells and makes your feel full) and **DECREASE GHRELIN** (secreted from the stomach and makes you hungry and crave more food). You can see they overlap with the checklist and will further help with your body composition goals.

- **Avoid MSG.** MSG (monosodium glutamate) makes your appetite spiral out of control. Your body loses its ability to tell that it's full because MSG suppresses leptin. You end up eating more than you normally would and get hungrier sooner. MSG is in ALL fast food and most processed food, even the healthy ones at Whole Foods.

- **Avoid Fructose.** Fructose prevents leptin and insulin from elevating to normal levels after a meal, while increasing ghrelin and triglycerides. This can lead to a dramatic increase in calorie consumption. While high-fructose sweeteners in soft drinks and snack foods are the biggest concern, it's also important to note that fruit, and especially fruit juice, consumption can lead to these shifts as well. Some authors suggest keeping fructose intake under 25 grams per day (about one piece of fruit).

- **Avoid Very-Low-Calorie Diets** (1000 Calories or Less Day). By eating more food, you'll avoid the diet hormone surges that trigger uncontrollable hunger and the inevitable weight gain that follows. The more a person diets, the hungrier they get. It is almost as if semi-starvation triggers gherlin to increase. This may be part of the reason that we regain weight lost by dieting (and then some). The secret is to stop dieting.

- **Fasting.** Ghrelin induces other metabolic actions, such as spikes in blood sugar, called the hyperglycemic effect. Therefore, modified fasting, which decreases ghrelin secretion and increases leptin, may provide an effective technique for treating obesity as opposed to low-calorie diets that increase ghrelin. The more you restrict your calories, the lower the baseline for ghrelin. Ghrelin levels tend to decrease naturally after you fast for a few days. That means that, after fasting for more than 48 hours, your hunger diminishes.

By decreasing the inflow of food and reducing caloric intake for as little as a few days, you can lessen the attendant cravings. This is an important tip to remember. When you are gaining weight, fast for two or three days and you will become less hungry and regain some control.

Stop dieting! By now, you have discovered that the desire for food is controlled by complex interactions between hunger/satiety and caloric or energy requirements. By slowing down digestion and increasing the length of time food stays in the stomach, it is possible to maintain equilibrium between ghrelin and leptin. Through fasting and chewing your food slowly, you can suppress ghrelin and hunger at its origin.

- **Eat High-Fiber Plant-Based Foods**. Ghrelin levels remain high until food stretches the wall of your stomach, making you feel full. High-volume, low-calorie, nutrient-dense foods reduce ghrelin and increase leptin levels long before you have overeaten.

Slow digestion abolishes hunger by providing a shortcut to the long-term satiety center in your hypothalamus. A salad or vegetable soup full of fiber and water stretches your stomach more than processed food.

- **Get at Least 7 Hours of Sleep Every Night.** Less than seven hours of sleep has been associated with higher ghrelin levels, decreased leptin, increased hunger, and higher body weight in research studies. This is why people who sleep less are heavier than those getting adequate sleep.

- **Eat Protein at Every Meal.** Protein takes longer to digest, and studies show it is the most effect food group at lowering ghrelin and losing weight. Research also suggests that protein improves leptin sensitivity. Just do not go over the recommended amount of .5-1 gram per pound of lean muscle.

- **Reduce Stress.** Stress is associated with higher body weight and ghrelin production. Reduce stress to enhance weight loss.

- **Increase Omega-3**. Eat a diet rich in omega-3 fatty acids to boost leptin. People who are overweight release too much of a group of molecules that the body uses to combat inflammation. These molecules reduce leptin's ability to communicate with the brain and are the primary cause of leptin resistance. Omega-3 fatty acids decrease the production of these molecules by reducing inflammation in the body. Foods high in omega-3 fatty acids include grass-fed meats, walnuts, salmon, anchovies, sardines, mackerel, trout, chia seeds, flax seeds, summer squash and kale.

- **Hydrate.** One glass of water before every meal decreases the amount you will eat by at least 8 ounces and suppresses ghrelin.

- **Heal Your Gut.** A healthy intestine can help control appetite and body weight. Conversely, leptin and ghrelin imbalances have been observed in gut disorders like colitis. Take probiotics and eat bone broths to heal the gut. Foods containing inulin (garlic, onions, leeks, artichokes, sunchokes, bananas) feed good gut bacteria, promoting their replication, and are more effective than supplementing probiotics.

Anything that helps intestinal health should be helpful for appetite issues.

- **Conclusion**. Leptin and ghrelin have evolved as a highly effective mechanism to keep us from starving to death in times of famine. Poor diet and lifestyle lead to the ultimate failure of this delicate signaling system, making weight loss an impossible task.

Master your appetite hormones by following a naturally evolved diet like the Modern Paleo diet and observe proper meal timing to reap the benefits of restored health and permanent weight loss.

Keep focused and motivated and you will be successful.

CHAPTER 4: EXERCISE - CREATED TO MOVE

That which is used develops. That which is not used wastes away. — **Hippocrates**

Walking is man's best medicine. — **Hippocrates**

We have discussed how our change in human behavior over the last hundred years and the advancement of technology has led to a society that is less motivated, moves less and is suffering the consequences of that loss of physical activity. What is very exciting is that there is plenty of evidence for the benefits of fitness.

Fitness and exercise have been shown to help slow or reverse most chronic diseases like hypertension, heart disease, obesity, diabetes, depression, sleep disorders, poor circulation, back pain and other orthopedic problems. That is why we call it medical fitness. It has a positive effect on medical health and healing.

A study in the Journal of Osteoarthritis Cartilage in 2016 concluded that, with patients suffering from the degenerative arthritis, those who lost weight over 48 months slowed the knee cartilage degeneration and improved their symptoms. Weight loss is helpful when treating pain and loss of activity from arthritis.[26] There are many studies concluding that those with chronic back pain who exercise have less long-term problems and less pain than those who choose a more sedentary lifestyle.

When it comes to exercise and healing, there are studies which also confirm that exercise is helpful. One study concludes that those who exercise preserve their muscle cells and can increase strength during the vulnerable aging years. Another study in 2011 showed that exercise improves stem cell bone formation.[34,35]

With all my patients I treat using PRP or stem cell treatments, we talk about exercise - both resistance and cardio - to help improve their stem cell or PRP procedural success. Other benefits of adding exercise is a change in body composition with an increase in lean muscle and a decrease in unwanted body fat.

Let's dive into exercise and break it down so that we can understand the different types of exercise and the benefits we can receive from it.

In general, exercise can be broken down into resistance training and cardiovascular training. Cardiovascular training can be broken down into anaerobic and aerobic type activities. Anaerobic activities are very intense and can only be sustained for short periods of time. They would be like high-intensity resistance training, sprinting and plyometric type workouts. The heart rate is elevated for short periods of time and they can have great impact on healthy hormone production, strength and power gains, as well as weight loss. Aerobic exercise is a lower intensity but a longer duration type of a workout. This would be like running, walking, skiing, swimming, boot camps and yoga. The heart rate is sustained at a relatively constant level and is good for endurance and sustained calorie burning.

Both types of cardiovascular exercise are important. Anaerobic exercise is important in short bursts to increase calorie utilization after the workout as well as production of growth hormone and testosterone. They are both hormones that will maximize strength and lean muscle gains and increase unwanted fat loss. Aerobic exercise can be used with weight loss but cycling anaerobic with aerobic exercise is actually best for weight-loss effects and overall fitness and health.

Depending on your goals, aerobic versus anaerobic activities based on your percentage of maximal heart rate can be used to achieve them. To calculate your maximum heart rate, you would take 220 minus your age. For example, if you are 35 years old, then your maximum heart rate would be 185 beats per minute.

From there, you can determine your percentage of maximum heart rate. If your goal is fat burning, then you want your percentage of maximum heart rate to be around 60 to 70%. This will increase the fat-burning pathways. For endurance games, you want your percentage of maximum heart rate to be about 70 to 75%. This will increase your aerobic energy sources and pathways. For a combination of both endurance and strength gains, your percent maximum heart rate should be around 75 to 80%. This will increase in your aerobic pathways but may not be an effective range for specific adaptions if you are looking for larger endurance or power gains. Again, it is the best route for overall fitness for the majority of us.

However, if you are an athlete and your goal is to train in your lactate threshold, then you would want your maximum heart rate to be about 80 to 90%. Not many of us need this type of workout but, depending on your sports performance goals, it can be utilized. This will increase your lactate threshold, aerobic and anaerobic energy pathways as well as your lactate clearance. If your goal is fast racing or peak performance, your percent maximum heart rate is 90-100%. This will increase anaerobic energy sources, fast twitch muscle fiber recruitment, and speed in your muscle coordination and firing.

Goals	% Max HR	Adaptions
Burn Fat	60-70	Increase fast-burning pathways
Endurance Gains	70-75	Increases aerobic energy sources and pathways
Endurance / Strength Gains	75-80	Increases aerobic pathways (may not be an effective range for specific adaptations)
Lactate Threshold	80-90	Increases lactate threshold, aerobic and anaerobic energy pathways and lactate clearance
Fast race/Peak	90-100	Increases anaerobic energy sources, fast-twitch fiber recruitment, speed and neuro-muscular coordination

With exercise, the body will adapt based on the stresses put on it. This is called gradual progressive overload, or GPO. For strength gains to occur with exercise, you need to slowly increase the training intensity and the resistance load. The body will adapt as you overload the muscles and then give them time to heal and recover. Not allowing adequate recovery can lead to injury and breakdown. The amount of recovery time needed will vary depending on the intensity and type of workout performed.

Cardiovascular training can usually be performed every day and adaptations will still occur. Strength training should have about 48 hours of rest to that muscle group before training it again. An example would be chest and arm workouts on Monday and Wednesday, then leg and back workouts on Tuesday and Thursday.

When I am prescribing exercise for my patients, I like to use this **F.I.T.T.** exercise prescription. The **F** is for frequency, which represents the number of sessions per week. The I is for intensity, which is the difficulty of the exercise. T is for time -the duration of the exercise. The second T is for type of exercise, meaning the mode of the exercise like strength, endurance, balance or flexibility. You can change up each of the above to achieve your specific goals.

A F.I.T.T. exercise prescription should be part of any office visit to a medical provider for any chronic metabolic disease like hypertension, diabetes, cardiovascular disease, high cholesterol or obesity for weight loss goals. It is the future of health care. Exercise is the best medicine and should be integrated into our medical model to decrease healthcare costs and increase our outcomes. It will also decreases our need for expensive medications that don't target the root causes of the diagnosis they are intended to treat. We need to create fitness to change our healthcare model to truly create health in ourselves, communities, nation and world. One of my missions is to change healthcare worldwide and a daily exercise, or medical fitness routine, is paramount.

GOALS	FREQUENCY	INTENSITY	TIME (Min)	TYPE
General Health Improvements	3 or more	Moderate	20 – 60	Mix cardio and strength
General Fitness Improvements	3 or more	Moderate to Moderately High	30 or more	Mix cardio and strength training, all muscle groups
Cardiovascular Endurance	Minimum of 3 to see improvement	Moderate to Moderately High	30 or more	Any exercise working large muscle groups for a sustained period of time
Strength and Power	1 to 5, depending on intensity	Mostly high	20 or more	Exercise that isolates muscle groups and rapidly fatigues them
Weight Loss	5 – 7	Moderate to high (once trained)	30-60 or more	Mostly cardio; strength important to maintain muscle mass

Goals and Training Intensity

In general, I encourage my patients to work out at least 4 to 5 times a week with moderate-intensity exercise. The duration should at least be a half-hour and can be a mix of cardiovascular and strength training. If your goal is weight loss, it is important to be active and work out at least 5 to 7 days a week. Intensity should be moderate with an increase to high-intensity once you are trained. The duration should be 30 to 60 minutes or more, focusing on activities that keep the heart rate elevated throughout the workout as this will facilitate fat loss and calorie burn.

To avoid fitness plateauing, it is important to add variation to your workout. You can start by changing the order and the intensity of the exercises you're doing. You can try new set systems like circuit training, supersets or antagonistic training. Antagonistic training is where you work out opposite muscle groups like biceps and triceps or chest and back at the same time without much downtime between exercises. Changing the amount of weight, or resistance, and the number of repetitions can also help to shock the muscles and encourage fitness gains. During a training session, you can mix strength, balance and endurance exercises together to increase your calorie burn and again add variation to your strength training. Adding instability, like standing on a Bosu ball or foam mat, can increase muscle recruitment during exercise. Decreasing the amount of rest time in between sets can also add intensity to your workout. It's important to continue to confuse your muscles and mix things up to avoid plateauing with your training.

Your workout should consist of three phases. The warm-up, the core workout and the cool-down. The warm-up should be a dynamic warm-up where you are doing large muscle movements, like lunges, gorilla walks, leg kicks or jacks. It is important to get the heart rate elevated and warm up the muscles during this time. You want to avoid static stretching during your warm-up as it may increase your risk of injury. Your warm-ups should last around five minutes, depending on the total duration of your workout. Next is the core workout. This is your strength training, circuit training or cardiovascular aspect of the workout. It is the bulk of your workout and, if doing a whole hour workout, should last about 40 to 45 minutes.

Finally, you enter the cool-down. Stretching can be done at the end of your workout to help with range of motion. You can also do balance exercises, like yoga and core exercises with your stretching. This should last 5 to 10 minutes and is a very important part of your total workout.

Your workout should be tailored toward your fitness goals. The workout should be a combination of strength training, cardiovascular and endurance training, balance and proprioception and flexibility.

Remember, exercise will eventually become a habit and a part of what you do and who you are daily. In the beginning, it will be very important that you schedule time and make it one of your weekly goals to get your exercise training in as part of your routine. Pick an exercise, sport or activity you enjoy, increasing the probability of your compliance and success. Let's get moving and start exercising to increase fitness and decrease risk of chronic disease.

Exercise is the best medicine.

CHAPTER 5: HORMONE OPTIMIZATION - THE SYMPHONY

A healthy outside starts from the inside. — **Robert Urich**

As mentioned previously, our hormone systems need to be well-balanced to create a synchronized, harmonious outcome that results in optimal health and healing. With this aspect of cell health, the goal is a life lived with zest and vitality, avoiding the aging effects of unbalanced hormones. The hormone symphony's main players include the thyroid hormone, the sex hormones and the adrenal hormones.

The first aspect to work on with hormone optimization is weight loss and a healthy lifestyle. This includes nutrition, exercise, sleep, adequate stress management and relaxation. If still needed, your hormone levels are then analyzed through detailed laboratory testing. Results are interpreted by a medical specialist who understands hormone optimization and your levels are returned to a healthier balance to optimize function in the body. It is also important to optimize the micronutrient environment with vitamins like vitamin D. Let's take a closer look.

THYROID HORMONE

The thyroid is a small gland that sits in the front of the neck. Its main function is to control our metabolism. Once thyroid hormone is released from the thyroid gland, it circulates through the blood and can have a profound impact on almost every cell in our bodies.

Take a look at the following symptoms related to deficiency of thyroid hormone. If you have some of these symptoms, it would be a good idea to be evaluated.

- Feeling tired
- Difficulty losing weight with a low metabolism
- Sluggish in the morning

- Low body temperature
- High cholesterol
- Dry skin
- Fluid retention
- Memory and focus trouble
- Decreased sex drive
- Cold hands and feet
- Thinning hair
- Hoarse voice
- Thicker fingernails
- Chronic aches and pains
- Muscle cramps and weakness
- Carpal tunnel syndrome
- Frozen shoulder
- Joint pain
- Other nerve entrapment syndromes

Does anything sound familiar? Thyroid deficiency is one of the most commonly missed diagnoses. Forty-five million people suffer the symptoms, and yet go undiagnosed yearly. Thyroid hormone affects everything from the skin, heart, brain, gut and muscles. It is important for optimal function in many aspects of our bodies.

Why are so many people not diagnosed or diagnosed incorrectly? Thyroid hormone deficiency symptoms can be very vague and not specific. Lab testing of the thyroid using the TSH blood test only has been shown to be inaccurate at times and can miss the diagnosis. It is important, when diagnosing the disorder, to consider the history and physical examination of the patient as well. New data shows that there may be different ways to diagnose the disorder more completely using a more expanded lab evaluation.

It is critical to get an accurate diagnosis by a skilled provider who understands how to diagnose an under-functioning thyroid. Once the diagnosis is confirmed, treatment and follow-up is important for optimal functioning of our body systems.

ADRENAL HORMONES

The adrenal glands are two small organs located on the top of both the kidneys. Their function is to control the effects of stress, pain and injury in our bodies. They release the hormone cortisol, as well as other stress hormones, in response to stress and injury. They function to increase energy and mood, fight inflammation, modulate the healing response, respond to acute stressors and also to decrease pain. The stress response is important to fight dangers in life-threatening situations, but prolonged stress responses can take their toll on their body.

PHYSICAL:	ENVIRONMENTAL:

• Pain
• Infection
• Allergies
   − Food (i.e. Gluten, Eggs, Wheat, Dairy, etc.)
   − Environmental (i.e., Pollen, Dust, Molds, Animals)
• Chronic illness and disease
EMOTIONAL:
• Family
• Work
• Relationship
• Financial
• Loss
	• Air Pollution
	• Water Pollution
	• Metal Toxicity
	• Food
	   − Preservatives
	   − MSG
	   − Aspartame
	   − Hormones
	   − Antibiotics
	• Chemical

Different Types of Stressors

Cortisol released from the adrenal glands follows a cycle. It is elevated in the morning and shuts down in the evening to allow for sleep. Prolonged stressors can lead to dysfunction in the adrenal cycle manifesting itself as sub-optimal health, fatigue, poor healing and amplified pain.

ACUTE STRESS	CHRONIC STRESS
Immediate danger response	Prolonged stressors
Increased blood sugar for energy to brain and muscles	Body shifts priorities from other areas for handling prolonged stressors
Heart rate and BP increases for O2 delivery to muscles	Cortisol production dominates other hormone production
Other functions decrease: hormones, bowel, kidney, immune	PMS, irregular periods, weight gain, Irritable Bowel Syndrome

Acute and Chronic Stress

With an acute stress, like an immediate danger, the body responds to create balance in the body and fight the stressor. During this time, there is an increase in blood sugar delivery for energy to fuel optimal function of the brain and muscles. The heart rate and blood pressure increase to help deliver oxygen to the muscles to help get out of the stressful situation or fight it. The body sacrifices function of the other organs to shunt the energy to these vital areas.

With chronic stress from a prolonged stressor, like chronic pain, unhealthy relationships, unhealthy living environments or excessive activity and exercise, there can be compensation and sub-optimal adrenal function. With prolonged stressors, cortisol function may dominate other hormone productions, like estrogen, progesterone, testosterone and thyroid hormone. Symptoms like PMS, irregular periods, poor sleep, weight gain and fatigue can all start to set in.

Over time, if the stressors are not dealt with, the adrenal glands eventually cannot support the chronic stress and the release of cortisol may then drop to sub-optimal levels of cortisol for adequate function in the body. This is sometimes referred to as adrenal fatigue with symptoms of apathy, depression, decreased energy and also the amplification of pain.

Let's look at different patterns in the release of cortisol.

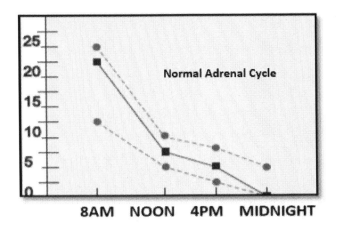

Normal Adrenal Cycle

8AM NOON 4PM MIDNIGHT

In a normal healthy state, release of cortisol is high in the morning to help wake you up and get the body turned on for the daytime stressors. It will slowly decrease throughout the day and, at night, the adrenal glands decrease the production of cortisol to allow for sleep induction and rest.

With a normal pattern, you awaken refreshed and have energy throughout the day. In the evening, when the body relaxes as the cortisol levels fall, and sleep is easily obtained. Adrenal cycles are set but can be altered with prolonged stressors. Chronic pain is a stressor that can modify the normal adrenal cycle as the body fights to maintain balance. If the pain persists, over time a pathologic adrenal cycle can develop.

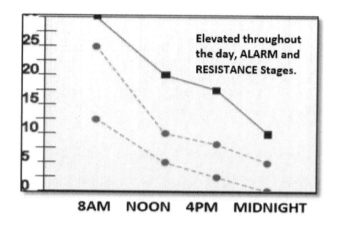

With chronic stressors, the adrenal glands can become hyperactive with elevated cortisol levels throughout the entire day. The physical presentation of this profile would be feeling wired, stressed out and agitated with poor sleep and insomnia. This type of profile is seen with prolonged stressors, as the body is fighting to survive by increasing cortisol levels. This type of pressured function can only last so long before the adrenal glands begin to shut down.

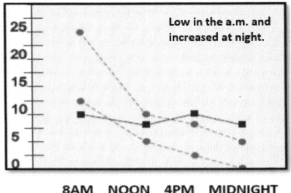

Low in the a.m. and increased at night.

8AM   NOON   4PM   MIDNIGHT

Next is another maladapted adrenal profile where the patient wakes up feeling very fatigued. They may feel somewhat normal around noon but then, in the evenings, feels agitated and has trouble sleeping. In this phase, the cortisol is sub-optimal in the morning but, as the day goes on, the cortisol level rises opposite of a normal cycle.

Finally, there is the chronic fatigue profile. This pathologic adaptation is seen after prolonged stress where the adrenal glands have lost the ability to keep making cortisol. The cortisol levels basically flat-line, leaving the patient fatigued, depressed and with an amplified pain response throughout the day. We see this pattern a lot with our chronic pain patients.

Chronic pain and arthritis can be a powerful physical stressor that leaves patients feeling hopeless and helpless.

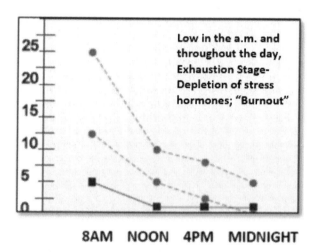

There are many ways to check cortisol levels. They can be checked through the blood and through saliva. Salivary cortisol levels have been shown to be very accurate and are used by NASA and the U.S. Air Force to test pilots during times of stress. If checking through saliva, four separate samples are given throughout the day starting at 8 AM, noon, 4 PM and finally before bed. When plotted out, this will give a good representation of the patient's cortisol and adrenal cyclic function. After lab evaluation, the patient may need treatment based on their profile type.

It is also very important to address the underlying stressors that are contributing to the problem in the first place. Treating the source of pain - utilizing procedures like Prolotherapy, PRP and stem cell treatments - can address the pain through healing the degenerating tissues. It is important to avoid using cover-up pain medications and steroid injections that may have a negative impact on health and the healing of the area of concern.

SEX HORMONES

When we refer to the sex hormones, we are referring to the hormones of estrogen, progesterone, testosterone and DHEA. All these hormones are found in both males and females and are needed for optimal function and longevity. Dysfunction in these hormones can occur, leading to imbalances and symptoms. Stress, physical over-training, menopause and in andropause in males can lead to abnormal balances of these important hormones.

First, let's look at the predominately female hormones - estrogen and progesterone. These hormones are made by the ovaries during the menstrual years and are also made in lower amounts in the adipose tissue and adrenal glands. These two hormones need to be in balance, with appropriate ratios, for the body to function optimally.

As women age, usually around age 35 or more, they will enter the perimenopause years. This is a time when women are usually still making hormones, but their ratios may become sub-optimal and out of balance. These changes can affect the mind and the body. The menstrual cycle may become erratic with less ovulation which creates disruption in the normal hormonal balance. This can lead to unwanted weight gain, anxiety and depression. It is important to understand what each hormone does to understand the problems that occur when these hormones are not balanced.

ESTROGEN. Estrogen is a hormone made by the ovaries and adrenal glands. It will communicate with different tissues and have a profound influence on them.

- UTERUS - stimulates growth and prepares for the implantation of a baby.
- BREASTS -stimulates growth (normal and abnormal cells).
- VAGINA - thickens the wall, moistens and lubricates.
- BONE - decreases breakdown rate and prevents osteoporosis.
- BLADDER - tightens muscle and prevents leakage.

- THYROID - decreases function and decreases metabolism, which if in excess causes weight gain.
- BRAIN - if too high or too low, can cause depression, anxiety, insomnia, loss of sex drive and poor concentration.

PROGESTERONE. Progesterone is made exclusively by the ovaries, so it is often low during the perimenopause and menopausal years. Low levels can also lead to weight gain. The body cannot make progesterone in adipose or adrenal tissue like it can make estrogen. The hormone effects the same tissue as estrogen, but the message is much different.

- UTERUS - if no pregnancy, stimulates shedding (menstruation) and decreases growth; also decreases uterine contractions (menstrual cramping).
- BREAST - decreases cell growth (can aid in decreasing cancer risk).
- BONE - stimulates new bone formation and prevents osteoporosis.

- THYROID - increases thyroid hormone activity and the metabolism of fat (weight loss).
- KIDNEYS - it is a natural diuretic (decreases water retention).
- BRAIN - normal levels decrease anxiety and depression and can increases sex drive.

Taking a closer look at the perimenopausal years reveals it is a time of imbalance. Most of the time during this period, the estrogen levels are elevated compared to a lower progesterone level. As the ovaries are not able to make as much hormone, the progesterone level will drop more quickly than the estrogen levels because the estrogen is still made in the adipose tissue and adrenal glands. This imbalance of excess estrogen with inadequate progesterone leads to problems.

Elevated estrogen levels can be due to the failure to ovulate during this time, external estrogens being consumed in animal fats, synthetic estrogen in pesticides and pollutants, the fact that body fat itself can increase its own estrogen production, and that most of our diets are low in fiber and high in fat and sugar which all leads to dysfunction with estrogen metabolism and excretion.

Breast tenderness	Depression and Fatigue
Fibrocystic Breasts	PMS
Fibroid Growth	Poor Concentration
Endometriosis	Decreased Sex Drive
Breast and Uterine Cancer	Thinning Hair
Water Retention/Bloating	Fat Gain in Hips and Thighs

High Estrogen, Low Progesterone Ratio

SYMPTOMS	COMMON TREATMENTS	PROBLEM	SOLUTION
Irregular Bleeding	Birth control pills Synthetic Progestins D/C or Hysterectomy	Synthetic Progestins block Progesterone	Balance elevated Estrogen levels with Bio-identical Progesterone
Increased Breast Tissue	Multiple Biopsies	Premarin and BCP increase cancer risk	Bio-identical Progesterone can decrease cancer risk
Loss of Bone Mass	Premarin	Increased Cancer and blood clot risks	Bio-identical Progesterone can increase bone mass
Depression Anxiety	Antidepressants Antianxiety	Side effects Dependence	Bio-identical Progesterone can balance Estrogen effects
Weight Gain Low Energy		High Estrogen blocks Thyroid action	Bio-identical Progesterone (also, a natural diuretic)

Perimenopause Symptoms, Misdiagnosis and Treatments

During the perimenopause time, a female will often go to her physician with some of the above symptoms. Treatments are often geared at covering up the symptoms of fatigue or depression with another medication. They may also be given a synthetic hormone that can have a much higher side effect profile than natural bio-identical hormones. Bio-identical hormones can be used to treat these menopausal years with much less risk than the commonly prescribed synthetic hormones.

Bio-identical hormones are structurally identical to those the body naturally utilizes, as opposed to synthetic hormones which are not structurally the same and have a much more profound risk and side effect profile. As with any medical treatment, it is important for those in the menopausal or perimenopausal years to be followed by a well-trained functional medicine practitioner who can monitor blood levels and assess for any side effects or changes needed in the treatment plan.

Next comes menopause. This occurs in women around age 48 to 52 years old. A variety of symptoms can predominate, from hot flashes to poor sleeping to uncontrolled weight gain. It can be a frustrating time of transition with many problematic symptoms. Like perimenopause, menopause is a problem with too much estrogen. It is even more dramatic than perimenopause because the ovaries are no longer making any progesterone, leaving her progesterone-deficient in estrogen dominance. This is a difficult transition with the loss of ovulation and symptomatic hormone imbalance.

The progesterone production stops but the estrogen continues to be produced by other tissues, including the adrenal glands and fat tissue. Remember estrogen is also consumed in food sources and from environmental chemicals. It is the elevated estrogen and low progesterone levels that lead to menopausal problems. Low progesterone has been found to be related to hypertension in menopause; progesterone treatments have been shown to lower blood pressure also decreasing the cardiovascular risks for strokes and heart attacks.[85]

Hot Flashes	Mood Swings
Insomnia	Hair Loss
Uncontrollable Weight Gain and Hypertension	Skin Changes
Vaginal Dryness	Decreased Sex Drive
Fatigue	Depression/Anxiety

Menopausal Symptoms

It is important to investigate menopause with a complete history and physical exam followed by detailed laboratory evaluation. Evaluation should include tests that look at the pituitary function as well as a full check of the different types of estrogens, progesterone and their metabolites.

It is also important to look at the estrogen to progesterone ratio so treatment can be tailored to optimize function and minimize any side effects. Depending on her symptoms and her labs, progesterone or a combination of progesterone and estrogen can be given back in different forms. Hormones can be given topically through creams on the skin or vaginal walls and progesterone can be also be given orally.

When progesterone is given orally at night, a restorative sleep can be induced, which is often disrupted during menopause. It is important to bring back the natural progesterone balance. Progesterone will balance estrogens' stimulating effects and bring back a synergy between the two hormones. Progesterone also mobilizes fat for energy and decreases water retention. It helps with estrogen-dominant depression and anxiety. Progesterone can also increase libido which can be a problem during this time. It also increases the effects of other hormones that can be given in a synergistic manner, including thyroid, testosterone and estrogen.

TESTOSTERONE. Testosterone is definitely not a male-only hormone. It has many effects in both sexes and is also very important to help create a healing environment in the body and maintain an ideal body composition. Testosterone is made in the testicles in males and the adrenal glands in females. Important functions of testosterone include helping maintain muscle mass, mood, energy, sex drive, memory and mental function, bone density, healthy-leveled cholesterol, blood flow and healing. It plays a role in reproductive sexual function. It is also important in preventing heart attack, strokes and in the prevention of certain cancers.

Andropause in males is analogous to menopause in females. Starting around age 30 and progressing from there, a gradual loss of testosterone production occurs in the testicles. Around the age of 45, symptoms of low testosterone can often be felt in men. These can range from decreased libido and mood to decreased muscle mass and decreased body hair. During this time, there is often a decreased sense of well-being with difficulty concentrating and a sense of fatigue and lower energy. Testosterone affects most organs and cells throughout our body and optimal levels are important for peak functioning and performance. Below is a list of symptoms associated with low testosterone levels. If you relate to this list, it would be a good idea to be evaluated and treated, if appropriate.

Injury/Infection to testicles	Aging
Obesity	Chemo or radiation treatments
Genetic abnormalities	Hemochromatosis
Pituitary problems	Medication side effects
Chronic illness	Liver and kidney disease
Stress	Overtraining
Alcoholism	Varicocele

Cause of Low Testosterone and Testicular Failure

It is also important to be aware of other causes of low testosterone that should be ruled out prior to treating low testosterone levels.

Again, if you are suffering from any of these symptoms, testosterone levels should be checked by a practitioner with the knowledge of how to diagnose and treat low levels.

Typically, a blood sample is taken in the morning when the levels are normally the highest. Treatment options for low levels would include injections, patches, gels, troches, creams and implants. With testosterone replacement, it is important to block testosterone's conversion to other hormones. The skin, subcutaneous tissue and fat can all convert testosterone to DHT or estrogen which can have unwanted side effects. Grape Seed Extract at 100mg a day and Saw Palmetto at 450mg a day can be given to block a conversion to DHT. High DHT levels is often associated with male pattern baldness and prostate issues. Zinc at 100mg a day can be given to block the testosterone conversion to estrogen.

Elevated estrogen levels in males can have unwanted side effects as well. Symptoms include sexual dysfunction like low libido, decreased morning erections and erectile dysfunction. Men with elevated estrogens can also develop enlarged breasts and urinary retention symptoms associated with benign prosthetic hypertrophy. Increased abdominal fat is also seen in males with elevated estrogen levels.

Males who are overweight and obese will have higher estrogen levels because the fat tissue converts their testosterone into unwanted estrogen. Estrogen levels as well as liver and prostate function should also be monitored in males receiving testosterone replacement.

I often get the younger population coming in and talking about testosterone levels and wanting their levels checked. It is much less common to have low testosterone in a younger male, but it can happen with chronic stress, over-training or the other medical conditions listed above. In this situation, it is critical to figure out why the testosterone levels are low in the first place.

Decreased sex drive	Decreased sense of well-being
Depressed mood	Difficulties with memory / concentration
Erectile dysfunction	Fatigue and low energy
Decreased muscle mass	Cholesterol issues
Decreased blood volume	Fragile bones (osteoporosis)
Decreased body hair	Decreased blood flow to organs

Symptoms of Low Testosterone

Once that has been determined, there are ways to naturally increase testosterone levels. These natural treatments will not elevate testosterone to unsafe levels or cause the testicles to shut down. Tribulus root extract taken at 250mg twice a day has been shown, through activation of the pituitary via a hormone called luteinizing hormone, to stimulate the testicles to make more testosterone on their own. Long Jack extract, DHEA and amino acids like glutamine, arginine and tryptophan can be taken before sleep to help increase the body's natural testosterone release at night.

Another way that all males can increase their testosterone levels naturally is exercising with increased intensity. When you exercise for short periods in the anaerobic range, you can actually increase testosterone release for hours after your workout. Sprint 8, Tabata and interval training are good ideas to incorporate into your core workout to maximize testosterone and growth hormone release, as well as increase fat-burning for hours after your workout. Resistance training of large muscle groups, like the back and legs, can also naturally increase testosterone production.

VITAMIN D. Vitamin D, although not formally called a hormone, acts much like a hormone in the body. In fact, its chemical structure is very much like that of other hormones like testosterone. Vitamin D is made in the skin in response to sun exposure and affects almost every cell in the body. Adequate levels are vital for optimal function in the body.

I grew up in North Dakota and I now live in Minnesota, so sun exposure in the winter months doesn't happen much. The farther North you live, the less vitamin D will be created because of the lack of sun exposure. Even in warmer climates, most people are clothed or indoors from 10 AM to 2 PM when optimal sun exposure allows for vitamin D production. Sub-optimal or low vitamin D can cause many signs and symptoms that overlap with many other chronic diseases. It is one of the most important things to optimize for those suffering from chronic disease, as well as those experiencing symptoms of fatigue, muscle aches and pains, poor concentration, sleep problems or weight gain and hypertension.

According to the Mayo Clinic, vitamin D deficiency has a direct link to hypertension and heart disease. I check the vitamin D level on most of my patients when they are in to have a regenerative procedure done or have symptoms associated with low vitamin D levels. Recent studies show optimal levels of vitamin D to be around 60-80 ng/ml. With certain medical conditions like cancer, it might be important to get vitamin D levels closer to 100 ng/ml. A study on athletes showed that those with vitamin D supplementation had around a 20% increase in strength. Once vitamin D levels have been checked and are optimized, a variety of beneficial effects are seen from increased strength, decreased cancer rates, decrease pain and arthritis, improved sleep, improved mood and concentration as well as increased energy and decreased weight.

Increased strength	Increased bone density
Increased mood/concentration	Increased energy
Decreased cancer	Decreased weight and blood pressure
Decreased pain and arthritis	Decreased autoimmune disease
Decreased Alzheimer's risk	Decreased bowel problems
Better sleep	Better tooth and gum health

Effects of Optimal Vitamin D Levels

Other vitamins, minerals, micronutrients, fatty acids and amino acids can be sub-optimal and impair the body's ability to heal and repair. Proton pump inhibitors, which are often prescribed for acid reflux and are also available over the counter, will impair proper absorption of nutrients and have a host of related side effects. Other medications can also impair the absorption of micronutrients in which case supplementation will be important. Statin medications for elevated cholesterol can decrease the liver's production of CoQ10, which leads to fatigue and muscle aches. Levels of these important substances can also be checked and supplemented to help regain health and set the body up for peak performance and optimal healing.

As you can see, optimal hormone and vitamin levels are important to enhance the healing environment! Along with having levels checked and augmenting their levels using bio-identical hormone replacement options, there are things you can do to naturally tune-up your hormone symphony. Getting at least eight hours of sleep leads to optimal hormone release. It is also important to avoid sleeping pills that induce an artificial sleep with less hormone production.

Also, studies show exercise increases hormone release. It is important to exercise at least four times a week and to utilize interval and intense burst-type exercises in your workout. Note that over-exercising can have a negative effect on hormones, like cortisol and testosterone.

Next, focusing on avoiding processed foods, high-sugar carbohydrates and vegetable oils, as well as getting adequate proteins and good fats can also lead to optimal hormone function and levels. Increasing your fiber intake can decrease excess hormones through excretion in the gastrointestinal tract. Optimal hormone levels are important if you are looking to optimize your health, longevity, chronic disease risk and create healing environment that allows regeneration to occur.

CHAPTER 6: INFLAMMATION - THE CORE OF CHRONIC DISEASE

Bad digestion is at the root of all evil. — **Hippocrates**

Inflammation - what is it? Inflammation is the natural response the body mounts to an infection, an injury or some type of outside invader or stress. This will cause an immediate reaction as the body responds to the stressor. Sometimes a chronic inflammatory reaction can burn secondary to a prolonged stimulus. Inflammation is not always bad. It is needed for important functions like defending against invaders like viruses, bacteria and fungi. It is also needed for detoxification of the body and for the healing of injuries, and after workouts and exertion. It is needed acutely, but chronic and uncontrolled inflammation can create problems.

Take the questionnaire below to see if you are dealing with excess inflammation.

Point Scale:

0 = Never or almost never have the symptom

1 = Occasionally have it; effect is not severe

2 = Occasionally have it; effect is severe

3 = Frequently have it; effect is not severe

4 = Frequently have it; effect is severe

HEAD

__Headaches

__Dizziness

__Insomnia

__Faintness

__TOTAL

EARS

__Itchy ears

__Ringing in ears/loss of hearing

__Earaches/ear infections

__Drainage from ear

__TOTAL

EYES

___Bags or dark circles under eyes

___Watery or itchy eye

___Swollen, reddened, or sticky eyelids

___Blurred or tunnel vision (excluding near- or far-sightedness)

___TOTAL

NOSE

___Stuffy nose

___Sinus congestion, sinus infection

___Constant sneezing

___Hay fever/allergies

___Excess mucus formation

___TOTAL

MOUTH/THROAT

___Chronic coughing

___Sore throat, hoarseness, loss of voice

___Gagging, frequent need to clear throat

___Swollen lymph nodes

___Swollen tongue, gums or lips

___Canker sores, mouth ulcers

___TOTAL

HEART

___Chest pain

___Irregular or skipped heartbeat

___Rapid or pounding heartbeat

___TOTAL

LUNGS

___Asthma, bronchitis

___Chest congestion

___Shortness of breath

___Difficulty breathing

___TOTAL

SKIN

___Acne or brown "age/liver spots"

___Hives, rashes, cysts, boils

___Shortness of breath

___Difficulty breathing

___TOTAL

SKIN

___Acne or brown "age/liver spots"

___Hives, rashes, cysts, boils

___Eczema or psoriasis

___Itchy skin/dermatitis

___Hair loss, hair thinning

___Body odor

___Excessive sweating

___TOTAL

JOINTS/MUSCLES

___Pain or aches in joints or lower back

___Arthritis

___Stiffness or limitation of movement

___Pain or muscle aches

___TOTAL

MENTAL/EMOTIONAL

___Poor memory

___Difficulty concentrating

___Mood swings

___Depression

___Anxiety, fear or nervousness

___Anger, irritability, or aggressiveness

___Insomnia

___TOTAL

ENERGY LEVEL

___Fatigue/low energy

___Restlessness

___Hyperactivity

___Feeling of weakness

___TOTAL

WEIGHT

___Underweight

___Overweight

___Difficulty losing weight

___Crave certain foods

___TOTAL

DIGESTIVE TRACT

___Nausea, vomiting

___Diarrhea

___Constipation

___Bloated feeling

___Belching, passing gas

___Heartburn

___Intestinal/stomach pain

___TOTAL

OTHER

___PMS

___Frequent colds, flus

___Food allergies/sensitivities

___Chemical or environmental sensitivities

___TOTAL

Add the numbers from each section and write the section totals in the spaces provided, then add all the section totals together and put that total in the space below.

___GRAND TOTAL

Interpreting Your TOTAL STRESS and INFLAMMATION SCORE:

15 or lower: You have a low level of inflammation.

16 to 49: You have a moderate level of inflammation and should have further investigation.

50 or higher: You have a high level of inflammation and should have further investigation.

ABOUT INFLAMMATION

Let's look at the different types of inflammation. First, we have acute inflammation. We have all experienced this after an injury or an infection. An example would be like after an ankle sprain, when you experience immediate swelling, redness, heat, pain, and loss of function. During this time, the body is sending healing cells that remove damaged tissue and start the healing process through stimulation of the immune system. This inflammatory phase of healing usually only lasts a few days.

Chronic inflammation occurs if the stimulus that started the acute response continues. This is more of a smoldering, low-grade response. Healing does not occur with chronic inflammation, and you may not experience outward symptoms but still be suffering damage on the inside. This can last for a long time if the root cause of the inflammation is not addressed, leading to body damage and disease.

So, what can cause inflammation to be ignited in the body? It can start from microbial infections from viruses, bacteria and fungi. Next, stress in the form of physical trauma, excessive exercise, burns and UV radiation can turn on inflammation. Inflammation can also start from chemicals found in pesticides and household products. Smoking is a very dangerous and powerful source of inflammation in the body.

High blood pressure can cause stress to the body as well as fuel inflammation of blood vessel walls, increasing risk of stroke and heart attacks. Different medications, including synthetic estrogen, increase inflammation and estrogens can also increase blood clot risk. Advanced Glycosylation End Products (AGEs), when consumed, can cause health issues and inflammation. AGEs are formed from over-cooking food, browning meet, burnt bread, and from excessive amounts of consumed sugar.

Free radicals, which signal negative health, are formed from our cellular by-products as well as environmental stresses, such as UV light. Obesity itself causes inflammation. You can also have allergies or hypersensitivity reactions to substances such as pollen, animals, gas fumes, medications, supplements or, most commonly, to food. Food sensitivities are a very common cause of systemic inflammation in the body.

When it comes to healing, the right amount of inflammation followed by the normal healing response is needed for function and optimal regeneration. Imbalance with prolonged inflammation can lead to damage, disease and degeneration. Our fast-food, stressful, unbalanced and often sedentary lifestyles lead to an overworked system which will eventually breakdown, and cause inflammation and chronic disease in our bodies.

Two common areas that contribute to imbalance in the body include the mind and the mouth. Poor sleep, work demands and unhealthy relationships all lead to *mental* stress. If our *mouths* are consuming too much sugar, over-cooked protein, fried foods, hydrogenated fats and vegetable oils, chemicals and food, that our bodies are sensitive to, it will feed the flame of inflammation in our bodies, causing disease and degeneration to flourish.

THE GUT

The gut is the first frontier when it comes to sources of inflammation. Everything we eat and drink goes through it. Without proper and complete digestion, large particles can remain in the intestines. These undigested particles are perceived by the body as a foreign invader and the body may mount an immune attack against them. Large fat particles can turn rancid, carbohydrates can ferment, and proteins can putrefy if not digested properly. This creates a breeding ground for invasive bacteria and fungi to overgrow.

It can also cause inflammation that can damage the intestinal linings by creating larger holes in the gut, which then allows the large undigested food particles to enter the bloodstream. Once in circulation, this creates a food sensitivity as the immune system then treats the particles as invaders and mounts an immune attack against them. When the body sees those types of foods again, it is primed to become inflamed, and that is the beginning of developing a food sensitivity. Inflammation can then spread throughout the body.

The body can create a food sensitivity to any type of food that most people would be healthy to eat. If that same food is consumed after the immune system has been primed against it, the body becomes inflamed. Those foods need to be temporarily removed from consumption, so the body can desensitize and no longer mount a response against them.

There are different factors that can increase a person's risk of developing a food allergy or sensitivity. Alcohol abuse, premature birth, anti-inflammatory medication and prescription drugs, ingestion of harmful foods like hydrogenated fats and vegetable oils, sugars, high fructose corn syrup and fried foods, gut bacterial and fungal overgrowth, and over-eating have been shown to decrease essential enzymes needed to breakdown food. This leads to partial digestion of food and the development of food sensitivities.

Research confirms a strong link between inflammation and food allergies and sensitivities. Reactions can occur towards food as well as environmental toxins and chemicals. It is estimated that around 60% of the population suffers from food allergies and sensitivities.

Food sensitivities can cause a wide variety of symptoms, many of which can go unnoticed. The following list shows the diversity of presentation of food sensitivities. How many of these symptoms relate to what you are experiencing?

Abdominal pain	Coated tongue	Infant colic	Rashes
Aching muscles	Colitis	Inflammation	Recurrent
Acne	Compulsive	Insomnia	Bronchitis
Addictions	thirst	IBS	Croup
Anemia	Constant hunger	Itching	Ear infections
Arthritis	Constipation	Itchy red eyes/ ears	Restless legs
Asthma	Coughing	Lethargy	Rhinitis
Athlete's foot	Difficult swallowing	Loss of appetite	Schizophrenia
Bad breath	Dizziness	Low back pain	Seizures
Bed-wetting	Eczema	Food malabsorption	Sensitivity to
Blackouts	Fainting	Menstrual problems	light and noise
Bloating	Flushing	Metallic taste	Sore tongue
Blood sugar issues	Food Cravings	Mouth ulcers	Sore eyes
Bloody stools	Gas	Multiple sclerosis	Sweating
Bladder infections	Gastritis	Muscle aches	SLE
Blurred vision	Gritty eyes	Muscle tremors	Temperature
Breast pain	Headaches	Nausea/Vomit	fluctuations
Bursitis	Heavy body odor	Palpitations	Thrush
Canker sores	High/low blood	Persistent cough	Tics
Celiac Disease	pressure	Poor balance	Weight gain or loss
Chronic fatigue	Hives	Postnasal drip	Wheezing
Chronic	Hyperactivity	PMS	
infections	Indigestion		

A food sensitivity will create inflammation throughout the body. It is a complex of syndromes resulting in the body sensitizing to one or more foods. The immune system recognizes another harmless food as a hostile invader posing a threat. The body then mobilizes its defense system and creates inflammation. This can range from mild sensitivity reactions to complete organ failure with allergies. These responses weaken the immune system and increase the risk for chronic disease. Most people do not realize that foods may be making them sick.

ALLERGY	SENSITIVITY
Rarely more than a few foods	Multiple foods can be involved
Small amount can cause severe reaction	Small or large amounts can cause reaction
Reaction occurs 2 or less hours after eating	Reactions occur 2-24 hours after eating
Rare in adults	Very common in children and adults
Addictive cravings never seen	Addictive cravings and withdrawal seen in up to 20% of cases
Offending good often diagnosed because of reaction	Offending foods are rarely diagnosed because of delayed reaction and multiple foods
A permanent fixed allergy	Many symptoms clear after avoidance for a few months and slow reintroduction
IgE and skin test positive reaction	IgE negative, IgG often positive
Mast cell release of histamine	Sensitized lymphocytes, eosinophils, platelets with release of leukotrienes (inflammation) present
When stop eating, no withdrawal or cravings	When stop eating, 30% get addictive cravings and disabling symptoms

Symptoms of Food Sensitivities:
Differences Between a Food Allergy and Sensitivity

"But there are persons who cannot readily change their diet with impunity; and if they make any alteration in it for one day, or every part of a day, are greatly injured thereby. Such persons, provided they take dinner when it is not their wont, immediately become heavy and inactive, both in mind and body, and are weighed down with yawning, slumbering, and thirst: and if they take supper in addition, they are seized with flatulence, termini and diarrhea, and to many this has been the commencement of serious disease, when they have merely taken in a day the same food which they have been in the custom of taking once." —**Hippocrates**

It is important to note the difference between an allergy and a sensitivity. The biggest difference is the power of the response to the offending food or environmental agent. An allergy is an IgE mediated immune response that tests positive to a skin prick test. A sensitivity will have a negative IgE reaction, but an IgG test is often positive. An allergy is an immediate response that happens very quickly and can lead to a severe reaction. A sensitivity can be delayed 2 - 24 hours after eating the offending food and has much more vague symptoms. With allergies, those foods are often avoided and rarely eaten because of the extreme response they provoke. With a sensitivity, it is often one of the person's favorite foods and they actually will crave them. An allergy is a fixed and permanent response and a reaction that never goes away, while a sensitivity can clear after avoidance for a few months with a slow reintroduction of that food. A food allergy or sensitivity can occur while eating many common foods, as well as from vitamin supplements, drugs, and herbs. Following is a list of common foods that provoke allergic responses.

Barley	Eggs	Sugar (all forms)*
Beef	Nuts	Tea
Chocolate	Peanuts	Tomatoes
Citrus	Rye	Wheat
Coffee	Seafood	Yeast
Dairy	Soy	

Common Foods Associated with Food Allergies

Let's review inflammation and food sensitivities as well as the formation of the leaky gut syndrome. First, the ingested food or allergen causes inflammation and an increase in immune cells called eosinophils in the gut wall. Eosinophils invade portions of the gut tract, irritating the surrounding tissue and attracting other immune cells. This causes the gut to swell and has an impact on digestion. Eosinophils then spread throughout the body and attack healthy tissue, causing degeneration and breakdown.

The weakened gut wall allows bacteria, metabolic material and drugs to enter the blood stream prior to being fully broken down. These toxins enter the blood stream and cause widespread inflammation and systemic disease. The gut lining is under constant attack from food allergies, preservatives and food additives, bacteria, drugs, and excessive sugars and high fructose corn syrup.

Antibiotics also kill the friendly protective bacteria that prevent fungi such as *Candida* from overgrowing.

There are many food additives that can cause inflammation and are toxic to the human body. They are found in many processed foods as well as preservatives to extend food shelf life; see the following chart for a list of these additives.

ADDITIVES	REACTIONS TO SUSCEPTIBLE PEOPLE:
Sulfites	Wine, dried fruit, pizza, cold drinks, fruit juice concentrate
Benzoic Acid and Parabens	Antibacterial and antifungal, prevent spoiling
Aspartame	Artificial sweetener is soda, drinks, gum and children's vitamins
MSG	Flavor enhancer in processed foods and fast food
Nitrites	Processed meat preservative and smoke, linked to cancer
Amines	Found in foods and can accumulate over time and cause reaction
Salicylates	Naturally in curry, herbs, tea, almonds, fruit skins and plant source

Additives That Can Cause Reactions

There are many symptoms related to food sensitivities. In the **gastrointestinal** system, individuals can experience bloating, diarrhea, constipation, irritable bowel syndrome and colitis. It can lead to malabsorption and nutrient deficiencies of iron, B12, and vitamin D. The **respiratory** system can be affected with increased asthma problems, chronic cough and sinusitis. The **skin** can be affected with eczema, psoriasis and keratosis pilaris (bumps on the side of the arms and legs). **Mental** manifestations include migraines, behavior problems, ADHD, memory, mood, and sleep issues. **Musculoskeletal** symptoms include arthritis, joint stiffness and tendinitis. **Endocrine** problems include infertility, irregular periods, weight gain, weight loss, thyroid disease and osteoporosis. The **immune** system is affected with increased allergies, decreased ability to fight infections and susceptibility to autoimmune diseases.

Susceptibility to food intolerances is dependent upon many factors. First off, genetics can make you more vulnerable. How well the liver detoxifies toxins through phase 1 and phase 2 of detoxification can contribute to susceptibility. The amount of food consumed and also the combination of food can contribute to developing food sensitivities. Stress with increased cortisol levels increases food sensitivities. Undigested food molecules invade the bloodstream and can also activate the immune system producing food sensitivities.

Food sensitivities seem to be more common - and why is that? Advances in food technology, including methods of processing, preserving and flavoring with use of dyes, pesticides and fertilizers, has altered food. Theses additives, in addition to foods' natural components, can cause a disruption in the immune system.

Further complication comes from the overuse of antibiotics in our meat sources, along with the dramatic increases in the amount of simple sugars and refined flour we consume regularly. These foods are often seen in a food-sensitive patients' diet. Also, an imbalance in the gut bacterial flora can lead to overgrowth of yeast (Candida). Yeast overgrowth irritates the mucosal lining of the intestines contributing to "leaky gut syndrome". As mentioned previously, food not fully digested can enter the blood, triggering an immune reaction.

Weight management and weight loss is also affected by the food we eat. After eating a food that the body has a sensitivity to, the blood levels of the neurotransmitter serotonin go down. Ingestion of highly refined carbohydrates and simple sugars cause a rapid release of insulin, raising blood levels of tryptophan which is a precursor of serotonin. In order to compensate for lower brain levels of serotonin - caused by eating offending foods -food-sensitive people crave foods which will increase serotonin in their brains. Inflammation is known to be a root cause of most chronic health conditions, including obesity. One of the major causes of inflammation in our body is consuming foods that our bodies are sensitive to – so, by avoiding foods that cause inflammation, we can lose weight and decrease the risk of chronic diseases!

By now, we understand that the food we eat, as well as environmental toxins, preservatives and artificial sweeteners, can all cause inflammation and disease progression in our bodies. Let's take a closer look at some of these causes of inflammation and how they have a negative impact on our health.

ADVANCED GLYCATION END PRODUCTS- AGEs.

AGEs are proteins or lipids that become glycated (coated in sugar) after exposure to high levels of sugars. AGEs are prevalent in the diabetic vasculature and contribute to the development of atherosclerosis. AGEs are also produced when proteins are heated at high temperatures during cooking such as browning, grilling, toasting, baking and frying. Excess sugars in our bodies can also have the same reaction, causing our body's proteins and lipids to become coated and sticky after being glycated. Since we consume over

160 pounds of sugar a year, including an average of 450 sugar sodas a year, this process is happening all the time inside our bodies. The high levels cause sugar to abnormally bind to proteins, thereafter causing direct tissue damage.

AGEs attack the body, creating low-grade inflammation. This can lead to a variety of disease conditions as follows.

Oxidative stress	Atherosclerosis and stiff blood vessels	Hypertension	Cataracts
Macular degeneration	Dementia	Uremia	Joint stiffness
Kidney damage	Diabetes	Inflammation	Increased blood clotting
Increased cancer	Skin damage	Alzheimer's disease	Rheumatoid arthritis

Diseases Associated with AGEs

The same reaction that is seen when browning meat occurs in our tissues and is irreversible with advanced glycation. Over time, these products can accumulate in the skin, eyes and the organs of the body. An over-consumption of eating browned meats and foods has now been linked to heart attacks, strokes and nerve damage.

TOBACCO. Tobacco is cured under intense heating creating AGEs. Smoking increases the body's AGEs, resulting in tissue damage. The smoke itself also increases inflammation which increases pain, increases cancer rates and increases heart attack and strokes. The day you quit is the day you start healing!

FREE RADICALS. Free radicals can be produced in many different ways. They are created by the normal aging process, excessive exercise or use of the body (i.e., distance cardio exercise), dietary factors, chemical factors and radiation exposure. Free radicals are molecules with a free electron which differs from a normal molecule. The free radical can attack cell membranes, interfere with protein synthesis, lower energy levels, prevent muscle-building and decrease essential enzymes leading to increased metabolic waste products.

The body needs small amounts of free radicals to function normally, but too many can overwhelm and cause destruction. The free radicals destroy cells by attacking unsaturated lipids, proteins, cell membranes and enzymes. The DNA blueprint in our bodies is damaged and can lead to increased risk of cancer. Free radicals also increase our risk of autoimmune disease that affect all our body's organ systems, joints and skin.

GENERAL	DIETARY FACTORS	CHEMICAL FACTORS	RADIATION
Aging	Additives	Air pollutants	Cosmic
Normal metabolism	Alcohol-excessive	Chemical solvents	Electro-magnetic
Stress-Cortisol	Coffee		Medical x-ray
Intense workouts	AGE's foods		
	Herbicides		
	Pesticides		
	Hydrogenated oils		
	Sugars		

Causes of Free Radicals

Illnesses Caused by Free Radicals

General: accelerated aging, cancer, autoimmune diseases, SLE, DM

GI: pancreatitis, liver damage, leaky gut syndrome

Brain: Parkinson's, Alzheimer's, MS

CV: high blood pressure, CADz

Lungs: asthma, emphysema

Eyes: cataracts, retinopathy, macular degeneration

Joints: RA

Skin: wrinkles, cancer

Treatment of free radicals includes, first and most importantly, avoiding exposure to elements that create them. It is important to consume pesticide- and allergy-free foods. Eating as little sugar and highly processed foods as possible is also very important. Drink purified water free of toxins. Avoid exposure to volatile chemicals and limit as much as possible the exposure to air pollution. Wear sun protection during mid-day to avoid free radical injury to the skin. Taking antioxidants, like vitamin C and resveratrol, can be used to neutralize free radicals through the donation of an electron to neutralize the free radical.

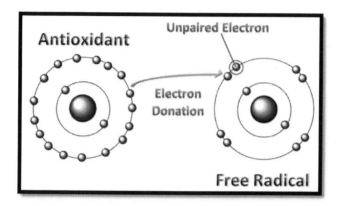

Antioxidants donate an electron to neutralize the unpaired electron of a free radical

With reversal of the cause of inflammation, we can also reverse many of the disease processes to which it contributes. Let's look at some of these diseases inflammation fuels.

ALZHEIMER'S DISEASE. Alzheimer's disease may result from loss of brain cells from oxidative stress and inflammation. Antioxidants have been shown to decrease rates of the disease. Those who exercise also show lower rates of Alzheimer's disease. Healthy lifestyle and dietary changes can have a positive influence on brain function.

BLOOD SUGAR PROBLEMS. Diabetes, hyperglycemia and metabolic syndrome all lead to high blood sugars circulating through the body followed by insulin spikes. The high blood sugars cause glycosylation (AGEs) and tissue damage in the heart, brain, eyes, kidneys, small blood vessels of our limbs, and also leads to an increased risk of infection.

CANCER. Recent research shows long-term inflammation is a cause of cancer. Inflammation pushes the abnormal growth of cancer cells. Precancerous inflammatory conditions include:

– Chronic infections (H. pylori, Hep. B, Schistomasomiasis)
– Free radical damage and oxidative stress (DNA damage)
– Stress – Physical, Emotional and Environmental
– AGEs (Associated with gastric cancers)

- Food allergies and sensitivities (many studies show association with cancers)

CANDIDA. Candida is a type of yeast and is present all over our body. If the balance of normal bacteria is disrupted, Candida can overgrow and cause problems. This is usually seen in areas of the mouth, vagina, skin, and intestines and all organs. Candida infections cause many symptoms that can mimic allergies. In the gut, yeast can burrow roots deep in the intestinal wall and contribute to "leaky gut syndrome." Again, this allows large particles of undigested food to pass into the blood resulting in an inflammatory reaction in the body.

Candida overgrowth is most often caused by the factors in the following chart.

Alcohol	Antacids and ulcer meds	Antibiotics
Birth control pills	Chemicals	Toxins
Chronic constipation or diarrhea	Diabetes	High sugar diabetes
Excessive stress	Repressed immunity	Parasites
Steroids	Thyroid disease	Chemotherapy

Candida overgrowth can cause a variety of **ALLERGIC** and **RESPIRATORY PROBLEMS:**

Blurred vision	Chemical sensitivity	Swollen lips and face
Body aches and tension	Chest pain	Urticaria (hives, welts)
Bronchitis	Coughing	
Burning and tingling	Ear aches	
Headaches	Hay fever (runny nose)	
Head/neck tension	Painful swollen joints	
Nasal congestion	Shortness of breath	
Numbness	Sore throats	

Candida overgrowth can cause **COGNITIVE** and **BEHAVIORAL PROBLEMS:**

ADHD	Fatigue	Poor concentration
Confusion	Feelings of unreality	OCD
Disorientation	Hyperactivity	Poor memory
Drowsiness	Anxiety	Irritability
Mood swings	Nervousness	

Candida overgrowth can cause **GENITOURINARY PROBLEMS:**

Bladder infections	Frequent urination
Burning on urination	Impotency
Cystitis (bladder inflammation)	Infertility
Fluid retention	Loss of sexual feelings
	Prostatitis

Candida overgrowth can cause **GLANDULAR** and **AUTOIMMUNE DISORDERS:**

Adrenal and thyroid	Hypoglycemia
Cold hands and feet	Hypothyroidism
Diabetes mellitus	Low body temperature
	Lupus

Candida overgrowth can cause **SKIN PROBLEMS:**

Acne	Fungus infection in nails
Athlete's foot	Impetigo (skin infection)
Dandruff	Inflammation of hair follicles
Diaper rash	Psoriasis
Dry skin	Seborrheic dermatitis
Excessive perspiration	Tinea versicolor (white patches on skin)
Facial rash	

Candida is associated with many **WOMEN'S HEALTH ISSUES**:

Cramps	PMS
Endometriosis	Recurrent yeast vaginitis
Menstrual irregularities	Vaginal burning, itching
Painful intercourse	

Candida can cause a plethora of other symptoms as well:

Chronic fatigue	Muscle pain
Conjunctivitis	Obesity
Eye fatigue	Symptoms worse with wakening
Excessive weight loss	Tingling and numbness
Insomnia	

As you can see, Candida overgrowth and infection can present in a wide variety of ways and mimic many other disease processes. If an infection is suspected, it is important to see a trained practitioner for diagnosis and proper treatment.

CANKER SORES AND MOUTH ULCERS. Many research articles show relationships between canker sores and food allergies. Other research shows an association with gluten-containing foods. Food allergy testing may prove helpful with avoidance of reactive foods that can lead to inflammatory problems.

CYSTIC FIBROSIS. Cystic fibrosis patients struggle with persistent infections and inflammation that damages the lungs. Some studies show a relationship to infections, food allergies, fungus and oxidative stress in CF patients.

EPILEPSY. Some research shows decreased seizures with the elimination of food allergies.

FOOD ADDICTIONS AND EATING DISORDERS. Sometimes we crave our favorite foods because our bodies secrete opioid-like endorphins when we eat them. If you crave a food and feel better afterwards, you may be addicted. If you feel worse after eating a food you crave, you may be allergic or sensitive to it.

Sometimes you will feel better for a while and then feel worse. In this case, you may be allergic and addicted to the food. There is a connection between obesity and food addiction. It is common for people to crave and over-eat on foods they're addicted to, even if they know about their addiction. If you are suffering from an inflammatory disorder, chronic pain or you are trying to heal an injury, try removing all sugar, wheat and dairy and see what happens. You may be surprised at how good you feel and how well you will heal.

HEADACHES. There is a direct correlation between headaches and inflammation. Elimination of the cause of inflammation may aid in the treatment of the headaches.

HEARTBURN. Reflux of acid from the stomach can come up into the esophagus and cause inflammation and breakdown of the lining. To avoid heartburn, it is important to avoid the cause of the inflammation. Chewing food very well, setting the fork down between bites, and eating small meals more frequently can help decrease distention of the stomach and leakage of acid into the esophagus. Taking digestive enzymes before meals can also help breakdown food and avoid an increase in acid released from the stomach. They may also allow you to get off your medications (Proton Pump Inhibitors) like Omeprazole, which have been linked to chronic problems like obesity, osteoporosis and micronutrient deficiencies.

HEART DISEASE. Research is showing that inflammation, and not cholesterol, may be the cause of heart disease. Some evidence now shows that infection may also be involved in heart attacks. CRP, an inflammatory marker, is elevated in heart disease patients. Lowering a patients' CRP decreases their risk of heart disease. Omega-3's, like fish oil and also alphalinolenic acid (ALA), have been shown to decrease CRP and heart disease.

HYPERTENSION. We already knew that hypertension is related to obesity which has long been known to be pro-inflammatory. New evidence is showing that hypertension is linked to inflammation of the body even without obesity and smoking.

INFLAMMATORY BOWEL DISEASE. Inflammation in the gut causes disease and breakdown. Inflammation in the bowel can be associated with infection, antibiotics and also stress. Inflammatory bowel disease is also associated with other inflammatory diseases.

KIDNEY DISEASE. The kidneys are vulnerable to an autoimmune attack where the body mounts an immune attack on itself, resulting in damage to the organ. Inflammatory reactions triggered by foods, chemicals or infections can stimulate these autoimmune attacks. Studies show a strong correlation with food allergies and autoimmune disease.

OBESITY. 27% of the United States is obese by their mid-30s; 61% of adults are overweight or obese. Obesity is directly related to inflammation and research shows that obese people have elevated inflammation levels measured by the CRP blood test. Fat cells release cytokines that produce inflammation that can spread throughout the body. They also have higher insulin, glucose and estrogen levels, which are all linked to increased inflammation. Obese individuals also have higher cancer rates with ovarian, colon, gallbladder, prostate, breast, kidney, endometrial and gastrointestinal cancers.

PERIODONTAL DISEASE. In periodontal disease, inflammation develops from infections in the gums and teeth. The inflammation then spreads to the rest of the body. It has been shown that there is an association with metabolic disease and diabetes, pneumonia, heart disease and stroke. These are all diseases associated with excess inflammation.

Smoking is also a major risk factor for periodontal disease. Smoking also depletes the body of systemic antioxidants, which further promotes inflammation and disease formation.

CHILDREN. Research shows that inflammation and food allergies are implicated in ADHD, autism, behavioral issues and learning disabilities in children. Avoiding wheat, dairy, sugar, MSG, aspartame, free radicals and AGEs may be helpful and improve mental symptoms in children. It is important to also try and improve gut health with probiotics and also test for yeast, bacteria and parasites. Omega-3 fatty acids are also import for optimal function of children's brains.

RESPIRATORY DISEASE. Chronic lung conditions like asthma, bronchitis, and emphysema have a direct relationship to food and chemical allergies and sensitivities. Avoiding the offending foods and chemicals may be helpful in the management of these inflammatory diseases.

JOINT DISEASE. Rheumatoid arthritis, osteoarthritis, systemic lupus erythematosus, fibromyalgia and other inflammatory joint diseases are all associated with excess inflammation. Studies show gluten and other foods contribute to inflammation causing joint destruction. The synovial fluid in osteoarthritis contains activated macrophages that destroy cartilage cells like little Pac-men. Studies show that the injection of autologous stem cells into the joint will deactivate the destructive macrophages that are destroying the cartilage and the stem cells also help rebuild new healthy cartilage.

When you are investigating and trying to treat chronic inflammatory conditions, it is important to see a practitioner trained in these investigations and treatment options. Tests that would be recommended in an inflammation investigation include the following.

- Blood inflammatory markers
  - ESR (sed. Rate), CRP
- Blood infection tests
- Yeast

- Blood or stool
- Allergy testing
  - ALCAT (Measures the bodies reaction to food and chemical stimulants)
  - RAST-IgE
  - Skin prick test
  - IgG test
- Heavy metal testing
  - Blood or hair

When treating inflammation, remember that uncontrolled chronic disease and illness can cause ongoing inflammation. It is important to treat any illnesses that are contributing to the inflammation. Also, think about side effects of medications, environmental toxins and pollutions as well. Don't forget the most common causes of inflammation are poor diet and lack of exercise.

The first step in treating any inflammatory disorder is tuning up the diet and starting an exercise program. It is critical to reduce inflammation and put out the fire in as many ways as possible. Decrease sugar consumption and eat whole unprocessed foods as much as possible. Nutritional supplementation is sometimes needed to increase antioxidants and to augment nutritional deficiencies. Exercise should be engaged in most days of the week but limiting chronic energy-depleting workouts to once or twice a week can be helpful if inflammation is a concern. Higher intensity weight and resistance training 2 to 3 times a week can be helpful. Daily light exercise, like walking or biking, is a great way to keep the metabolism burning fat as well as a great way to decompress and relax. It is critical to stop smoking and reduce alcohol intake while striving to maintain a healthy weight. It is important to reduce stress and eliminate stressors in your life.

Things you can do that are healthy and help reduce stress include the following.

- Exercise and healthy nutrition
- Engage in your passions, interests and hobbies
- Sleep around eight solid hours a night

- Laugh often
- Relaxation techniques
    - Meditation and Deep breathing
    - Guided Imagery
    - Yoga and Tai chi

FOOD SENSITIVITIES AND ALLERGIES

Another important step in reducing inflammation is to avoid food sensitivities. This can be done through an elimination diet. An elimination diet without lab testing involves avoiding the most highly allergenic foods and watching for the response. These would include sugar, vegetable oils, gluten, wheat, dairy, eggs, corn, soy and food products containing them.

Traditionally, four weeks is often thought of as sufficient to see results, but you may need to limit these foods for six months or more before reintroducing them back into your palate. Reintroduce foods back slowly and one at a time. You can also have a food sensitivity blood lab evaluation performed that will give a detailed analysis of foods that are potentially inflammatory to your body.

Your gut is the first line of defense. When it is injured from toxins, food sensitivities, infections or antibiotics, it can lead to inflammation in the body. It's important to take steps to help heal and repair the gut if you are going to try to eliminate inflammation. Avoid eating on the run as it compromises healthy food digestion.

Following are some gut-healing supplements that are essential to healing.

- **Digestive Enzymes** - Take 3 times a day with larger meals.
  - Enzymes that break down FATS, PROTEINS AND CARBS
- **Probiotics** - 10-20 billion organism of broad spectrum, one with breakfast and one with dinner.
  - Medications, stress and poor diet allow overgrowth of bad bugs.
  - Abnormal gut flora leads to inflammation, weight gain and illness.

- **L-Glutamine** - 2,500mg twice a day
  - Amino acid that is the food for the cells that line the intestinal wall.
  - Aids in healing of the G.I. tract.
- **Quercetin** - 500mg twice a day
  - Potent anti-inflammatory.

DETOXIFICATION

Another important step in cleaning the body and eliminating inflammation is to deal with all the toxins that are stored within us. We are constantly surrounded by toxins. Four billion pounds of chemicals are released into the earth each year. Two billion pounds of air emissions are released each year. Two and a half billion pounds of pesticides are used each year. Thousands of chemicals and preservatives are added to foods to preserve and flavor them. The average person living in United States eats an average of 14 pounds of food additives and 160 pounds of sugar a year. There are 167 chemicals that have been found in the blood that are not healthy to optimal body function, of which 76 cause cancer, 94 are toxic to the brain and nervous system, 79 cause birth defects or abnormal development.

Toxins are everywhere. They are found in our air, food and water. The body is constantly detoxifying as we are exposed to hundreds of toxins daily. A high-toxin burden contributes to illness, inflammation and difficulty losing weight. Detoxification is the body's process of mobilizing toxins and eliminating them. Most of this is done in the liver, where fat-soluble toxins enter the liver and go through a phase 1 detoxification pathway. They then enter a phase 2 pathway, where they become water-soluble and are eliminated from the body via the gallbladder through the bile and stool, or through the kidneys via in the urine.

There are some detoxification helpers that can aid your body and liver in in processing toxins and eliminating them through your stool or urine as follows.

- **Water**
  - Drink half your ideal body weight in ounces a day.
- **Eat more**:
  - Cruciferous vegetables (broccoli, cauliflower, kale, cabbage)
  - Garlic, Green tea, turmeric, whole eggs
  - Cilantro, celery, parsley, dandelion greens, citrus peels, pomegranate, rosemary
- **Omega-3 Fatty Acids** (2,000-10,000mg a day)
- **Vitamin C** (3,000mg or more a day)
  - Especially with periods of increased detoxification (weight loss and exercise).
- **Fiber** (15 grams) twice a day in addition to vegetables and fruits.
- **NAC (N-acetyl-cysteine)** (600-1000mg twice a day)
  - Increases Glutathione and aids in detoxification.
  - It is protected from digestion and not broken down like Glutathione.

- **Glutathione**
  - It can also be taken orally but is broken down by digestion.
  - NAC is a form that can increases levels after digestion.
  - It is found naturally in Asparagus, Avocado, Fish, Meat, Walnuts.

Detoxification can also be enhanced through heat and sweat therapy. Sweating has been found to increase heavy metal detoxification. Heat and sweat therapy have been shown to decrease weight, lower blood pressure and reduce stress.

Infrared heat has been shown to have many health benefits. It has been shown to raise core temperature, resulting in a deep detoxification. It helps relaxation and deep sleep. Infrared heat induces a deep sweat that increases blood flow and decreases blood pressure. It has been shown to help with antiaging of the skin and wrinkles through the stimulation of collagen production. It is important for cell health through the stimulation of the circulatory system which improves oxygen- and nutrient delivery as well as increases the transfer of toxins out of the body. Infrared heat has also been shown to help with weight loss, pain relief and healing, as well as improve circulation. It is important to remember that toxin mobilization may make you feel worse before you start to feel better.

A checklist prior to utilizing heat and sweat for detoxification includes the following.

- Check with your doctor if you are on medications and have chronic disease.
- Drink 16 ounces of purified water prior to sauna or workout.
- Drink another 16 ounces after sauna or workout.
- Start with three and increase to 5-7 sauna treatments a week.
- Start with a 10-minute duration and increase to 30-45 minutes.
  - Take break with a cool rinse every 10 minutes to remove toxins.

- For intense detoxification, use daily for six weeks, then weekly for maintenance.
- INFRARED heat has more health benefits without the extreme heat of other saunas.
- Rinse again after the sauna to rid the toxins off the skin (soap and skin brush).
- Increase vitamin C and other antioxidants during detoxing.

In summary, realize that inflammation can come from a variety of sources and is linked to many chronic diseases. Identify what is causing inflammation in your body and take the steps necessary to decrease exposures. Start and maintain proper detoxification. Most importantly, you need to be patient. It took years to get here and it will take some time to heal and reverse the damage. Reducing inflammation is another step towards optimizing your body's healing environment and maximizing your regenerative potential.

CHAPTER 7: WATER - FOUNTAIN OF YOUTH OR SWAMPY MARSH?

Water is the only drink for a wise man. — **Henry Thoreau**

Water is involved in almost every function in our bodies and it is essential for optimal health. Water transports vital nutrients and oxygen to our cells and muscles and lends a supportive structure to our organs and musculoskeletal system. It can also be a source of toxic metals and contaminants, so it is important to drink enough but also to drink clean water sources.

Let's start by looking at some water facts:

- Water is around 70% of weight in men and 60% of the weight in women.
- The sedentary adult needs at least 2.4 L to maintain proper function in the body.
- Sweating rates of 1.5 L liters per hour are common in sports. Athletes can lose 2 - 4% of their water with vigorous workout. Marathon runners can lose

6 - 8% or more during their long runs and workouts. With greater than 2% dehydration, a decrease in sports performance will occur.

- Dehydration can be a burden to our systems. First, it can be a thermal burden. With every one percent of water lost, a one to two-degree increase in temperature is found. This is from decreased skin vasodilation and decreased sweating. It's also a cardiovascular burden as dehydration puts more stress on the heart to pump a lower blood volume, resulting in a decreased stroke volume and an increased heart rate.

Most of us are not drinking enough water throughout the day which can lead to many problems. At 1% dehydration, we will start to feel thirsty. By 2%, we will feel a vague discomfort, as well as a decreased appetite. At 3 to 4% loss of water volume, our blood cells start to concentrate, we feel slow, have flushed skin and feel apathetic. By 6%, we will have tingling in our extremities, stumble and enter heat exhaustion with an increased temperature, heart rate and breathing rate. With 8% dehydration, we will feel dizziness and confusion. Greater than 10 to 15% water loss leads to delirium, dim vision, deafness and cracked skin. Greater than 20% loss of water volume is not compatible with life. Following are some symptoms associated with chronic dehydration.

Allergies	Heart pains
Asthma	Chronic fatigue syndrome
Constipation	Depression
High blood pressure	Increased cholesterol
Osteoarthritis	Ulcers

Symptoms Associated with Chronic Dehydration

On the flip side, too much water can cause problems as well. An over-abundance of water without electrolytes will dilute our sodium and hyponatremia can occur. This is a decrease in sodium level in the blood, which leads to headache, nausea, confusion, muscle spasm and even death. Muscle cramps with exercise or activity is often on early sign of low electrolyte levels. When drinking and replenishing large amounts of water, it is important to add electrolytes to the water to avoid diluting your electrolytes.

There are three important properties of water that help us sustain life and optimize health. First, water acts as a solvent that can keep things suspended in it, enabling water to transport oxygen, nutrients and waste. Next, it is incompressible and helps us support our body structure, giving shape and volume to our cells and blood. It also holds in heat to help us maintain adequate body temperature. Adequate water intake can lead to many health benefits, including improved bowel function, increased energy and mental alertness. We can also experience increased exercise stamina as well as increased weight loss.

Because water is a solvent, many things can be dissolved into it. Some substances are very helpful, like nutrients and oxygen, but some can also be harmful. Let's take a closer look at what else can be dissolved in tap water.

CHLORINE. Chlorine is added at 98% of water utilities as disinfectant to kill microorganisms. The problem with chlorine as it can combine with natural substances like bark, leaves and sediment to create trihalomethanes (THMs). This by-product is known to be a carcinogen and can cause birth-related complications.

FLUORIDE. Fluoride is also added to water because of early studies showing benefits in preventing tooth decay. Excess amounts can actually cause bone and tooth fluorosis, which is a breakdown of the tooth enamel. Many organizations are now questioning if the risk to benefit ratio favors adding fluoride to water sources. Fluoride also inhibits many enzyme activities in our body preventing optimal functioning.

MICROORGANISMS. Microorganisms, or unwanted bacteria, are also found in our tap water. These come from animal and human waste and can cause infection and diseases. Chlorine kills most but not all microorganisms. It is important to use a home filtration system to remove what is missed by city facilities.

HEAVY METALS. Water is the most common source of heavy metal toxicity, including mercury, lead, cadmium, aluminum and arsenic. Heavy metals have many negative effects on the body, including inactivating critical enzymes, increasing free radical damage, causing a decreased immune system function, a lower IQ in children, and an increased risk of cardiovascular disease and cancer. It is important when dealing with pain, fatigue or inflammation to have your heavy metals checked and then get appropriate treatment if metal toxicity is an issue contributing to your symptoms.

What's in the well? Many rural homes still use well water as their source of water. With our increasing environmental pollutants, well water may not be as clean as it once was as contaminants near the well, including fertilizers, pesticides, gas and oil, and other hazardous chemicals, can leak into the ground contaminating the well. If you use well water, it should be tested annually for radon, bacteria and nitrates.

It is recommended that most well and city water be treated to take out any toxins or impurities that might be harmful to your health. Three methods that have been shown to be successful in removing toxins are reverse osmosis, deionization (ion exchange), and steam distillation.

METHOD	MECHANISM	PROS	CONS
REVERSE OSMOSIS	High pressure water through membranes	Consistent and priced more affordably	Requires a lot of water. Needs frequent cleaning
DEINOIZATION (ION EXCHANGE)	Done after RO	Expensive	Pure, neutral water
STEAM DISTALLATION	Water vaporized to separate out pure water	Pure and clean	All minerals are left behind so need to supplement if used or water will steal from body sources

Water Purification Methods

There are a lot of different bottled water options available. It is sometimes difficult to know exactly what you are drinking and what makes one better than the other. Following is a summary of the different types of bottled water.

TYPE	
ARTESIAN	Water from a well between rock layer
DRINKING	Water that may be just filtered tap water
MINERAL	Minerals from the natural source of the water, cannot be added
OZONIZED/UV	Pathogens killed from oxygen or UV light exposure
SPRING	Water collected from underground natural source that flows to the surface
WELL	Water from a hole that taps an aquifer

Types of Bottled Water

Amazingly, 25% of bottled water is just bottled tap water. If buying bottled water, it is best to buy water labeled 'purified' and identify how it was treated. From an environmental standpoint, buy a clear polyethylene container and use your own filtered water to decrease the use of plastic bottles. You should sip clean and filtered water throughout the day and avoid drinking greater than 2 - 4 ounces at one time as it will cause diuresis through increased urination. Try to drink around 4 - 8 ounces before a meal and sip water throughout the meal.

Your goal is to drink one-half your body weight in ounces a day for maintenance. If you weigh around 160 pounds, you will need 80 ounces of water per day and more if you are active, exercising or in a hot climate. Drink 12 - 20 ounces two hours prior to exercise and drink another 8 - 12 ounces thirty minutes before exercise. You should strive to drink 4 - 8 ounces every fifteen minutes during exercise. It is important to stay hydrated during a workout to maximize your fitness outcomes.

If you find it hard to drink that much water, it might be helpful to flavor your water to help encourage more consumption. Following are a few tasty options you can infuse into your water to make it more appealing.

- Lemon, lime or citrus
- Cucumber
- Mint leaves

- Honey (few drops)
- Green tea
- Stevia
- Ice

Also, with fruit- and vegetable-infused water, you not only get good flavors but also some of the antioxidant properties out of the food. Water is the basic foundation for cell health. It is involved in most cell functions and, when we are dehydrated, our cells, muscles and organ systems don't function optimally. Let's drink to health, happiness and hydration... Cheers!

CHAPTER 8: STRESS AND SLEEP - MINIMIZE ONE, MAXIMIZE THE OTHER

Sleep is a healing balm for every ill. — **Menander**

We live in a fast-paced, on the go, tightly scheduled and sleep-deprived world. It seems we are always trying to catch up with our to-do lists, which are always growing longer and longer and never finished. Stress can be categorized as physical stress, emotional stress or environmental stress. We are getting hit daily from a combination of all these sources. Stress is attacking us from all directions - at work, at home, from friends, from environmental pollution and toxins, from the food we eat, or from physical and play activities. We do not take time to decompress, unwind and set up an environment for sleep and restoration. We often do not get the good, deep, restorative sleep which is needed for cellular restoration and body repair.

Steve is a patient of mine who came in because of chronic pain in his knee. He had seen an orthopedic surgeon who recommended a total knee replacement. Steve is only 55 years old, and his dad had a knee replacement at a young age as well. His dad ended up having a revision of the knee replacement and never did return to a full-level function afterwards. He wanted to know if we could do something on the regenerative side of things that may help him avoid a knee replacement.

Steve also told me he was dealing with decreased energy, feeling very irritable and moody. He was your typical Type A personality, working long hours as an executive. Despite being very successful, he never took vacations, and he spent his weekends working without any scheduled downtime in his life. He had stopped working out three years ago because of lack of time and now had lack of motivation. He ate on the go, often driving through fast food on the way to and from work. When I asked him about his vegetable intake, he jokingly said, "*Is ketchup a vegetable?*"

He slept around six hours a night because he needed to get up early to get his emails done prior to starting the day. He felt that his life revolved around work and, since he was a private business owner, his success was dependent on his performance. He did admit to feeling stressed, and also confessed he wasn't currently not doing anything to change his patterns. I told him, "*Steve, we can definitely help you out with your knees. I don't think you will have to have that knee replacement as you are a good candidate for stem cell injections but, before we head down that road, we need to make sure we have addressed your lifestyle and stressors, so we can set you up for optimal outcomes. Not to mention decrease your risk for stroke and heart attack!*"

Steve made some healthy lifestyle choices and addressed each one of his stressors, started to schedule downtime and vacations, got back into the gym and started eating healthier and sleeping longer. He then went on to have his procedure done. He ended up having a great result and returned to playing competitive tennis again. As you can see, everything is related. By dealing with his stress and stressors, he not only set himself up to heal better, but also decreased his risk for other stress-related ailments like stroke, heart attack and hypertension.

Next is a questionnaire from the International Stress Management Association. This stress test is intended to give you an overview only. Please see a physician or provider trained in stress management for a more in-depth analysis. Answer all the questions either yes or no. Answer yes even if only part of a question applies to you.

Once you have completed the test, review the questions where you scored yes so you can:
- See if you can reduce, change or modify this trait.
- Start with the ones that are easiest and most likely to be successful for you.
- See that you should only expect small changes to start with, it takes daily practice to make any change.

- Gain support from friends, family, and colleagues will make the process easier and more enjoyable.
- Find the professional help that is always available - your physician is a good place to start.

Most of us can manage varying amounts of pressure without feeling stressed. However, too much or excessive pressure, often created by our own thinking patterns and life experiences, can overstretch our ability to cope, and then stress is experienced.

Take your time, but please be completely honest with your answers when answering the following questions with a yes or a no.

1. I frequently bring work home at night.
2. Not enough hours in the day to do all the things I must do.
3. I deny or ignore problems in the hope they will go away.
4. I do the jobs myself to ensure they are done properly.

5. I underestimate how long it takes to do things.

6. I feel there are too many deadlines in my work / life that are difficult to meet.

7. My self-confidence / self-esteem is lower than I would like it to be.

8. I frequently have guilty feelings if I relax and do nothing.

9. I find myself thinking about problems even when I am supposed to be relaxing.

10. I feel fatigued or tired when I wake after an adequate sleep.

11. I often nod or finish other people's sentences for them when they speak slowly.

12. I have a tendency to eat, talk, walk and drive quickly.

13. My appetite has changed, have either a desire to binge or have a loss of appetite / may skip meals.

14. I feel irritated or angry if the car or traffic in front seems to be going too slowly/ I become very frustrated at having to wait in a queue.

15. If something or someone really annoys me I will bottle up my feelings.

16. When I play sport or games, I really try to win whoever I play.

17. I experience mood swings, difficulty making decisions, concentration and memory is impaired.

18. I find fault and criticize others rather than praising, even if it is deserved.

19. I seem to be listening even though I am preoccupied with my own thoughts.

20. My sex drive is lower, I can experience changes to menstrual cycle.

21. I find myself grinding my teeth.

22. Increase in muscular aches and pains especially in the neck, head, lower back, shoulders.

23. I am unable to perform tasks as well as I used to, my judgment is clouded or not as good as it was.

24. I find I have a greater dependency on alcohol, caffeine, nicotine or drugs.

25. I find that I don't have time for many interests / hobbies outside of work.

A yes answer score = 1 (one), and a no answer score = 0 (zero).

TOTAL your score here: _____

4 points or less: You are least likely to suffer from stress-related illness.

5 - 13 points: You are more likely to experience stress related ill health either mental, physical or both. You would benefit from stress management / counseling or advice to help in the identified areas.

14 points or more: You are the most prone to stress showing a great many traits or characteristics that are creating unhealthy behaviors. This means you are also more likely to experience stress and stress-related illness (e.g., diabetes, irritable bowel, migraine, back and neck pain, high blood pressure, heart disease/strokes, mental ill health (depression, anxiety and stress)). It is important to seek professional help or stress management counseling. Consult your medical practitioner for further analysis and management.

© International Stress Management Association U.K.

STRESS

We touched on stress and adrenal function earlier - now let's dive deeper into how stress can affect our health. 43% of adults suffer from stress-related health effects. 75 to 90% of visits to primary care physicians are for stress-related complaints or disorders. Stress has been linked to all leading causes of death including strokes, cancer, lung disease, accidents, liver cirrhosis and suicide. An estimated one million workers are absent each day with stress-related complaints. Stress is responsible for more than 25 billion workdays lost annually because of absenteeism. Following is a list of stress-related illnesses.

MAJOR ILLNESS	OTHER
Cardiovascular	Muscle-tension, aches and pains
Cancer	Allergies
Depression	Colds
Heart Disease	PMS
Rheumatoid Arthritis	Warts
Hypertension	Skin rashes
Ulcers	Loss and graying of hair
Obesity and weight gain	Gout
	Herpes

Stress-Related Illnesses

To better understand the effects of stress on our bodies, let's look deeper into the stress response system. First, in the brain, the hypothalamus and pituitary gland will respond to stressors and release hormones to help us survive the stressors. Cortisol and DHEA, as well as other hormones, are released from the adrenal glands to fight the stress. Cortisol is the main player in this response. The release of cortisol affects the function of all other hormone systems, including thyroid hormone, sex hormones, growth hormone, adrenal glands and the kidneys. Cortisol, when released from the adrenal glands, has the responsibility to defend us against the stressors. It has anti-inflammatory properties: it regulates glucose, amino acids and fat used by the body, increases oxygen supply to the tissue, and is important for the short-term response to stress. If cortisol remains elevated for too long a period because of constant stressors, this can lead to imbalance and disease. Earlier we saw different cortisol patterns that can occur with chronic and constant stress.

Let's recap what happens in the body as a response to incoming stressors. First, there is the **alarm reaction**. This is a quick increase in cortisol levels where the stress system is activated to fight. Next, during the **resistance stage**, adaptation takes place and the body can fight the stressors with relatively balanced hormone levels for a limited amount of time. If the stressors continue, eventually there will be a depletion of the stress hormones cortisol and DHEA. This is called the **burnout stage**. With repeated exposures to stress, the body will go through these predictable stages.

Stress-related symptoms include weight gain, fatigue, poor sleep, anxiety, high blood pressure, depression, heart disease and irritability. It is important with stress and stress-related symptoms to implement strategies to decrease the stress. This includes evaluating what environmental, physical and emotional stressors are feeding the fire and taking steps to decrease them. You may also need a medical evaluation for adrenal dysfunction and have your cortisol and stress hormone levels checked to see if other treatment options will be helpful.

Let's go through some practical steps that can help your combat stressors in your life.

1.   **Know what stresses you**. Take time to evaluate your life - what goes in your mouth and mind and how your treat your body. Avoid excessive sugar, get better sleep, fight chronic inflammation from the gut, and avoid food allergies and sensitivities. Evaluate mental and emotional stressors, like new experiences, unpredictable events, threatening situations and times when you feel a loss of control.

2.   **Take control of your stress response**. First, control your health and get a full evaluation and diagnosis of your aches, pains and arthritic issues. Control your chronic disease including arthritis, gum disease, inflammatory bowel disorders, sinusitis, allergies and obesity which all increase your risk of

hypertension, diabetes, heart disease and most other chronic diseases. Pledge to yourself to get healthy!

3.   **Control your work**. Work is a source of stress for most people. Do not skip meals to get more done. Resolve issues with coworkers as soon as possible. Recognize what you can and cannot control and "forget about it". Organize your office space and schedule for efficiency. Learn new skills as needed to maximize your work outcomes and set yourself up for advancement. Finally, and most importantly, schedule as much vacation time as you can - you are more productive when you let your mind take that tropical break it deserves. When you do get away, leave work behind if possible.

4.   **Control your finances**. Financial stress is one of the most common sources of stress in families. It can be helpful to get a good financial advisor. Set priorities in your spending and plan for the future. Finally, save money monthly, as you never know when you may need it.

5.   Control your rest and relaxation. Make sure you have a plan for downtime during your work days and on weekends. Treat yourself to the spa and get a massage. Plan time with quality friends who you enjoy spending time with and who care about you deeply. Get away and combat the stress. Plan a 15-minute or a one-week vacation. Learn to practice meditation to help your mind relax and get refocused. Set up environments that are familiar, predictable, safe and where you are in control.

6.   Control your relationships. You only have so much time and it is critical that you spend time with those that build you up, make your feel better about yourself, and inspire you. Make a list and then make a call to those you enjoy being with and plan time to hang out. Say "Thank you," to someone! When you thank someone and "pay your debt of gratitude", it releases stress and makes both of your feel better. Pay it forward and compliment someone or do something kind for them. It will release some very positive healthy endorphins. Resolve your disputes.

Do this as soon as possible so things don't start to fester.

Finally, ask for forgiveness and also be willing to receive it. This will relieve a large burden from you and allow you to then start focusing on how wonderful you are and how blessed you are to be surrounded by those who care for you! Have someone on your emergency call list that you can call anytime who knows and understands you and can be supportive in your health journey.

7.   **Get off the sugar rollercoaster.** Constant ups and downs of your blood sugar level is very inflammatory and a stressor to the body. As discussed previously, high sugar levels are very damaging to tissue. Also, the lows after the highs are stressors to the brain. Eat food that promotes sugar stability. Choose low glycemic index, high-fiber foods to stabilize blood sugars. Most of your diet should be fruits and vegetables that are high in antioxidants and energy-sustaining carbohydrates that help heal and

repair the body. Increase your omega-3s and anti-inflammatory good fats and try to reduce the omega-6s found in corn products, vegetable oils and over-the-counter processed foods. Get regular physical activity, relax and remember that stress and poor sleep triggers unhealthy eating of comfort foods.

8.   **Get to bed.** Sleep is needed to repair the body. It is the foundation of good stress management, healing and rejuvenation. Let's dive deeper into sleep. Stretch and yawn... aaaaahhhhhhhh.

SLEEP

Sleep is critical to our health and to the healing ability of our bodies. It is the time when our bodies repair and regenerate after the stress and breakdown from the day. Reparative hormones are released that stimulate muscle and soft tissue repair. Our minds are also rejuvenated through a deep restorative sleep. Many of us do not fall sleep easily and do not reach a restorative state during sleep.

The prevalence of non-restorative sleep (NRS) is estimated to be 10% to 25% of the general population. NRS presents as a feeling that sleep was restless, light, of poor quality, or awakening feeling unrestored or unrefreshed. It can manifest with or without difficulties initiating and maintaining sleep. Therefore, feeling unrefreshed upon awakening is a common complaint associated with a variety of medical, sleep, and psychiatric conditions.[79]

Sleep is the foundation for health. We spend one-third of our life in this blissful state. I love good sleep. I love the feeling of crawling into my pillow-top bed, feeling the softness of the sheets around me, kissing my wife good night and letting my mind drift off into a deep slumber. My mind shuts off, my body takes over releasing those healing hormones that restore my brain and body.

Studies show that healthy sleep is needed for health and disease prevention, including diabetes, obesity, hypertension, stroke prevention and hormone balancing. 50 to 70 million Americans have a sleep disorder with 10% taking medication for it. Short sleep, less than 7 - 8 hours, is linked to difficulty losing weight. Make it a goal to get at least eight hours of sound restful sleep per night. You say, "*But, I can't fall asleep and I wake up feeling unrested.*" Something is affecting your circadian cycle and there is something we can do about it.

Your circadian cycle is a daily rhythm of the body. It's what regulates your sleep and your wake patterns. Your hormones also cycle throughout the day with fluctuations in growth hormone, testosterone, cortisol, and DHEA and melatonin. Your rhythm can be fine-tuned or disrupted by external stimuli including light and dark, sound, and even the moon and sun cycles.

If you suffer from poor sleep, let's look at what could be keeping you up and offer some tips that can restore your normal circadian sleep cycle.

1. Certain health conditions like obstructive sleep apnea, pain, anxiety and night sweats make it very difficult to get deep restorative sleep. Drinking caffeine in the evening also keeps the mind turned on, preventing the normal mental shut off needed for sleep. The bedroom environment may not be dark enough or you may have to many noisy distractions. Your partner may sound like a bulldozer and have a snoring issue that constantly is waking you up. By avoiding carbohydrates in the evening, you may be getting low blood sugars at night that increase the cortisol too soon, leading to early awakening.

2. It's important to have a complex carbohydrate, like a half of an apple mixed with a protein source, to help you get into a deep sleep cycle. Sometimes when people engage in intense exercise later in the evening, it will also increase their cortisol levels. Again, high cortisol levels keep the body awake. Consistent regular exercise earlier in the day is actually very helpful in maintaining a normal

circadian cycle and helps to fall into a deep sleep later.

3. You may suffer from low progesterone levels or low and inadequate melatonin levels. Melatonin is a hormone made by the pineal gland that is essential for shutting off our brains and orchestrating the rest of the hormone symphony during sleep. Having your hormones evaluated for sleep issues may be helpful to restore healthy sleep.

4. Sunlight is needed for a normal circadian rhythm. You can use natural sunlight outside or through a window to help your naturally wake up in the morning. In the evening, use lowlight levels in the house to help to start to prepare you for sleep. Natural sunlight also increases vitamin D levels which is needed for health in many ways. Try to sleep in complete darkness.

5. Beware of cycle shifters. Activities like long plane rides, night- and shift-work can all cause disruption in the normal sleep-wake cycle. Disruption of the circadian rhythm can lead to obesity, diabetes, hypertension and cerebral vascular disease.

6. Nap when needed. Naps can be a quick way to restore your mind and catch up on lost sleep. It is still most important to get a regular night's sleep of about eight hours but, if you miss that goal, try to get a short, up to 10-20 minutes, nap. Between 4 and 5 pm is the optimal time for a quick nap.

7. Make weekends and vacations count. Set yourself up for some real rest and relaxation. On your vacation, try not to over-plan and set no obligations. Avoid "working" during your vacation as this does not allow your mind to release and keeps the stress right on the surface. Plan times during your vacation where you have nothing scheduled so you can truly rest. Have fun, laugh

and spend time with family and friends you enjoy thoroughly. Put the phone and computers away!

8. Walk and connect with your environment daily. Get outside and go for short walks throughout the day. Being outside, even in short bursts, increases vitamin D from sun exposure. Walk barefoot through the grass or in the sand. Being outdoors also stimulates the imagination, helps you to relax and de-stress. Walking also decreases insulin resistance and helps with weight loss and metabolism.

9. Artificial light in the evenings, including LEDs, fluorescent bulbs and incandescent bulbs, can all interrupt normal sleep patterns. The normal circadian rhythms are regulated by the amount of light and dark the body is exposed to during the day. Circadian rhythms control the timing of many physiological processes that take place in our bodies daily. They determine sleeping and feeding

patterns, as well as brain activity, hormone production and cell regeneration.

When the body is exposed to only to the natural light of the sun, the hypothalamus area of the brain sets its sleep patterns according to when it is light outside and to when it is dark. When the sun falls, and it starts to get dark outside, the hypothalamus tells the brain to start creating sleep hormones, like melatonin, and to decrease the body temperature to prepare for sleep. With the sunrise the next morning, light is sensed, and the body stimulated to make hormones like cortisol that wake and warm the body up.

When artificial light is added to a human's day, and especially during the evening and night hours, the body's natural rhythms become mixed up. It is not sure if it should be waking up or getting ready to shut down. A recent study in the Endocrine Society's Journal of Clinical Endocrinology and Metabolism found that, when compared with dim light, exposure to room light during the night suppressed melatonin by around 85 percent.[123]

Fluorescent and LED bulbs create a two-fold problem when it comes to sleep. First, they produce artificial light. Second, they produce blue light. Blue light wavelengths produced by electronics and overhead lights increase attention, reaction times and mood which is great during the day, but counterproductive at night when it is time to wind down and sleep deeply.

Research has found that exposure to blue light decreases the production of melatonin more than any other type of light. It is believed that the shorter wavelengths in blue light is what causes the body to produce less melatonin because the body is more sensitive to this type of light. A study by the University of Toronto found that people who wore glasses that blocked the blue light wavelengths produced more melatonin than those who didn't during night shifts. Other studies have found that blue wavelengths suppress delta brainwaves, which induce sleep, and increase alpha wavelengths, which create alertness.[124]

To get better sleep, it would be ideal to avoid using artificial light, but that is not a reality in our modern world. There are some things you can do to decrease exposure in the evening to artificial and blue light. To prevent sleeping problems, avoid any exposure to blue light 30 - 60 minutes prior to bed - no TV, tablets, computers or smart phones. Try to reside in an environment that is dimly lit so your brain starts to produce that slumber-inducing hormone - melatonin.

To help encourage the body's natural sleep/wake cycle, turn your computer and cell phones to the night mode that increase the warm tones and decreases the blue light on the screen. In addition, wearing blue light-filtering glasses during the evenings and when watching TV or on your "screens" can also be helpful. You can also get "smart" lights that you can program with your phone to increase warm tones in the evening and even start to dim to get your brain ready for sleep.

Use the following questionnaire to evaluate your sleep and how restorative it is on a daily basis. This was developed by the American Academy of Sleep Medicine.[79] It is a good assessment of how well your sleep is doing to restore your body daily.

RESTORATIVE SLEEP QUESTIONNAIRE
DAILY VERSION

Please complete this survey about half an hour after you get up in the morning and start the day. Try to complete the survey with as little distraction as possible. We want to know how you feel every day even if how you feel each day is the same.

What time did you wake up from sleep and start the day?

☐☐ : ☐☐
Hour : Minutes

What time is it right now?

☐☐ : ☐☐
Hour : Minutes

For each question below, please circle the number that best indicates how you feel (circle only one number for each question).

To what extent do you feel...	Not at All	A little bit	Some	Very much	Completely
1. tired? (R)	1	2	3	4	5
2. sleepy? (R)	1	2	3	4	5
3. in a good mood?	1	2	3	4	5
4. rested?	1	2	3	4	5
5. refreshed or restored?	1	2	3	4	5
6. ready to start the day?	1	2	3	4	5
7. energetic?	1	2	3	4	5
8. mentally alert?	1	2	3	4	5
9. grouchy? (R)	1	2	3	4	5

(R) = Reverse Scoring

Scoring: A total score is calculated as the average of the questionnaire items. The total score ranges from 0 to 100, with higher scores indicating better restorative sleep. A minimum of five items must be completed, otherwise the scale is considered as "missing." Item 9, grouchy must be reversed scored. To convert the average score to a 0-100 scale, the following transformation is used:

RSQ-D Total Score = {RSQ-D Average Score Across Completed Items – 1}*25

American Academy of Sleep Medicine

Now use the following questionnaire to evaluate your sleep and how restorative it is on a weekly basis. This was also developed by the American Academy of

Sleep Medicine.[79] It is a good screen as to how well your sleep is doing to restore your body weekly.

RESTORATIVE SLEEP QUESTIONNAIRE
WEEKLY VERSION

The following questions ask about how you felt when you woke up and started the day during the past 7 DAYS. When answering the questions think of how you felt about thirty minutes after getting out of bed to start the day.

For each question below, please circle the number that best indicates how you feel (circle only one number for each question).

To what extent do you feel...

	Not at All	A little bit	Some	Very much	Completely
1. tired? (R)	1	2	3	4	5
2. sleepy? (R)	1	2	3	4	5
3. in a good mood?	1	2	3	4	5
4. rested?	1	2	3	4	5
5. refreshed or restored?	1	2	3	4	5
6. ready to start the day?	1	2	3	4	5
7. energetic?	1	2	3	4	5
8. mentally alert?	1	2	3	4	5
9. grouchy? (R)	1	2	3	4	5

(R) = Reversed Scoring

Scoring: A total score is calculated as the average of the questionnaire items. The total score ranges from 0 to 100, with higher scores indicating better restorative sleep. A minimum of five items must be completed, otherwise the scale is considered as "missing." Item 9, grouchy must be reversed scored. To convert the average score to a 0-100 scale, the following transformation is used:

RSQ-W Total Score = {RSQ-W Average Score Across Completed Items – 1}*25

American Academy of Sleep Medicine

There are some sleep aids and tips that will help you fall asleep and stay asleep longer. Use this as a checklist before crawling into bed. Try different things from this list to see what works best for you.

1. Sleep in complete darkness. Even small amounts of light from windows or alarm clocks can turn on your wake cycle and increased cortisol. Use sleeping masks that block out all light. This will increase your melatonin release and inspire a deeper sleep. It is helpful in the summer months when the sun rises very early, causing your brain to increase cortisol that starts to wake you up that early.

2. Avoid TV or stimulating books before your fall asleep. This can stimulate the brain and disrupt your sleep cycle.

3. Wear socks if you have cold feet.

4. Keep the room temperature below 70°. Studies show that people sleep better at temperatures in this range.

5. Participate in a spiritual activity before you go to bed. Studies show that those who pray, meditate,

engaged in yoga or tai chi, or simply just give thanks, fall asleep faster and get more restorative sleep. This puts your mind in the right mindset for restorative, healthy sleep.

6. Avoid a loud alarm clock. Find an alarm setting that has a gentle sound that slowly wakes you from sleep. Loud and abrupt alarms cause a stress response and elevates cortisol.

7. Go to bed early and allow the body to recharge. Get into a bedtime routine doing activities that set your up for good rest and relaxation. Brush your teeth, have a pleasant conversation with your spouse or partner, meditate or say a prayer giving thanks for all your blessings, take some deep breaths, snuggle, and tuck in the kids and then go to bed.

8. Take a hot shower or bathe with magnesium Epsom salt. This elevates the core body temperature and facilitates sleep while the

magnesium relaxes the muscles. Adding some lavender oil to the bath or pillow spray can help calm the mind before sleep.

9. Make your bed a place for sleep only. Try to avoid watching TV, checking your emails or playing around on your phone. Do this in a separate area of your room or house prior to crawling into bed.

10. Decrease your exposure to blue lights in the evening with blue-filtering glasses and use the night settings on your screens. Dim the house lights before sleep and limit screen time before bed.

After going through this list of helpful tips, see what works for you and assess how your feel in the morning. Do your feel fully rested with adequate energy? Does your energy sustain you throughout the day? Are you falling asleep easier at night with less night awakening?

If yes – great! If not, it would be worth your time to see a medical practitioner who can check different lab levels, including cortisol and your hormone levels, to see if there's anything else impairing your ability to sleep.

They can also review your medications to make sure you are not having any sleep-related side effects. Medications like asthma medications, blood pressure medications, and synthetic progestins have been shown to disrupt sleep.

They can also assess your level of nutrient deficiencies that interfere with sleep, like niacin, magnesium, copper, iron, tryptophan and B vitamins.

They can investigate chemical exposures as over 100 chemicals are known to interfere with sleep. It is important to avoid over-the-counter and prescription sleep medications as they have been shown to be associated with more long-term health consequences due to a lack of a deep restorative sleep. Over-the-counter supplements can be used to help you relax at night and get into a better sleep cycle.

Supplements that can help with sleep include the following.

- **Chamomile tea or chamomile extract** - 3 to 6ml or 300 to 400mg of extract three times a day. If you are on a blood thinner, make sure you see your healthcare provider.
- **5-hydroxy-tryptophan (5-HTP)** - 100 to 200mg once a day at bedtime. Do not take with vitamin B6 and consult your healthcare provider if you are taking antidepressants.
- **Gamma- amino-butyric acid (GABA)** - 300 to 900mg once a day at bedtime. This will calm you down and make your drowsy so make sure you are ready for bed.
- **Magnesium** - 600mg once a day at bedtime. See your healthcare provider if you have kidney disease. Discontinue if you have any of abdominal pain. Too high a dose may cause diarrhea, so you may need to decrease the dose.

- **Melatonin** - 1 to 6mg a day. This should be taken before bedtime. Start with a lower dose and increase until you find a dose where you sleep through the night and do not wake up groggy.
- **Passion flower** - 1 to 2g of dry plants or in tea. You can also do 200 to 400mg of solid extract once a day. Do not take if on an MAO inhibitor.

Along with all the strategies for an optimal sleep environment, first try chamomile tea combined with magnesium before bedtime. From there, you can try adding melatonin and then 5-HTP. Add the others as needed until you find the combination that works best for you. These natural remedies will help you get into a deep and restorative state of sleep. A sleep disorder, like obstructive sleep apnea or narcolepsy, should be ruled out with poor sleep if simple remedies do not help.

Sleep is a vital piece of the healing and restoration puzzle. Strive to improve your sleeping habits and get into a deep consistent sleep cycle enabling you to

maximize your healing and improve your health.
Schedule and plan for healthy deep restorative sleep.
Good night and sleep well.

CHAPTER 9: RELAXATION TECHNIQUES TO DE-STRESS

The best cure for the body is a quiet mind. — **Napoleon Bonaparte**

You have had a busy and demanding work day. Your kids are driving you crazy. You have a huge to-do list and you didn't have time for your workout. You need to relax. You need to schedule relaxation into your day. It is an essential part of stress control, health and inflammation management. Your body will regenerate and heal better when you learn to cool down. We've talked about relaxation during the cool-down of your workout. Other times during the day, it is important to find times to focus and develop skills that relax you and reset your thermostat.

We live in a high-stress society. There is research on the relationship between stress and overall health. As we've talked about previously, stress is linked to digestive disorders, high cholesterol, hypertension, artery damage and heart disease, decreased immunities and increase infection, and a poor healing response. We don't want poor healing - we want restoration and rejuvenation!

Let's look at some key points and habits that should be learned to help you fully relax.

1. **Breathing**. Part of the fuel our body needs to live is oxygen. Giving the body a generous supply of oxygen with special breathing techniques during the day will help alleviate tension and stress.

2. **Relaxation practice**. Practice makes perfect. It helps to know different relaxation techniques that you can use to relax your mind and body.

3. **Focus on your body**. Listen to what your body is telling you. Your subconscious knows exactly what your body needs and gives you signs as to what that is for you. Sometimes during meditation and prayer, you can figure a lot of things out.

4. **Stretching**. Stretching exercises can be used to release tension, facilitate improved muscle contraction and improve flexibility.

5. **Fascial release**. Fascial release from massage or foam rolling is important for healthy muscle function. It is also a time to wind down the mind as well. It is a great activity prior to bedtime.

6. **Exercise**. Light physical exercise and specific types of exercise, like yoga and tai chi, can be very helpful in clearing the mind and resetting the body for performance. They have also been shown to lower blood pressure and decrease cortisol levels.

7. **Calming and relaxing the mind**. Your mind may need a break on occasion just as your muscles do. Take time out during the day to clear your mind. Try to think of little or nothing for a few minutes. Let your mind wander wherever it wants to go.

8. **Confidence**. Focus on positive self-affirmation. You were made unique and special and are perfect just the way you are - figure out your purpose in life and utilize your gifts to do good for others. This will give you confidence and, when we are confident about ourselves, we worry less.

9. **Care for ourselves**. Do something special just for you. You work hard, and you deserve to celebrate yourself and your accomplishments. Reflect on your blessings and the positive things in your life that you cherish. It is okay to spoil yourself once in a while.

There are many relaxation techniques that you can use to help decrease stress and reset, like the following.

Deep diaphragmatic breathing	Progressive Muscle Relaxation
Guided Imagery	Biofeedback
Autogenic training (self-suggestion/statements)	Yoga
Meditation	Infrared sauna
Exercise/stretching	Massage

Relaxation Techniques

DEEP DIAPHRAGMATIC BREATHING

You would think that breathing just naturally happens the right way. It's often the last thing we think about as a means to achieve health. The problem is many people have learned the wrong way to breathe. They're breathing through their nose. They use the upper chest and accessory muscles of the neck and often breathe in a slumped posture. Improved breathing techniques can be used during your workouts, during the cool-down, after workouts, before bed to relax and get ready for sleep, or anytime during the day when you have time to reap the benefits of healthy breathing.

There are five advantages to using the diaphragm in breathing as follows.

1. **Oxygen**. The bottom part of the lungs is where most of the gas exchange takes place and, when you use your diaphragm to breathe, you're able to get the air and oxygen to the

base of the lungs. This results in a more effective delivery of oxygen to the tissues. This is critical for health and healing.

2. **Less tension.** Deep breathing relaxes the muscles in the neck and shoulders. This is important for posture and also to decrease the stress on the brachial plexus and nerves passing through the neck. Less stress on the nerves means less muscle spasm, less pain and more healing.

3. **It helps you chill.** Deep diaphragmatic breathing tells the nervous system to relax. This reduces the heart rate and breathing rate and has a calming relaxation effect. It can also decrease elevated cortisol levels from chronic stress. The less sympathetic stimulation, the lower the blood pressure and stress to the heart and blood vessels as well as helping prepare the body for sleep.

4. **Organ massage.** Deep diaphragmatic breathing gently moves the abdominal organs, aiding digestion and helping with lymphatic drainage. Much of our lymphatic and immune system is located in the bowels just below the diaphragm. Improved digestion is important for all healing, detoxification and weight loss.

5. **Better posture.** The diaphragm is related to core muscle strength and needs to be worked properly. Overworked and tight abdominal muscles can decrease the abdominal cavity's ability to expand and allow for the lungs to lower during breathing.

How to perform deep diaphragmatic breathing

First, put one hand on your upper chest and the other hand over your belly button. Take a big breath in and observe which moves first. Ideally, you want your belly to expand first to allow for the diaphragm to drop and the lungs to fully inhale. To practice and train your body in diaphragmatic breathing, lie flat on your back and rest your knees over a pillow so that your abdominal muscles can relax. Observe that your belly button is rising and falling as you breathe. You can put some weights over your belly button and watch it rise and fall. The upper hand on your chest should not be the primary movement. You can put your hands behind your head to further encourage this movement. Once you can perform deep breathing in this position, you can do this technique in any position - from sitting, standing and even moving. Don't hold the air in but, after inhalation, slowly exhale. The more you practice this technique, the easier it will become as the diaphragm is a muscle and will become more efficient and stronger in its movement.

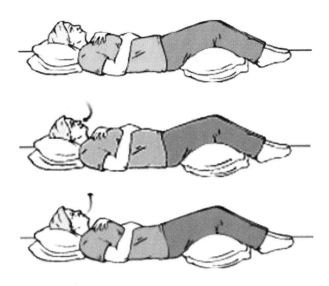

Deep Diaphragmatic Breathing Technique

Trained opera singers and musicians use this technique to give them good vocal control and breath support for long, sustained notes and phrasings during songs.

GUIDED IMAGERY

Mental or guided imagery is a type of meditation that can be used as a technique to focus and direct the imagination in ways they can get us to relax and improve our performance. You can combine your own spirituality and faith with this technique as well. I recommend if you have a faith in God or believe in a higher power than yourself, use that strength with your guided imagery to increase its power. Athletes, actors, public speakers, politicians and anyone who wants to improve their focus and performance can use these techniques. It can be as simple as imagining yourself doing the activity, doing it well, and getting the response that you want out of it. Guided imagery can involve all our senses and not just our vision and imagination. Through engaging all the senses, it becomes not just a mental activity, but can have a powerful impact on our nervous system and other systems in our body on a cellular level.

Guided imagery is a technique that has been around for many years, and recently there's been some good research showing its positive effects on health, creativity and performance. It has been shown that, in many instances, even just ten minutes of guided imagery can reduce blood pressure, lower cholesterol and glucose levels in the blood, and improve our nervous systems. It can decrease headaches and pain. It can increase our performance and skills from sport activities to acting and singing. You can accelerate weight loss, reduce anxiety and sharpen your focus on your goals. It has been used in chemotherapy to decrease nausea, depression, soreness and fatigue.

Those who utilize these techniques often notice heightened emotion, increased laughter, more sensitivity to music, openness to spirituality, improved intuition, better abstract thinking and empathy.

It can be an essential part of conscious goal setting as it can bring more clarity and passion behind your core reason for creating a healthy change. The more you utilize these techniques, the more powerful they can become in changing your unconscious thought process to a more positive and goal-oriented state of mind and body.

Guided imagery can be simple once you let your mind go and let your imagination and subconscious mind take over. You can invent your own imagery, or you can listen to imagery that has been created for you. Either way, your imagination will take over and create the images in your mind allowing your inner creative, awesome and powerful self to appear.

The Three Principles of Guided Imagery

1. **The mind-body connection**. To our bodies, what is happening in our mind is like a dream state which can feel as real as the actual event itself. The mind does not always see the difference. Try this... imagine in your hand a ripe, juicy, yellow lemon. Cut it open, and then see yourself opening your mouth to take a huge bite out of it. Feel its juice bathing your tongue. Did you squint your eyes or taste a sour sensation in your mouth? That is the power of guided imagery. You can create physiological change in your body from an imagined stimulus. Guided imagery can also be

used to decrease your pulse, relax the body and melt tension away through imagining the feeling of warm sand, cool waters or relaxing touch on the body.

2. **The relaxed focused state.** In the relaxed focused state, we can learn faster and perform better. We can actually shift our body chemistry and brainwave activity. Our moods, feelings and ability to focus can change. We can do amazing things that we may not be able to do in our normal mental state, like lifting a heavy object off a child or composing beautiful and powerful music. You can replace the fear of pain with a sense of safety, optimism and calmness. Our mind wanders in and out of altered states of consciousness throughout the day. You may find yourself daydreaming when you work out or go for run. This is an altered state of consciousness. I often find when I'm working out that my mind can be clear and creative and I can solve problems without thinking about them.

3. **The state of being in control**. With guided imagery, we have a sense of being in control which makes us feel more powerful and optimistic about the challenges we face. Being in control is associated with higher optimism, self-esteem and the ability to tolerate pain, confusion and stress. Research in psychotherapy shows that when we have a sense of mastery over our environment, we will feel better about ourselves, have more self-confidence and perform better in difficult situations. On the contrary, when we feel a sense of helplessness, we have lower self-esteem, a decreased ability to cope and have less optimism about the future. The fact that you can use guided imagery at any time puts you in control, knowing that you have a technique that can help you master difficult situations.

Here are some excerpts from two books on guided imagery. First, here is an excerpt from **Invisible Heroes: Survivors of Trauma and How They Heal** by Belleruth Naparstek.

What to Expect from Guided Imagery

Here are some general facts and user-friendly tips about how to best use guided imagery techniques, and what to expect from it.

Your skill and efficiency will increase with practice. You'll improve from whatever skill level you start with. Guided imagery functions in a way that is the opposite of addictive substances the more you use it, the less and less it will take for it to work.

Imagery works best in a permissive, relaxed, unforced atmosphere. So, try not to get too intense about "doing it right". There are many ways to do it right.

Your choice of imagery content needs to be congruent with your values, so don't try to impose imagery on yourself that doesn't sit right. Let your own images come up and work for you. Don't get stuck in somebody else's way.

It's best to engage all the senses, especially your kinesthetic or feeling sense. Remember, only a little over half of the population is strongly visual.

Imagery is generally more powerful in a group setting, mainly due to the contagious nature of the altered state. So, a support group, special study group or healing group is a nice place to work with it (and try to sit next to a yoga instructor or some other heavy-hitter meditator!).

Music, when properly chosen, will increase the effects of imagery. You will intuitively know what music is right for what you need. A small percentage of people prefer no music at all.

Imagery that elicits emotion is generally more effective than imagery that doesn't. Responding with emotion is a good sign that the imagery is working for you in a deep way.

If you're using self-talk with your imagery, try to avoid

the imperative verb form on yourself, so that inadvertently "bossy" language doesn't get your back up and marshal unnecessary resistance.

You do not have to be a "believer" in order for imagery to help. Positive expectancy helps, but even a skeptical willingness to give it a try can be quite sufficient.

Touch may be the most powerful accompaniment to imagery you can employ, both to help with relaxation and to increase the kinesthetic power of the images. Imagery combined with therapeutic massage, energy work, or other kinesthetic modalities is very potent, and more than the sum of its parts.

Using the same posture cues, gestures or hand-positioning with each imaging session creates an "anchor" that conditions you to respond immediately to the posture. You can then adopt the posture in a meeting, or while waiting in traffic, or while resting, and your body will respond the way it did during the imagery.

If you aren't used to being both relaxed and awake at the same time, you will routinely fall asleep during an imagery session, especially if you're listening to a tape. If you want to stay awake, you might try sitting up, standing, walking or listening with your eyes half-open.

Even asleep, though, you'll benefit from repeated listening, as demonstrated in test results with sleeping diabetics and unconscious surgery patients.

Don't worry if you keep "spacing out" or losing track of a guided imagery narrative. This is not an indicator that you're listening wrong. On the contrary, a wandering mind often comes with the territory.

You may tear up, get a runny nose, cough, yawn, feel heaviness in your limbs, get tingling along the top of their scalp or in your hands and feet, or experience minor, involuntary muscle-movements. These are entirely normal responses.

Other indicators of a strong response to imagery are unusual stillness, increased coloring in the face, and an ironing out of lines and wrinkles. After some imagery, your voice will be deeper and lower, slower and more relaxed.

Usually an imaging exercise, regardless of what it's for, will clear a headache, relieve stress, lift mood and reduce chronic pain."

Next is an excerpt from **Staying Well with Guided Imagery,** also by Belleruth Napartek.

EIGHT TYPES OF GUIDED IMAGERY CONTENT

There are many kinds of effective healing imagery, and, because people respond differently to different kinds, it's good to be aware of the range of possibilities.

FEELING STATE IMAGERY

This is simple imagery that changes mood, such as seeing yourself in your favorite place, or recalling a happy, peaceful time. Any imagery that can genuinely elicit feelings of love, care, safety and gratitude, will crowd out feelings of fear, anxiety, resentment and anger. All of this qualifies as feeling state imagery.

END-STATE IMAGERY

This is imagery that uses for its content any desired outcome or goal, in all it's realistic particulars. So, imagining a strong, cancer-free body; a perfectly played, confident, relaxed, focused game of tennis; or the sound of a perfectly registered high C note just before singing it, would all be end-state imagery, sometimes called "mental rehearsal" in hypnosis.

ENERGETIC IMAGERY

This is imagery, taken from Ayurvedic and Chinese medicine, as well as quantum physics, that uses the notion of plentiful, coherent, free-flowing, unblocked energy as the underlying dynamic of good health.

Illness, in this paradigm, would be seen as stuck energy, or energy that is withheld from the general flow. This can be imagined as moving dots, a kind of sound, or an internal feeling of motion.

CELLULAR IMAGERY

This imagery focuses on the healthy interaction of the cells, and requires accurate technical knowledge, so it isn't for everyone. For asthma, it would be imagining the mast cells being less reactive to neutral particles floating by; for diabetes, it would be insulin attaching to energy hungry cells, so they can take in glucose from the bloodstream; and so on.

PHYSIOLOGICAL IMAGERY

This is imagery that focuses on larger healing processes in the body, such as sensing the widening, softening and clearing of the arteries for heart disease; imagining the feel of tumors shrinking in the body with cancer; and seeing the opening of swollen, constricted passageways in the lungs for asthma.

This too requires accurate knowledge of how the body naturally operates to heal each condition.

METPHORIC IMAGERY

This is imagery that works with symbols instead of concrete reality, such as seeing a flower opening its petals as a metaphor for enhanced creativity blossoming again; or seeing a tumor as an enemy encampment, being decimated by a powerful supply of tanks, missiles and guns; or sensing insulin "keys" unlocking the "doors" to hungry cells for people with diabetes.

PSYCHOLOGICAL IMAGERY

This is imagery that specifically addresses a person's psychological issues by providing corrective emotional content. So, for instance, it might consist of imagining being surrounded by loving friends and allies to interrupt a sense of isolation and despair; or seeing oneself through kind and loving eyes, for someone who is relentlessly self-attacking; or perceiving the presence of a beloved, recently lost parent to alleviate grief.

SPIRITUAL IMAGERY

This imagery evokes the wider perspective and peaceful or transcendent feelings provided by mystical states of consciousness and prayer. This might involve sensing assistance from angels, guides, power animals, God, or specific religious figures and symbols; or imagery that fosters a sense of oneness and connection with all things; or any imagery that deeply opens the heart."

If you have a faith and believe in God, use this as a tool to help.

As you can see, guided imagery is a powerful way to use your imagination to create health and healing in the body.

AUTOGENIC TRAINING (Self-Suggestions / Statements) and MEDITATION

As you now know, chronic stress to our bodies without proper recovery and relaxation can contribute to many chronic diseases. It is like a silent killer. Stress is associated with mental health from depression and anxiety, to all forms of chronic disease. It is critical that we know how to decompress, relax and let loose a little.

Autogenetic training is a simple and effective way to teach your body to relax and respond to your commands. You can gain control over different body functions such as heart rate, blood pressure, digestion, body temperature and breathing. It is not fully understood how it works but it seems to be a form of self-hypnosis. In this state, you become more open to suggestion and train your brain to get into a deep relaxed state, similar to deep sleep. When you are under stress, your sympathetic nervous system kicks in. Autogenic training can turn on your calming, parasympathetic nervous system to decrease your stress response which will have healthy outcomes in decompressing and treating chronic disease. Autogenic training balances the two nervous systems and brings them into a state of optimal performance.

Autogenic training is simple and can be done anytime and anywhere. It is effective and can be done in less than ten minutes. Here's an example of how to do a session.

First, find yourself in a comfortable relaxed position, either sitting or lying down flat. Next, uncross your arms and legs, and have your arms comfortably by your side. Take a few slow, deep diaphragmatic breaths and then say to yourself the following statements slowly. Repeat each statement 3 - 6 times before moving onto the next. Use imagination to visualize what is happening to your body with each suggestion (combined with Mental Imagery).

1. *My arms are heavy. My left arm is heavy. My right arm is heavy. Both of my arms are heavy.*
2. *My legs are heavy. My left leg is heavy. My right arm is heavy. Both of my arms are heavy.*
3. *My arms are warm. My left arm is warm. My right arm is warm. Both of my arms are warm.*
4. *My legs are warm. My left leg is warm. My right arm is warm. Both of my arms are warm.*
5. *My heartbeat is calm and regular.*
6. *My breathing is calm and regular.*
7. *My abdomen is warm.*
8. *My forehead is cool.*

Next, take three more deep diaphragmatic breaths and slowly open your eyes. As you can see, it is very simple yet can have a very powerful effect on helping your body relax and calm down. *Insight Timer* and *Headspace* are two good apps that can help with mindset and meditation. Another good app you can download is *Autogenic Training and Progressive Muscle Relaxation*. It can be downloaded from the Apple App Store or at the Google Play Store.

You can also do an internet search for *"autogenic training, mindfulness or meditation"* to find streamable versions.

EXERCISE/STRETCHING

Exercise and stretching can be an effective means to decrease stress and release tension in the body. Most people, after exercising, feel they have been more fruitful in their day, feel more relaxed and at ease, and are more productive when they get back to work. Those who exercise during the day will also sleep better at night, as muscles use that time to heal and recover.

We've previously referenced our format for workouts. With our exercise programs, we start with the **dynamic warm-up**, followed by the **core workout** and then we end with a **functional cool-down**. During this functional cool-down, we implement deep breathing techniques, guided imagery, yoga and stretching to get the body and mind back into alignment and ready for the rest of the day.

YOGA AND TAI CHI

Yoga and tai chi are not only great forms of exercise for strengthening the body, but they also help with range of motion, balance and mental relaxation. Studies show that they are beneficial with arthritis pain as well as a decrease in stress hormones. Again, we blend many of the movements and philosophies of yoga and tai chi into our functional cool-down at the end of a workout to reset the body after the stress and strain of exercise. Yoga and tai chi can also help to warm up, and stretch the different fascial lines prior to a workout, to help with range of motion and improved functional movement.

INFRARED SAUNA

Infrared saunas can be an effective tool for healing and disease prevention. Infrared light can penetrate human tissue and, in turn, produce a host of anti-aging health benefits. In fact, after our regenerative PRP and stem cell treatments, we recommend infrared heat because of the influence it has on healing. Following are some of the health benefits of infrared saunas.

Detoxification. Sweating is good for you. It is the body's safe and natural way to heal and stay healthy. Infrared sauna benefits the body by heating it directly, causing a rise in core temperature resulting in a deep, detoxifying sweat at the cellular level where toxins reside. You really do "sweat it out."

"Detoxification is important because it strengthens the body's immune system and helps the body's biochemical processes function efficiently so that we are better able to digest the nutrients in our foods. Detoxification has also been shown to be helpful with colitis, chronic fatigue, fibromyalgia, auto-immune disease, immune deficiency states, autism, ADD and ADHD." - Dr. Rachel West

Relaxation. Relaxation is more important to health than most people realize. The American Institute of Stress estimates that 75 to 90% of all visits to primary care physicians are for stress-related problems. Long-term stress is the cause of countless physiological effects on the body, including increased blood pressure, weight gain and weakening of the immune system. Unlike traditional saunas which operate at extremely harsh temperatures, infrared is a gentle, soothing and therapeutic heat that promotes relaxation and improved sleep. Infrared sauna therapy helps you relax while receiving an invigorating deep-tissue sweat, leaving you fully refreshed after each session.

Weight Loss. Maintaining a healthy weight is important to your overall quality of life. In fact, a 10-year study published by the New England Journal of Medicine discovered that the circumference of your waist alone is a critical factor for assessing the risk of premature death. In other words, by maintaining a healthy weight, you may be able to live a longer, healthier life. Studies have shown that the benefits of an infrared sauna session can burn upwards of 600 calories per hour... and that is while you relax! As the body works to cool itself, there is a substantial increase in heart rate, cardiac output and metabolic rate, causing the body to burn more calories. It has also been shown to increase human growth hormone which also contributes to weight loss and healing effects.[115]

Pain Relief and Healing. Infrared heat penetrates tissue, joints, and muscles to relieve anything from minor aches and pains to chronic pain conditions, such as fibromyalgia. Infrared sauna heat works by penetrating joints, muscles and tissues, increasing circulation and speeding oxygen flow. By reducing soreness on nerve endings, infrared heat reduces muscle spasms and helps the body heal itself naturally. The more blood flow to an area the better - the body will heal because of increased oxygenation and nutrient delivery to the area of injury or after a regenerative procedure. Studies show a positive effect on low back pain with infrared heat.[116] We recommend infrared heat after all PRP and stem cell treatments.

Lower Blood Pressure. Infrared saunas induce a deep sweat to make the heart pump faster which, in turn, increases blood flow, lowers blood pressure and helps circulation. Scientific evidence shows that using an infrared sauna a couple of times a week lowers blood pressure.

Improved Circulation. Heating the muscles with infrared rays produces an increase in blood flow similar to that seen during exercise. Regular infrared sauna use can significantly stimulate blood flow up to twice the normal rate. Again, the more blood flow, the more healing and faster muscle recovery after a workout. An infrared sauna treatment is a great way to finish a workout as it will increase calories burned as well as improve circulation to help with workout recovery. In our gym at Rejuv Medical, we have infrared saunas in the locker rooms as well as an entire workout studio heated with infrared panels in the ceiling. This is where we do a heated workout, from Pilates to Yoga, for improved circulation, recovery and healing.

Anti-aging. The infrared wavelength is the most effective wavelength for healing the epidermis and dermis layers of the skin. Infrared wavelengths stimulate collagen production to reduce wrinkles and improve overall skin tone. A study published in the Journal of Cosmetic and Laser Therapy showed significant improvements in skin appearance after just 12 weeks of sauna skin therapy using near-infrared technology. Participants experienced a reduction in wrinkles and crow's feet, as well as improved overall skin tone, including softness, smoothness, elasticity, clarity and firmness.

Wound Healing. Skin plays a vital role in the protection of our bodies from the external environment. When broken, it is important to repair it quickly to prevent infection or further problems. Scientific research has concluded that infrared heat greatly enhances the skin's healing process by promoting faster cell regeneration and human tissue growth. Human cell growth increases to repair wounds and prevent infection. This is another reason we use infrared heat with injury and regenerative procedures like PRP and stem cells.

Cell Health. Infrared heat aids in cell health, muscle recovery and overall immunity defense. Infrared therapy stimulates the circulatory system to more fully oxygenate the body's cells. Better blood circulation means more toxins flow from the cellular level to the skin's surface to be removed and excreted. [114, 115]

MASSAGE

Massage therapy is also an effective tool to help the body and mind relax as well as improve musculoskeletal health. A trained massage therapist can help release fascial adhesions to restore healthy functional movement. It helps with rehydration of the fascia and restores blood flow to help with healing.

Take advantage of one or all the different discussed relaxation techniques. They all have therapeutic value and are powerful tools in regaining your health and augmenting your healing potential with injury or after a regenerative orthopedic procedure.

CHAPTER 10: FUNCTIONAL MOVEMENT & FASCIA - STAY CONNECTED

When everything is connected to everything else, for better or for worse, everything matters. — **Bruce Mau**

We have seen how cell health is instrumental in creating an environment that allows the body to repair and also helps to maintain optimal function once healing is achieved. The next element in the C.F.A.N. model is functional movement. Functional movement has to do with how all the parts of the body function together as a whole to create balance, symmetry, coordination, flexibility and stability. It involves all the supportive and structural elements in the body, including the spine, joints, fascia, tendons and ligaments.

Many different factors can affect our functional movement. The aging process in and of itself will create loss in range of motion, tight and stiff muscles, decreased neurological function with loss of balance and proprioception, and fascial adhesions which all contribute to dysfunctional movement patterns. For the body to withstand all the physical stresses imposed on it, it is important we address healthy functional movement so that the body can function optimally with the least amount of wear and tear.

When we see a patient for regenerative procedures, or for fitness and weight loss, we begin their health journey with a functional movement screen we call an Integrated Movement Assessment™. The screening assesses how their body moves, where they might have flexibility and tight fascial issues, and where they might have a lack of supportive strength. Dysfunction in these areas can all lead to breakdown of the body. From there, corrective exercises are shared via their Intergraded Movement Plan™, and fascial mobilization and muscle stretching are implemented to restore healthy movement patterns.

The **3F's** need to be addressed with functional movement to ensure optimal performance. They are **FLEX** (muscle strength), **FLEXIBILITY** (muscle, tendon, ligament and joint strength and range of motion) and **FASCIA** health (how the fascia supports movements and allows transfer of information through its connective structures). Each of these areas need to be analyzed for dysfunction and then corrections and treatments done to return them to a healthy state. Each of these areas is vulnerable to breakdown and dysfunction, which will lead to abnormal stresses on the joints, nerves and spine. When this happens, the body will breakdown, leading to degenerative chronic conditions like tendon injury, muscle tears and strains, and joint and spine arthritis. The good news is we can have positive influence over our muscles, joints, ligaments and tendons, and fascia.

Functional movement is critical for optimal performance in our bodies. Degeneration of the spine and peripheral joints sets in with dysfunctional movement and instability. When you have injury, over-use or aging to muscles, joints, tendons and ligaments, instability sets in. This will cause dysfunctional movement in that area. Chronic repetitive dysfunctional movement leads to abnormal wear and arthritis. With over-use, injury or aging, fascia can develop adhesions which leads to restricted movement patterns. This can then also lead to abnormal wear patterns in the body. Often, it's a combination of both - instabilities of joints and restricted fascial movement - that leads to the end product of degeneration.

An example would be with an injury to a peripheral joint. A sprained ligament - if not fully healed - can lead to instability of the joint. Over time, instability causes dysfunctional movement of the joint which causes accelerated degeneration. A high school football player who is tackled may develop a sprain to his MCL, the inside ligament that stabilizes the knee. He misses the rest of the game but partially heals after a couple weeks and finishes off the season. He continues to have mild discomfort in his knee but is still able to be active. Years later, he starts to develop more pain and swelling in his knee. He comes to see me at age 30 and we get an x-ray showing he has moderate arthritis or degeneration of the inside aspect of his knee joint. The arthritis developed because of the years of abnormal movement in that joint after the earlier sprained ligament.

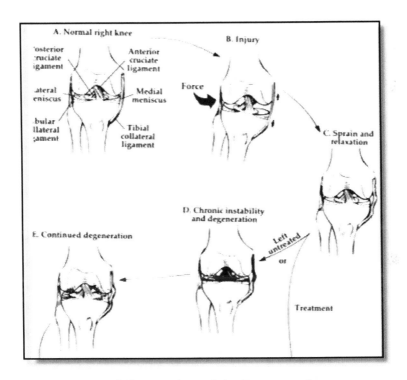

Instability Leads to Joint Degeneration

A similar process can happen in the spine. I see patients every day who come in with chronic back pain and the MRI reveals significant degeneration of the spinal facet joints and the intervertebral discs. When discussing their history, many of them have an injury in the remote past - sometimes greater than 10 years ago - which created instability and was the catalyst which started the degeneration.

During a whiplash injury, like a motor vehicle accident, the spine goes from a protected extended position into kyphosis, which is a flexed and vulnerable position of the spine. This injury sprains and loosens the ligaments and fascia that hold the spine together. The injured patient will experience pain initially from the sprain, but even more significant is the degeneration that ensues after abnormal movement patterns take over the spine. Continued instability leads to friction between the joints, causing facet arthritis and disc herniations. This is painful in and of itself, but also the disc can put pressure on the nerve roots. When the nerve roots have pressure from the herniated disc, they create pain that radiates down the extremity all the way to the foot. Injury and aging create instability. Instability creates dysfunctional movement. Dysfunctional movement creates degeneration.

All three components of the 3 F's are important to prevent dysfunctional movement patterns: Flex (muscle core strength), Flexibility (the ability of muscles, ligaments and tendons to allow healthy functional range of motion in the joints and spine) and Fascia (connects it all together).

FLEX

Core muscle strength and function is essential for a body that performs optimally. Muscles have multiple functions. Our body has over 650 muscles that aid in movement, like walking, talking, sitting, standing, eating and other internal functions that we don't even think about like breathing and digestion. Muscles are also critical for maintaining posture, distributing forces throughout our body and also in blood circulation. Skeletal muscles are arranged in synergistic chains that work together in both creating movements and supportive stability. Muscles are surrounded by fascia which, together, merge with ligaments and tendons to distribute forces along these body chains. Muscular imbalances and weakness caused by injury or disease can lead to dysfunctional movement patterns, contributing to joint and spine breakdown and degeneration.

Also, the lack of core strength and support along the axial spine and pelvis creates a weak and unstable platform for the muscles and the joints to work off. A movement and strength assessment is an important tool in analyzing the body for dysfunctional patterns contributing to a patient's degenerative process. Once core weakness and peripheral muscle imbalances are identified, a plan to correct the assessment is needed.

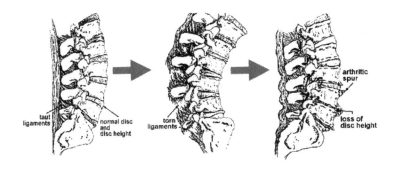

taut ligaments / normal disc and disc height / torn ligaments / arthritic spur / loss of disc height

FLEXIBILITY

Flexibility is important for normal spine and joint function. Optimal range of motion leads to decreases stress in the joints. With increased range of motion, it is important to have good muscular control over that movement. Flexibility comes from appropriate tension in the muscles and tendons with stability given from the ligaments connecting the joints. Loss of range of motion comes from tense muscles, fascia adhesions and joint capsular tightness. Flexibility issues need to be addressed for optimal function.

FASCIA

"The fascia forms the largest system in the body, as it is the system that touches all other systems."
- James L. Oschman, PhD

"The muscle-bone concept presented in standard anatomical description gives a purely mechanical model of movement. It separates movement into discrete functions, failing to give a picture of the seamless integration seen in a living body. When one-part moves, the body as a whole respond. Functionally, the only tissue that can mediate such responsiveness is the connective tissue (fascia)."
- Feitis Schultz

The most recent definition of fascia, by the Fascia Research Congress in 2012, characterizes fascia as *"fibrous collagenous tissues which are part of a body wide tensional force transmission system."* Fascia is that dense white connective tissue that is seen around muscle. It envelopes the muscular system and blends with tendons and ligamentous structures throughout the body. It is one continuous overlapping organ that has many functions. There are both superficial and deep fascial layers. There's also meningeal fascia around the nervous system and visceral fascia that surrounds and supports our organs.

Contraction of the muscles transmits forces through all these layers. With normal function, this creates a synergistic movement pattern that amplifies stability, power, posture and strength. With dysfunction of the fascial layers, breakdown and pathology can be seen in the muscles, tendons, ligaments, joints and throughout the peripheral nervous system. The superficial layer, which surrounds and supports the muscles, also surrounds the nerves and blood vessels of the body.

Fascial adhesions, where these peripheral nerves pass through and around muscles, are vulnerable areas for the formation of compression syndromes.

These adhesions develop over and between muscles where repetitive muscle movement causes the fascial layers to stick together. Fascial adhesions are a common cause of muscle strain and nerve entrapment syndromes. Carpal tunnel syndrome, in the wrist, and suprascapular nerve compression, in the shoulder, are two examples of situations where nerves are passing through fascial tunnels and become compressed. Fascial treatments like massage, myofascial release and various foam rolling techniques all address this layer.

So, essentially, fascia is the connective tissue the links the body together. Muscles, bones, nerves and organs are all connected to each other via the fascia. Fascia has superficial and deep layers.

The superficial fascial layer has many major features, including the following.

- Contains lymphatic channels.
- Has a shock-absorbing type of function, like the plantar fascia in the foot and heel.

- Acts as a heat insulator and thermal regulator.
- Stores energy in the form of triglycerides.
- Provides channels and tunnels for veins and nerves and contains many mechanoreceptors that aid in movement and proprioception but also in the sensation of pain.
- Contains elastic fibers that lets the skin stretch and then return to its original resting state.
- Connects the deeper fascia with the body surface.
- Contains the ground substance that fills the space between cells and is made up of collagen and fluids that support movements like gliding and sliding of the tissues.
- Contains contractile fibers that can also aid in musculoskeletal movement.

Superficial fascia is made up of various cell types with differing functions as follows.
- Adipocytes for fat storage.
- Fibroblasts for connective tissue formation. Fibroblasts, along with mast cells, secrete

proteoglycans. This is the glue that holds connective tissue together and allows the transfer of forces. If your connective tissue and fascia has a lack range of motion with disuse of after an injury, it dehydrates and thickens, becoming gel-like and sticky. This creates adhesions that can cause dysfunctional movement, and it can cause compression around nerves that are running through the fascial layers.

- Blood cells that a part of our immune system, including neutrophils and macrophages, are found in fascia. They are also involved in the process of healing and remodeling.
- Mast and plasma cells are immune cells found in fascia.
- Sweat glands are found in fascia.

In the fascia, the interaction of all the cell types is critical for optimal function. Fascia has functions in healing, structural support, information communication, protection and lubrication. Force transfer during muscle contraction is a very important responsibility of fascia. With regards to force transmission and load transfer, Schleip describes fascia as "... *the dense irregular connective tissue that surrounds and connects every cell, even the tiniest myofibril, and every single organ of the body forming continuity throughout the body*".[118]

We usually think of muscles as moving in directions like flexion or extension, but with the additional three-dimensional structure of fascia, force transmission is not only in two directions – it can be transferred in any 360° motion with muscle contraction. This is because the muscle is intimately involved in all planes of motion through the fascia surrounding it. We find that muscle contractions in the upper extremity is transferred through the thoracolumbar fascia and can affect the movement in our trunk, legs and the rest of our lower extremity. This is due to the interconnectedness of the muscle with the fascial planes that run throughout the body from side to side and top to bottom.

A philosophical question which has been asked is, do we really have 600 muscles, or do we have one muscular contractile structure enveloped in 600 fascial pockets? Chew on that a bit.

Fascia envelopes the muscles and augments force transmission

Connective tissue and fascia are constantly remodeling slightly based on strain and stress patterns that are read by the cells in the connective fascial tissue. The cells respond by augmenting, reducing or changing the cellular elements in that area within the limits of nutrition, age and protein synthesis. This is remodeling. There's constantly a balance between bone, ligament, tendon, and fascia formation and reabsorption. We need to be in states of movement with enough activity and stress to promote this healthy remodeling.

When treating fascial and musculoskeletal dysfunctions, we need to first look at global movement patterns. From there, we can look at the isolated local problems, like joint arthritis, and do things like PRP and stem cell treatment to heal the degenerating joint. After we have induced healing into the local joint, we need to go back again and analyze global movement patterns to make sure those have been corrected through fascial treatments and physical therapy to ensure the dysfunctional movement patterns do not recur and cause the joint to again breakdown. This approach to musculoskeletal healing incorporates what we call a model of bio-tensegrity.

Bio-tensegrity is the concept that dysfunction in movement patterns from injured fascia and ligaments leads to breakdown in the rest of the body. On the contrary, healthy fascia, muscle and ligaments protects the joints and spine and decreases the aging and degenerative process.

A model that shows the interaction between fascia, joints and movement throughout the body is a concept of myofascial meridians. Thomas Myers, author of Anatomy Trains, does a brilliant job explaining the different fascial lines that transmit forces throughout the body. There are twelve specific fascia lines that interact to transfer forces, support, and protect the musculoskeletal system.

The different fascia lines described by Myers are:

- SBL - superficial back line
- SFL - superficial front line
- LL - lateral line
- SL - spiral line
- DFAL - deep front arm line
- SFAL - superficial front arm line
- DBAL - deep back arm line
- SBAL - superficial back arm line
- BFL - back functional line
- FFL - front functional line
- IFL - ipsilateral functional line
- DFL - deep front line

Myofascial Meridians... *"make up the "fascial net",* *which holds everything together. Connective tissue* *(fascia) binds every cell to the next and even bonds* *the internal network of each cell to the mechanical* *state of the entire body. These meridians are able to* *store and communicate information throughout the* *body as a whole."* —Thomas Myers

Some of the benefits of addressing postural compensation, resulting in pain and dysfunction, throughout these myofascial meridians include:

- Skeletal alignment and support.
- Increased range of motion.
- Reduced pain.
- Reduced effort and stress in standing or moving.

Another overlooked function of fascia is information conduction. Information is communicated throughout the body via **NEURONS, CAPILLARIES** and also **COLLAGEN** (fascia). **Neurons** utilize the nerves to conduct impulses from the brain, to the spine, to the peripheral nervous system and then back to the brain.

Capillaries use blood to transport hormones, nutrients and oxygen. Fascia uses **collagen**, through the fascia net, to conduct tension throughout the body. Fascia transfers information the fastest of all the different cell types. It transfers information at a rate of 720 mph, which is the speed of sound. Any disruption to the fascial net will delay information transfer and cause compensation and dysfunctional movement patterns. The area of pain and breakdown is not the only area needed to treat. We also need to treat restrictive fascial planes and address those compensatory movement patterns to restore normal movement and prevent structural breakdown of the spine and peripheral joints.

FASCIAL BREAKDOWN

There are many influences that can cause dysfunction in the fascial connective tissue system. Over-use, mis-use, dis-use, abuse and inflammation can all lead to dysfunctional fascial planes; this creates dysfunctional movement and structural breakdown.

OVER-USE can occur from repetitive motions and actions. This would be like a baseball pitcher who does the same motion over again. This over-use pattern can cause fascial strain and tearing, leading to a painful shoulder and excess strain on his rotator cuff.

Next, dysfunction can occur with **MIS-USE** through poor posture or ergonomic insults. This would be like sitting at work with poor posture with the desk too high. Over time, this can cause neck, back and shoulder pain from dysfunction in the fascial planes.

DIS-USE, through lack of exercise, aging or protection after an injury or pain, can also lead to weakening of the fascia connective tissue lead to breakdown and dysfunction. If you don't use a joint, muscles and fascia will weaken and tighten with restricted range of motion. This leads to further breakdown and degeneration.

ABUSE, like with trauma or an acute injury, can lead to weakening and tearing in fascial planes. This would be like the blunt trauma of a football helmet striking the thigh of an opponent. The injury can tear the quadriceps fascia and cause local bleeding. The bleeding can cause scarring and restricted motion if the injury is not treated appropriately.

Finally, **INFLAMMATION** from internal inflammatory sources or external invasion from infection can lead to dysfunction.

All these influences usually will act in combination to create the painful problem. The first thing that may develop would be either fascial plane adhesions or weakening and tearing. The combination of either of these forces leads to dysfunctional movement which can block force transmission, restrict movement and cause pathologic posturing. It can also lead to nerve entrapment syndromes, causing nerve pain in the area of constriction. With continued dysfunctional movements, the joints will degenerate with arthritis, and the tendons will develop tendinosis and tearing. Treatment options for functional movement disorders revolve around bringing back normal movement patterns, restoring tensegrity and then restoring joint and spine stability. Treatment often starts with a functional movement assessment, followed by the prescription of corrective muscle strengthening and flexibility. Physical therapy is often utilized to correct postural dysfunctional muscle movement patterns. Manipulation from a trained professional can be performed for joint and spine alignment. Ligament and joint instability, from chronic injuries and breakdown, can be strengthened through Prolotherapy and PRP. This will aid in restoring stability around the spine or joint.

There are different ways to treat fascia to attempt to restore a more functional movement pattern along the fascial meridians. Treatments would include: foam rolling, massage therapy, myofascial release, trigger point injections and dry needling, muscle energy techniques, instrument-assisted soft tissue mobilization, fascial unwinding and Rolfing. When it comes to foam rolling, I like to use the Rolga foam roller as it is the only roller on the market that is designed to contour to the curved shapes in our body.

I combine different rolling techniques with stretching and yoga to address all the movement and fascial planes. This type of movement pattern is a great warm-up for sports or fitness to get the fascia and muscle groups ready for optimal function and performance. Other topical creams can be used on the skin to help with myofascial pain. Some initial research on the TRPV1 pain receptors (ion channel), which are found throughout fascial tissue, seems to be showing that topical mannitol (a sugar analog), dextrose and vitamin D may have positive effects in decreasing the pain from a stimulated TRPV1 receptor by blocking its action.

Fascial manipulation and foam rolling helps with healing in a few different ways. First, a study in

Medicine and Science in Sports and Exercise 1999 showed that fascia manipulation and mobilization caused improved fibroblast healing.[41] Fibroblasts are the cells that repair after an injury or PRP procedure. Rolling enhances this essential healing response.

Next, a study in 1989 showed fascial manipulation caused decreased pain and. more importantly, increased blood flow to the area that was treated. Increased blood flow will help with detoxification of the area as well as delivery of vital nutrients needed for healing to the area.[42] This is another great reason to foam roll with an injury or a regenerative procedure to increase circulation and healing.

Furthermore, a study in 2012 showed fascial manipulation increased hydration of the tissues and helped with renewal in detoxification.[43] Fascial treatments also improve balance and proprioception around the area treated. This gets the nerves firing more effectively after an injury which will enhance recovery. Because of the healing properties associated with fascial treatments, we are starting to use light fascia manipulation and foam rolling after regenerative procedures to aid in fibroblasts healing, blood flow to the area, hydration and to improve nerve function and muscle movement patterns.

Fascia is only a part of healthy functional movement. Optimal functional movement is achieved from strong core strength and peripheral muscles (FLEX), optimal flexibility of the joints (FLEXIBILITY) and healthy FASCIA. Dysfunctional movement from the 3 F's needs to be assessed and a plan to improve any findings needs to be implemented to decrease degenerative influences on our peripheral joints and spine.

CHAPTER 11: ARTICULATION - IT IS ALL ABOUT THE JOINT

Wherever the art of medicine is loved, there is also a love of humanity. — **Hippocrates**

The articulation is all about the joint. The knee, hip, elbow, ankle, fingers and spinal facets are all joints that are vulnerable to injury and breakdown. This is one of the main reasons people fly in to see us at Rejuv Medical from all around the world. It is because they've been told they need a joint replacement or a surgery and are wondering if there's something else they can do before going down that extreme route. They don't want surgery if it is not needed and they have heard about other options, like Prolotherapy, PRP and Stem Cell treatments. They want their lives back. They want to be able to hike, play, and enjoy life to its fullest. Not only do they want less pain and freedom from prescriptive medications, but they want the body to heal itself, if possible. This is the point in the conversation when we spend time talking about cell health. Along with the skills of the injector, optimization of cell health is critical to having great outcomes with regenerative procedures.

You have now learned how to optimize cell health and healing. Before we can regenerate the articulation, we need to optimize the healing environment, so we get a robust response to our procedures and so that the healing that does occur will last. At our clinic, we start by teaching corrective exercise, healthy eating, working on dysfunctional movement patterns, dealing with their stresses, improving their sleep patterns, and avoiding toxins that break down the body. When they return for their regenerative joint treatments, they are 30 to 40 pounds lighter, have more energy, already have decreased pain scales, and are in a position to optimize their regenerative outcomes.

So, let's look at articulation. The articulation is the joint where two bones come together, and movement and transfer of forces occurs. Joints are covered by a **HYALINE CARTILAGE** that aids in smooth movement. It is the shiny, slippery substance that coats the joint and aids in smooth, friction-free movement. You want your cartilage to be healthy and thick. With instability and dysfunctional movement patterns, this cartilage can start to wear thin. This is what arthritis is - thinning of the articular cartilage.

Next, **DISK AND LABRAL CARTILAGE** are supportive structures that are found in the joint, whose job is to guide movement and absorb forces. They are stabilizers and spacers. In the knee, an example of disk cartilage would be the meniscus, which is held in place by the small wispy coronary ligaments. The meniscus can be torn or breakdown by an acute injury or from chronic wear and tear. New studies are showing that the meniscus is very valuable, and that surgery to remove part of it leads to more instability, with a definite increase in risk of arthritis development. You want to keep your meniscus and, if possible, do things like PRP or Stem Cell treatments to heal and regenerate as opposed to surgical removal.

In the wrist, there is a similar type of structure called the TFCC (Triangular Fibrocartilage Complex). It is a cartilage complex at the base of the wrist that absorbs forces and transfers them into the wrist. It is vulnerable to wear and breakdown with weight-bearing exercises like weightlifting, as well as wrist-weight-bearing sports, like cheerleading and gymnastics, as well as a fall on the wrist. The cartilage is also stabilized by the wrist ligaments that can also be weakened, making the TFCC more vulnerable to breakdown.

In the shoulder and hip, there is a ring-like structure called the labrum that extends off the joint socket with the goal of guiding movement and providing stability to the joint. It can be torn from over-use or acute stress and strain. Studies on labral surgery have shown the surgery to not be very successful. Regenerative treatments can be performed to both hip and shoulder labral tears using PRP to create a healing response at the site of the tear. It's always better to keep your original anatomy and return it to a more functional repaired state instead of removing a structure that is integral to the joint's function.

Next, the **JOINT CAPSULE** is like a connective tissue 'saran wrap' that encases the facet joints of our spine and the peripheral joints. Its goal is to guide joint movement and provide stability. The capsule can be stretched from trauma or from over-use and dysfunctional movement patterns in occupation or sports.

Finally, there are **LIGAMENTS** inside and outside the joints that stabilize movement and support the articulation. In the knee, we have the ACL and the PCL inside the joint, with the MCL and the LCL outside the joint. If they are injured and become loose, instability sets in leading to accelerated degeneration. Within the ankle are the sinus tarsi ligaments. Outside the ankle joint are stabilizing ligaments on the medial and lateral side of the joint that prevent excessive movement, like rolling the ankle. With recurrent sprains, these ligaments loosen allowing abnormal movement that leads to degeneration of the joint. The hip joint has an internal ligament called the ligamentum teres. The shoulder has big broad strong ligaments that prevent anterior and posterior translation of the joints during activities like throwing a ball or swinging a tennis racket. If these strong, stabilizing ligaments are loosened from trauma or over-use, a dysfunctional movement pattern will lead to tendon breakdown and arthritis in the joint. We need healthy ligaments to maintain a healthy joint. The good news is we have treatments like PRP and Prolotherapy that can be injected into the ligaments to promote healing and stability.

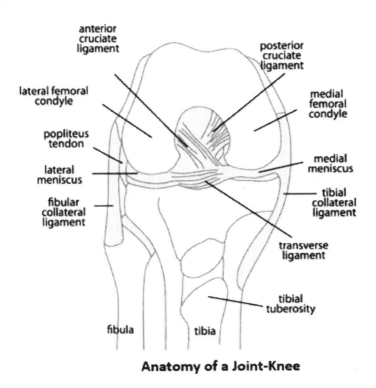

Anatomy of a Joint-Knee

REGENERATIVE ORTHOPEDIC TREATMENTS

There are three types of regenerative treatments that can be used to regenerate ligaments, tendons, fascia, joint cartilage, meniscus and labrums. They have all been researched and show good evidence for healing, pain relief and improved function.

1.   **PROLOTHERAPY** has been around the longest and uses hypertonic dextrose, which is injected into a ligament, tendon or joint, to stimulate the healing process. Webster's dictionary describes Prolotherapy as "the rehabilitation of an incompetent structure such as ligaments or tendon, by the proliferation of new cells." Proliferation = new growth. The procedure uses dextrose injected in to the joint, ligament, fascia or tendon, which acts as a slight irritant to the tissue injected. This attracts the body's natural healing cells to start a repair process. It is a catalyst for regeneration. It has been used safely for years for the management of pain and arthritis without negative or harmful side effects.

2.   Next, **PRP**, or platelet rich plasma, uses blood taken from the patient to create a platelet-rich healing solution. After a simple blood draw, the platelets and growth factors are separated from the rest of the blood and the concentrated platelets are then re-injected into the injured or degenerating area to stimulate repair.[10] PRP can be concentrated up to 5 to

20 times the baseline levels, depending on the age of the patient and the area of the body needing regeneration.

Research on PRP's mechanism of action shows that, after the platelets are injected, they release several different growth factors that stimulate the healing response. They also enhance the body's own stem cells migration and proliferation at the site injection.[11] There are many different growth factors found in PRP that help promote healing, cartilage repair, blood vessel formation and bone repair.[12, 13]

GROWTH FACTOR	PHASE IN WHICH MOST ACTIVE	FUNCTIONS
IGF-1	Inflammation, proliferation	Promotes proliferation and migration of cells, stimulates matrix production
TGF-B	Inflammation	Regulates cell migration, proteinase expression, fibronectin binding interactions, termination of cell proliferation, stimulation of collagen production
VEGF	Proliferation, remodeling	Promotes angiogenesis
PDGF	Proliferation, remodeling	Regulates protein and DNA synthesis at injury site, regulates expression of other growth factors
bFGF	Proliferation, remodeling	Promotes cellular migration, angiogenesis
EGF	Proliferation, remodeling	Stimulates proliferation and differentiation of epidermal cells, stimulates angiogenesis

Growth Factors Found in PRP

Once the PRP has been injected, it stimulates the body to go through the stages of healing with the goal of repairing the broken-down area. The first stage of healing is the **INFLAMMATION** phase. During this time, platelets become activated and the body sends other healing cells to the area to help with repair. This phase will last from the 1st through the 10th day after injection, throughout which fibrin and fibronectin are deposited by the platelets. The platelets release growth factors that influence healing and attract other cells to the area. Stem cells are recruited and can differentiate into tendons or cartilage at the site of the injection.

The next phase of healing is the **PROLIFERATION** phase. This starts from after the 2nd or 3rd day and it will last for 4 to 6 weeks. During this time, collagen is starting to be formed as fibroblasts synthesize new tissue.

The last phase is the **MATURATION** phase. This starts around the 3rd week and continues for six or more months after the injection. During this time, the collagen matures and there is an increase in the tensile strength of the tissue. It is important through all phases of healing to focus on your cellular health to optimize the body's ability to fully repair the tissue. That is why cell health is the foundation for all healing. PRP has been used in many medical subspecialties safely for more than 30 years. It was originally used in Dentistry, ENT surgeries, Neurosurgery, Ophthalmology, Urology, wound healing, Cardiothoracic surgery and, now, in Orthopedics and Sports medicine.

3.   Next, mesenchymal **STEM CELLS** can be used successfully for healing and regeneration in the body. They are the most powerful treatment available for orthopedic regenerative procedures. Stem cells have been found to augment healing through reducing pathologic inflammation, and with the ability to differentiate into bone, cartilage and tendon cells.[14] The stem cells utilized for the procedures are harvested from the patient's own body. They are

harvested either from bone marrow or fat. They are not cells from an embryo, placenta or donor source. The cells are taken directly from the patient's body and are not manipulated. They are concentrated and re-injected with precise guidance to the area of degeneration to repair and regenerate. Research is showing that the best and safest cell line for orthopedic use are those cells taken from the bone marrow of the patient themselves.

Stem cells are very powerful cells, and they do their work in a variety of ways at the area injected. First, they increase mitochondrial transfer to the damaged cells. The mitochondria are inside every cell and are the powerhouse of the cell. Stem cells injected around unhealthy cells will transfer their healthy mitochondria to the damaged cartilage cells. The healthy mitochondria then recharge the damage arthritic cells.[15]

Next, when injected into a degenerating joint, they can control the destructive inflammation found in arthritic joints. Severe arthritis in the joint creates a thick synovium filled with destructive macrophages. These cells become overactive and begin to destroy healthy cartilage cells furthers damaging the joint. Stem cells, when injected, detect the overactive macrophages and deactivate them, thus protecting the healthy cartilage from further damage and breakdown. They also instruct the macrophages to start to release helpful growth factors that aid in the repair and regenerative process.[16]

Stem cells also help stimulate repair by responding to signals released by the damaged cartilage cells. The stem cells respond to the damaged cells' signals and initiate a coordinated healing response to help them. The stem cells release growth factors that guide the healing process and recruit more cells to the area to help with the healing.[17]

Another fascinating way stem cells work is through teaching the arthritic or degenerating cells to start creating healthy proteins that can aid in tissue repair.

They do this by secreting exosomes. Exosomes are pods carrying messenger RNA (mRNA). Messenger RNA encodes for protein synthesis. The exosome leaves the stem cell and enters the damage cell and donate its healthy mRNA. The healthy mRNA then starts to code for healthy regenerative proteins in the damage cell. The stem cells help convert unhealthy damage cells into healthy protein creating healing cells.[18] It is pretty amazing what stem cells can do by converting unhealthy cartilage into healthy cartilage. We can regenerate!

REGENERATIVE EVIDENCE

Research in the field of regenerative orthopedic medicine is growing in both the basic sciences and clinical research. There is good research behind both the efficacy and the safety of these procedures. We have already looked at the negative and detrimental effects of intra-articular and spinal epidural steroid injections. Steroids at a normal orthopedic dose, when injected in the joint, are actually toxic to cartilage cells. Steroids damage and weaken the joint or tendon where they are injected. A single dose of steroid or cortisone with a spinal epidural, increases the risk of spinal fracture by one-third.[118] It is critical that we analyze, research and utilize procedures that are healthy and safe, and promote healing and regeneration over tissue destruction and degeneration. Let's look at the evidence for healing and repair using regenerative procedures.

First, do no harm. —Hippocrates

PROLOTHERAPY

Starting with Prolotherapy, there are many areas of the body studied using level one evidence, which is the top level of research, showing positive outcomes utilizing dextrose Prolotherapy injections into joints, ligaments and tendons.

- **Knee OA:** Dextrose injection is more effective in improving function than either saline injection or at-home exercise. [119]

- **Knee OA**: Dextrose injection is more effective for pain reduction and functional improvement than exercise alone.[120]
- **Knee OA**: Dextrose injection improved knee ROM and subjective swelling more than lidocaine injection. Improvements increased over 1-year follow-up. [121]
- **OSD**: Dextrose injection is more effective than lidocaine or usual care in symptoms elimination in OSD. [122]
- **Hand OA**: Dextrose injection is more effective than steroid injection for thumb arthritis. Dextrose injection is more effective than lidocaine injection in pain reduction and range of motion improvement in finger arthritis. [123]
- **Tennis Elbow**: Dextrose/Sodium Morrhuate is more effective than saline in improving pain and strength. [124]

A randomized controlled study in the *Annals of Family Medicine* in 2013 concluded significant sustained improvement of pain, function, and stiffness compare with blinded saline injections and at-home exercises.[57] Prolotherapy, when injected into the area of degeneration, has been shown to have positive effects on cartilage, tendon and ligaments.[19]

PLATELET RICH PLASMA (PRP)

Next, with PRP, there is a plethora of evidence showing its efficacy and safety in ligament, muscle, and cartilage and arthritis conditions.

- Achilles Tendon
    - Lyras et al, *Foot Ankle Int* 2009
    - Virchenko & Aspenberg, *Acta Orthop Scand* 2006
    - Gaweda et al, *Int J Sports Med* 2010
- Plantar Fascia
    - Barrett & Erredge, *Podiatry Today* 2004

- RTC
    - Scarpone et el, *Glob Adv Health and Med,* *March 2013*

- Elbow
  - Mirsha et al, *Am. J. Sports Med. May 2006*
  - Peerbooms et al, *AJSM 2010*
- Knee
  - Kon et al, *Injury* 2009
  - Sánchez et al, *Clin Exp Rheumatol* 2008
  - Carcangiu et al, *Am J Sports Med 2012*
  - *Am J Phys Med Rehabil.* 2012 May
  - Patel et al, *Am J Sports Medicine 2013*
  - Gobbi, Karnatzikos, Knee Surg Sports Traumatol Arthrosc. 2014
  - Chang, Hung, Aliwarga,Wang, Han. Arch Phys Med Rehabil. 2014
- Hip
  - Sanchez, *Rheumatology 2012*

The research with PRP and arthritis is very exciting, showing we now have non-surgical, non-steroid, treatments that don't just cover up the problem, but actually modulate destructive inflammatory conditions and promote regeneration. A randomized controlled trial in the Journal of Stem Cells and

Regenerative Medicine in 2016 looked at the combination of hyaluronic acid (lubricating) injections with and without the PRP injections into the knee of arthritic patients. The study concluded that PRP is an effective treatment for osteoarthritis and that, when you combine PRP with the lubricating injections, there were better outcomes than the lubrication injection alone and with fast resolution of pain at 30 days.[58]

In practice, I tend to start with lubricating injections first to help hydrate the cartilage and decrease friction in the joint. Then I will follow-up with a regenerative procedure of PRP or stem cells around a month later. This seems to work well and, during the month after the lubricating injection, we focus on all the different aspects of cell health to optimize healing after the regenerative procedure.

STEM CELLS

Of all areas in medicine, stem cell research has really been exploding over the last few years. We will focus here on some of the recent studies showing evidence for stem cell procedures in orthopedics. Stem cell evidence in orthopedics looks promising in knee arthritis, hip arthritis, rotator cuff tears and tendinosis, lumbar degenerative disc disease, and ACL disruption. Often with these and other conditions, PRP is used along with the stem cell treatments to stabilize the surrounding ligaments, tendons and fascia.

Again, where we once thought you have to live with the pain and disability of arthritis, take chronic pain medications or have surgery to replace the joint, we now see evidence of stem cell transplantation into the joints leads to increased cartilage and meniscus volume. A study released in 2016 concluded that "*stem cells play an important role in the treatment of many orthopedic conditions. It may increase cartilage and meniscus volume and individual human subjects. The results show adequate safety and minimal complications associated with mesenchymal stem cell transplantation.*"[14]

Another study in 2016 in the *Journal of Genetics and Molecular Research* studied the effects of PRP with stem cells in a rabbit model of arthritis. The combination showed benefits in articular cartilage regeneration with osteoarthritis. A groundbreaking study in *Pain Physician* in 2008 studied the effects on cartilage volume in the degenerative joint disease using autologous mesenchymal stem cells. The study concluded that, after the stem cell procedure, there was significant cartilage growth, decreased pain and increased joint mobility.[60] This is exactly what patients are looking for - they want to have the freedom to live life again with improved movement and less pain. They want to return to activities that they once enjoyed like walking, playing with the grandkids and adventuring on a vacation.

Another knee arthritis study in 2013 concluded, *"mesenchymal stem cell therapy may be a valid alternative treatment for chronic knee osteoarthritis. The Intervention is simple, does not require hospitalization or surgery, provides pain relief, and* significantly improves cartilage quality."[59] There are many other studies showing similar results on osteoarthritis both in safety and in efficacy.

It is important to note that not all PRP and stem cell procedures are created equal. The success of these procedures lies in the quality of the PRP and stem cells prepared and, more importantly, in the experience, skills, accuracy and thoroughness of the provider performing the procedure. I've written a book entitled *Regenerative Injections: The Art of Healing.*[20] This book is a teaching manual for other physicians to learn accurate and precise injection techniques. It is used by the American Association of Orthopedic Medicine and the Hemwall-Hackett-Patterson Foundation as their training manual when teaching other physicians around the world. The book shows how complex these procedures can be to fully treat all the areas of breakdown and instability.

Also, for optimal outcomes, much detail has to be taken, starting from the history and interview with the patient, to a detailed examination searching for the source of pain and pathology, followed by appropriate imaging studies. Once the source of pain and proper diagnosis is obtained, skill and experience are needed to deliver a treatment using the bio-tensegrity model. This model looks at all the dysfunctional movement and degenerative influences causing the breakdown of the joint. Each one of those areas is treated, while at the same time optimizing cell health for optimal outcomes.

This is an exciting time in orthopedics. The 80's were a good time for music and hair styles. It was also the days of cortisone shots, anti-inflammatory and prescription pain medications, and an abundance of surgeries and joint replacements. We are not living in the 80's anymore - technology, science and medicine has advanced with new innovation and research showing a different pathway for orthopedics - **Regenerative Orthopedics**. We now have the ability to return zest, vitality and a great quality of life back to our patients, without the risks of surgery or using cover-up injections or medications. Through injections of Prolotherapy, PRP and Stem Cells, we now have the ability to truly **REGENERATE.**

With PRP and Stem Cell "clinics" popping up more frequently, it is important if you are seeking out this type of treatment that you are informed about the options. It is also important that you have an understanding of how to optimize your outcomes when pursuing this type of treatment.

At Rejuv Medical, through our **INNOVATIVE** and **INTEGRATIVE** approach, we can **OPTIMIZE** your outcomes through our **Rejuv REGENERATIVE PRP**plus **and STEM CELL**plus **ADVANTAGE** using your body's own PRP and STEM CELLS. We don't just inject into the joint but inject all the structures involved in the stabilization of the joint or spine.

The Rejuv REGENERATIVE PRP^{plus} and STEM CELL^{plus} ADVANTAGE

Healthcare is broken. Too many surgeries, cortisone injections and pain medications are making our healthcare expensive and often not addressing the root cause of the problem. This is a new era in healthcare and it is time to heal and regenerate. At Rejuv Medical, we are redefining healthcare and how we treat chronic pain, injury and arthritis of the joints and spine. We are national leaders in the field of Regenerative Orthopedics. We teach injection procedures to other physicians worldwide and have authored a book that is being used as the standard for injection technique.

The **Rejuv REGENERATIVE PRP^{plus} and STEM CELL^{plus} ADVANTAGE** will maximize your regenerative results through the integration and optimization of healthy lifestyle changes and movement patterns. We analyze every aspect that will have a positive or negative effect on your success and optimize each parameter

---

to maximize your regenerative potential. It sets us apart and is why patients fly in from around the globe to be treated by our talented and passionate Regenerative team. Once we have optimized our healing environment, Prolotherapy, PRP or Stem Cell procedures are used to **REBUILD** our patients' degenerated bodies. This process can reverse degeneration and enable our esteemed patients to enjoy life to its fullest.

INNOVATION

Rejuv Medical uses the most leading-edge technology to treat degenerating areas with precise image guidance and a comprehensive injection technique to advanced cell processing in our Regenexx certified lab.

Advanced PRP and STEM CELL Lab Cell Processing by Regenexx[TM]

Innovative cell processing by our Regenexx™-trained technicians uses advanced lab techniques that maximize cell numbers and quality. Our **PRP**plus and **STEM CELL**plus processing is based on the most up-to-date technology and research that is conducted at the Regenexx research lab in Colorado. All stem cells are hand-processed in our regenerative lab. This sets us apart from the standard "kits" that are being used in other clinics and hospitals that have lower cell counts and whose quality and quantity are not controlled.

All the cells used are from our patients' own blood with PRP and from their own bone marrow with STEM CELLS. We are NOT using cells from placenta, embryo or adipose. Those clinics that advertise STEM CELLS often are using cells that are not your own from placenta or embryo. Independent research has shown that, under a microscope, these products DO NOT contain live or viable cells. Due to the process needed to allow it to be injected into a human, the cellular structures are destroyed and you are left with debris and not live cells.

The best cells are your own live viable cells from your own bone marrow, after you have optimized your Cell Health through the recommendations in this book. We have some of the best regenerative outcomes in the nation, and I believe part of it is due to how we optimize the health of our patients prior to and after the procedures. Also, based on the research, bone marrow-derived cells are superior to adipose cells when it comes to orthopedic use.

Additional Cell Biologics, in addition to your **PRP** and/or **STEM CELLS,** are used with all our procedures. These cells are used to enhance regenerative outcomes of our **Regenerative**plus **Procedures** and is unique to our process at Rejuv.

Platelet Growth Factors in Platelet Lysate (PL)
Advanced Platelet Lysate derived from our patients' own Platelets are created in our Regenexx™ lab that enhances the healing and regenerative effects of individual PRP procedures. Through a patented freezing technique, these powerful Growth Factors are

released from the platelets and harvested by our technicians for use. These Growth Factors act as a fertilizer to increase the tissue healing and repair. We can also use Platelet Lysate to inject around nerves and in the epidural space to decrease pain and help heal damaged nerves.

PPPP (Platelet Poor Plasma Prolotherapy)

This solution combines the regenerative and pain-modulating effects of Dextrose with additional Growth Factors found in patient plasma to inject weakened and dysfunctional tissue, ligaments and muscle. Research is finding additional Growth Factors in the Plasma that can be used to enhance patient regenerative outcomes of fascia, muscle, ligaments and tendons.

Precise Image Guidance

Image guidance is used during the injection of patients' healing cells into the damaged or degenerative structures. This will ensure accuracy and decrease the risks. Precision is critical to confirm a successful delivery of our solutions to the targeted areas. Our physicians are highly skilled and thoroughly trained in image guidance of the joints and spine.

BioTENSEGRITY Injection Technique

Patient success is dependent on how comprehensively we can diagnosis and subsequently treat ALL their affected areas of dysfunction. It is important to a successful outcome to not just inject the joint, but also focus on the entire complex of structures that support the joint. Through a comprehensive injection strategy to the fascia, ligaments, tendons, cartilage and joints, we not only address the local joint degeneration, but also the root causes that contribute to the breakdown.

This approach will increase the outcomes and longevity of our patients' treatment. Dr. Baumgartner has authored a book on the injection technique that is being used by multiple training organizations worldwide to increase the accuracy and thoroughness of these complex procedures. We are also teaching our comprehensive injection model to other physicians around the world. Our mission at Rejuv Medical is *"Redefining Healthcare Worldwide."*

INTEGRATION

We have created the **Rejuv Regenerative^plus Advantage** to empower our **C.F.A.N.** model for optimal outcomes. This model is **INNOVATIVE** with state-of-the-art technology and **INTEGRATES** fitness, nutrition and lifestyle changes to **OPTIMIZE** health and regenerative outcomes. In the **C.F.A.N.** model, the **C** stands for cell health. This includes a healthy nutrition plan we call Rejuv4Life, engaging in healthy exercise and movement, balancing of internal hormones and micronutrients, and also how we deal with life stressors and sleep.

The **F** represents functional movement. To have healthy functional movement, we must have proper core strength, flexibility and balance. Without healthy functional movement, our bodies are more prone to injury, breakdown and degeneration.

Next, the **A** is for the articulation. This is the joint, the joint capsule, the joint cartilage and the ligaments that hold the joint together. These structures, when injured or unstable, lead to arthritis from abnormal wear patterns in the joint. Until recently, the only treatments available for chronic pain and degeneration were cortisone injections, pain medications or surgery. Fortunately, advancements in regenerative orthopedics have given us the tools to actually REGENERATE the broken body. **Rejuv REGENERATIVE PRP**plus **and STEM CELL**plus procedures can reverse these degenerative processes without the side effects of cover-up medications or risks of invasive surgeries.

Finally, the **N** is for nerve health. A healthy nervous system is critical for proper function and musculoskeletal movement in the body. Every nerve that leaves the spine eventually passes by and has an effect, either positive or negative, on the muscles, ligaments, tendons and the joint that they innervate. They have a direct effect on the function and also the ability of that joint to repair and heal after an injury.

Through optimization of each of the elements of the **C.F.A.N.** model, true health and healing is obtainable and a new model for healthcare emerges, changing the landscape of medicine from disease control to disease prevention and reversal.

Integrated Movement Analysis™

Our **Integrated Movement Assessment™** (IMA) and **Integrated Movement Plan™** (IMP) are used to analyze patients' functional movement and guide fitness progression before and after regenerative procedures to optimize outcomes. Dysfunctional movement patterns are what have contributed to degeneration and, if not addressed fully, pain and degeneration will return. With our state-of-the art fitness gym, patients will have access to our **Levels of**

Fitness™ to guide them on their way to a healthy and fit body.

Integrated Health Analysis™

Our patients' power to heal is based on the health of your body's cells. The healthier the internal environment, the more robust the response patients will have to the procedures. It is important to do a comprehensive analysis of patient health and subsequent potential to regenerate. Our patented **Bioscore**™ is used, along with our Cell Antioxidant Level Scanner, Bio-Impedance Analysis and Heart Rate Variability Test, to analyze patient internal and external cell health. This will help us to predict their potential for a successful procedure based on objective data of how healthy their cells are and their ability to heal, protect and regenerate.

Functional Medicine Evaluation is performed, if indicated, to ensure we have ruled out other causes of pain and inflammation in our patients' body. This often includes a comprehensive evaluation of labs to make sure all the body systems are optimized for regeneration and repair. It is critical to decrease any inflammatory or degenerative influences and enhance regenerative influences prior to procedures. This process increases regenerative outcomes and long-term success.

OPTIMIZATION

Once patient movement and health have been analyzed, our systems will optimize all parameters to promote an optimal environment for healing and regeneration.

Healthy Lifestyle Optimization

Rejuv4Life Nutrition Plan. Optimal outcomes can only be obtained with nutrition that decreases inflammation and increases healing. Nutrition is also used as a tool in weight management to decrease the degenerative and inflammatory effects of excess body weight.

Physician-Grade Evidence-Based Supplements are recommended to enhance the regenerative outcome and promote healing throughout the body.

Lifestyle Optimization is taught to encourage a healthy environment before and after the procedure to prolong the regenerative state and maximize the healing effects of the procedure. This includes stress management, relaxation and hydration.

Mindset Optimization is implemented to teach strategies to get our patients' mind ready for the journey. Their success is based on their ability to adhere to the program, set goals and deal with obstacles that will come their way. They will learn to eliminate the toxic mindset that has the power to derail their goals while enhancing their strengths to give them the fuel needed to succeed.

Functional Medicine Optimization is implemented based on our patients' thorough *Functional Medicine Evaluation*

This will not only screen for other chronic causes of inflammation and degeneration, enhance our patients' regenerative outcomes, but will also optimize their long-term health and risk for chronic disease.

Functional Movement Optimization

Based on their **Integrated Movement Assessment** (IMA), a **Physical Therapy** plan is implemented that focuses on the cause of their problem with a graduated progression that brings increased activity back as our patients' tissue heals. The goal is to improve strength, flexibility and coordination of the involved structure that contributed to the degenerative process in the first place.

Our patients are sent home with an **Integrated Movement Plan** (IMP) tailored to their joint and movement dysfunctions that will safely progress them back into the active lifestyle they once had prior to their degeneration or injury. We also utilize joint unloading and **Functional Bracing** based the degenerative patterns in their body. This will unload and protect the vulnerable area before and after their regenerative procedure to give them the optimal healing advantage.

It is exciting to be a physician at a time when we have new and innovative regenerative options that we can use heal and regenerate our patients. We no longer have to give outdated advice on treatment options and can offer hope for those suffering from joint and spinal pain and degeneration.

CHAPTER 12: NERVES AND THE NERVOUS SYSTEM

Look well to the spine for the cause of diseases. —
Hippocrates

We have covered the importance of having a healthy body and focusing on cell health to optimize healing. Then we took a closer look at functional movement and how it needs to be addressed to prevent injury recurrence and give joint stability. This results in decreased wear and tear, and less degeneration of the body. Next, the articulation and the regenerative effects of Prolotherapy, PRP and Stem Cells were explored, revealing an optimal treatment for pain, injury and arthritis. There is one more often overlooked but very important concept to discuss in our quest to regenerate.

The more I read of Hippocrates, the more I realize how much wisdom and insight he really did have when it comes to healing the human body. He was correct when he speculated that one of the causes of disease is the influence the nervous system has on our bodies. Nerves don't just tell us when something is hot or cold or tell us to pull away from something that is sharp or painful. We are finding that nerves have an influence on the ability of the area they innervate to actually heal and repair.

John Hilton, a scientist and anatomist from the 1800's, spent hours dissecting the human body and following the nerves from the spinal cord to the peripheral muscles. He found that every nerve passing a joint or muscle sent a branch of that nerve into the joint and also to the skin surrounding it. The nerve had influence over the joint that it passed by. *Hilton's law: The principle that the nerve supplying a joint also supplies both the muscles that move the joint and the skin covering the articular insertion of those muscles.*

Also, remember we covered (in the section on functional movement and fascia) that nerves can get trapped in the fascia tunnels they passed through. Nerves are very vulnerable at sites where they change direction (like at the elbow), go through tunnels (like the carpal tunnel), or go through muscles and fascia holes when traveling from a deep to a superficial position. Nerves exit from between muscles where they pierce the fascia and run on top of the superficial fascia layers. At the point where they exit through the fascia, they are vulnerable to compressive and strangulation type forces. Dr. John Lyftogt calls this a CCI, or a chronic constrictive injury, where the nerves pass through these fascia buttonholes. Nerves can get compressed and strangulated in deep compressive tunnels as well as in these superficial buttonholes.

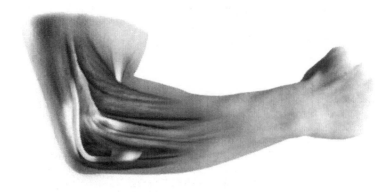

Ulnar nerve passing over the elbow and through a fascial tunnel

Let's examine Hiltons Law as the nerves pass over specific joints and can have an influence over the healing of those areas.

SHOULDER. In the shoulder, two nerves pass by the shoulder and give articular branches that influence the healing and function of the shoulder. Those nerves are the **Suprascapular** and the **Axillary** nerves. It is important to think about impingement in these nerves when treating shoulder degenerative conditions like shoulder and AC arthritis, labral tears and rotator cuff pathology.

ELBOW. In the elbow, four nerves have an influence over the muscles and tendons as well as the joint itself. Those nerves are the **Radial, Musculocutaneous, Ulnar** and **Median** nerves. Compression and tunnel syndromes of these nerves contribute to the pathology of elbow arthritis, osteochondritis dissecans, elbow tendonosis / tendonitis and elbow instability.

HIP. In the hip, three nerves have an influence over the structures in and around the hip. Those nerves are the **Femoral, Obturator** and **Sciatic** nerves. Compression and tunnel syndromes of these nerves can cause hip and pelvis pain and also contribute to hip arthritis, hip labral tears, hip tendinosis and hip instability.

KNEE. In the knee, four nerves pass by and innervate the surround muscles, tendons and knee joint. Those nerves are the **Anterior Femoral Cutaneous, Peroneal,**

Tibial, and **Obturator** nerves. Compression and tunnel syndrome of these nerves can cause knee, leg and thigh pain, and also contribute to knee arthritis, meniscal tears, baker's cysts, patellofemoral syndrome and patellar tendinosis.

ACHILLES TENDON. The Achilles tendon has three nerves that pass by and innervate the muscles that form the Achilles tendon as well as the tendon itself. Those nerves are the **Peroneal, Tibial** and **Sural** nerves. Compression and tunnel syndrome of these nerves can contribute to Achilles tendinosis and tearing. A study out of New Zealand actually showed healing the Achilles tendon through treating the nerves only.

PLANTAR FASCIA. The plantar fascia has two nerves that pass by and innervate its tissue. Those nerves are the **Posterior Tibial** and **Sural** nerves. Compression and tunnel syndromes of these nerves contribute to plantar fasciitis and plantar fascia tearing.

SPINE. The lumbar spine has small holes called foramen where the nerves exit from the spinal cord. This is a vulnerable area where a nerve can be compressed from stenosis secondary to arthritis of the facet joints as well as compression from disc bulging and herniations. When the nerves are compressed in these areas, this will lead to abnormal signals being sent into the lower extremities which can affect the joint of the lower extremities. It is important to evaluate the lumbar spine for these issues with lower extremity pathology of the hips knees and ankles.

For example, I find that, most of the time, those suffering from moderate to severe hip arthritis have issues of nerve compression in their lumbar spine. By treating both the lumbar spine using non-cortisone epidurals and regenerative procedures, and then treating the hip joint with a comprehensive Stem Cell procedure, my outcomes have greatly improved.

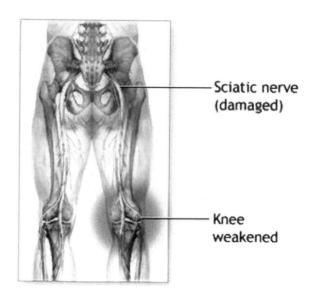

Sciatic nerve
(damaged)

Knee
weakened

Compression of the Sciatic Nerve Weakens the Knee and Contributes to Pathology

NERVES: Pain, Inflammation and Degeneration

To better understand how these nerves, when compressed and inflamed, can lead to degeneration of the tissue they surround, let's take a closer look at what happens with dysfunction around them. Nerves will become dysfunctional with continued compression or tension forces on them. Think of the nervous system like the wires running through your house. Wires are encased and protected by the walls and structures of your house. The mechanical interface is anything that is next to the nerve whose movements the nerves must follow. These would include tendons, muscles, bones, intervertebral disks, fascia, and blood vessels. The nerves must travel around and through those structures, where they can be damaged with stretch and compression forces imposed by the mechanical interface. Then the nerves, just like the wires in your house, must travel to innervate and influence something. In your house, the wires might innervate the appliances, while the nerves in our bodies innervate tissues. They innervate fascia, tendons, muscle and bone which are the same tissues that can turn around and impinge and compress them. Mechanical forces acting on the nerves can lead to physiological changes in the nerve. The mechanical forces influencing the nerve include tension, sliding and compressive forces. Those are the same forces that are found in various tunnel syndromes throughout the body.

The physiological response to these mechanical forces include; changes in intra-neural blood flow, impulse conduction, axonal transport, inflammation and mechanosensitivity. When mechanical forces have negative physiological effects on the nerves, breakdown of the innervated tissues occurs in the skin, bone, muscle, ligaments, tendons and fascia. To work normally, nerves must function in its musculoskeletal house through movements and stresses involving tension, sliding and compression. All these forces are acting on our nervous system continuously and, in combination, they can affect the nerve, causing pathology.

TENSION

First, let's look at tension functions. The nerves have fixed attachment points on two ends. One from the spinal cord and the other in the tissue it innervates like a muscle or joint. Tension occurs on the nerve through the movement of the extremities. Joints are the key site of elongation and stretching forces on the nerve. The *perineurium* is the fascial covering that guards against excessive strain. From tension forces, perineurium is a dense connective tissue surrounding nerve bundles, and it allows 18 to 22% strain before failure occurs.

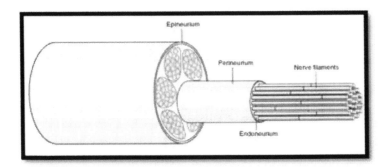

Epineurium, Perineurium and Endoneurium are the Fascia Layers that Protect the Nerves

SLIDING

The next mechanical function that takes place with nerves is sliding. Sliding can occur in a perpendicular direction to the nerve (transverse) or in a parallel direction with the nerve (longitudinal). Longitudinal sliding serves to dissipate tension through equalizing the tension along the entire track of the nerve. Transverse sliding helps nerves take the shortest course to avoid tension. This type of sliding takes place with the tension of muscles pulling on tendons and ligaments. An example would be the median nerve in the carpal tunnel with flexion and extension of the wrist. With sliding forces, the *mesoneurium* is the connective tissue fascia that allows for intra-neural sliding. With excessive sliding, the tension forces can become too great resulting in decreased blood flow to the nerve. The loss of blood blow causes nerve dysfunction.

COMPRESSION

The third mechanical factor acting on the nerve is compression. Compression creates a change in shape on the nerve from surrounding pressure. This is the type of force seen in many compressive tunnel syndromes. Compression is created with flexion of the joints. This is seen in the wrist with the median nerve and carpal tunnel syndrome. It also can occur near the elbow with the ulnar nerve. Spinal extension and ipsilateral flexion closes the foramen down on the nerve roots in the back. Muscles, bones, tendons and fascia can all cause compressive forces on nerves. Athletes with muscle hypertrophy can cause compressive forces where nerves are sliding between two muscle groups. Fascial adhesions can be seen from scars, trauma, and from repetitive over-use and micro-trauma. Internal lesions from masses, cancer and tumors can also cause compression of nerves. External factors that compress nerves include tight-fitting clothes, braces or prolonged sitting on a hard chair. The *epineurium* is the connective tissue fascia that pads the nerve and protects the axons from excessive compressive pressure.

There is tensegrity within the nervous system as well. The nervous system is a continuum of tissue surrounded by muscles and fascia. The nerves curve around joints and bony structures. Neck movement changes tension in the lumbar spine. Wrist extension produces tension in the brachial plexus of the neck. Ankle flexion moves the sciatic nerve. During the early range of motion with joint movement, slack is taken up in the nerve. During mid-range, nerve sliding takes place. At end range of motion, tension builds up. Mechanics of the nervous system are complex as they need to slide, stretch and resist compressive forces to function normally.

Nerves can become vulnerable with dysfunctional movement patterns, postural weakness or fascial adhesions. Tension and compression forces on the nerve will change blood flow to the nerve. The nervi vasa nervorum is a "nerve to the nerve" that will change the blood flow to the nerve in response to tension and compressive forces. It takes about 8 to 15% elongation and tension on the nerve to cause blood flow to the nerve to stop. With compression, 30 to 50mmHg will lead to decreased blood flow and hypoxia, as well as loss of normal nerve conduction and axonal transport. Both tension and compressive forces acting synergistically will increase the pathophysiology. Compression, stretch, injury, acidity and heat all stimulate and turn on the activity of the TRVP 1 ion channel. When this ion channel is turned on, it initiates inflammation and degeneration by releasing the pro-inflammatory neuropeptides, CGRP and Substance P. Substance P and CGRP in the surrounding tissues leads to degeneration, pain and swelling.

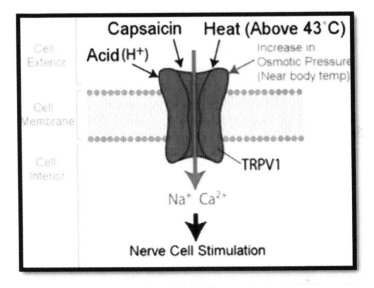

Stimulation of the TRPV 1 Ion Channel

These inflammatory neuropeptides cause degenerative effects on the tissues they innervate.

CGPR release causes:

- **Neovascularization** - The abnormal blood vessel formation seen in degenerating tissues.
- **Collagenolysis** - The breakdown of collagen structures, like ligaments and tendons, leading to tendinosis and tendon tears, like those seen in the rotator cuff and Achilles tendon.
- **Calcification** - The pathological and abnormal laying down of calcium in a tendon or muscle seen in chronic degenerative conditions like chronic tendinosis.
- **Osteoclast activity** - the osteoclast is a cell that causes bone breakdown leading to weakening of the bone structure and stress fractures.

Substance P release causes:

- **Vasodilation** and **swelling** from fluid and protein leakage in the area of nerve compression.[80]
- **Increased compartment pressures** which further cause nerve pathology and localized structure breakdown.

- **Neuropathic pain** with hypersensitivity to touch in the skin and structures innervated.
- **Depression, anxiety** and **stress** are also seen with high Substance P secondary to its central brain effects.[79]

Many of the consequences of chronic degeneration, including bone breakdown, tendon and ligament breakdown, swelling, pain, as well as the neuropsychiatric problems felt with pain, injury and arthritis, can be linked to the degenerative effects unhealthy nerves can have on the tissues they innervate.

In summary, injury - both acute and from chronic over-use - can lead to tissue damage and dysfunctional movement. Tension and compressive forces can cause damage to the nerve. This leads to stimulation of the TRPV 1 ion channel and release of CGRP and Substance P. The release of these pro-inflammatory neuropeptides leads to tissue and joint degeneration. Hilton and Hippocrates were correct - nerves can have an influence, both positive and negative, on the tissue and joints they innervate.

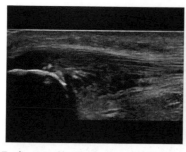
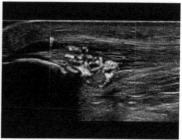

Tendinosis and breakdown from CGRP effects on the tendon.

Neovascularization from CGRP effects on the tendon.

The worn-down faces of pain and degeneration seen when patients walk through the door can be replaced by the faces of health and healing once proper treatment is initiated. Neuropathic pain, stimulated by TRPV 1 ion channel activation, can be reversed by blocking the ion channel and stopping the destructive effects of the inflammatory neuropeptides. It is speculated that sugar analogues, like mannitol and dextrose, may act as an antagonist to the TRPV1 ion channel and reverse the degenerative effects of CGRP and Substance P.

New treatments for neuropathic pain involve the injection of substances like dextrose, mannitol or glycerin, sometimes combined with a very diluted anti-inflammatory. They have been shown to cause immediate pain relief once injected around the pathologic peripheral nerve.

A study published in PMR in 2015 looked at topical mannitol reducing capsaicin-induced pain. Capsaicin is found in hot peppers and causes immediate pain when applied to the lips. It also stimulates the TRPV 1 ion channel. In this double-blinded, randomized controlled trial, mannitol was effective at alleviating the pain induced by capsaicin through blocking the ion channel that causes the neuropathic pain.[22] A recent study out of Mayo showed a hydro-dissection of the median nerve using dextrose is an effective treatment for carpel tunnel syndrome without having to use surgery.

When treating neuropathic pain caused by activated peripheral nerves, it is important to target the peripheral branches of these nerves as well as the deeper areas of nerve compression in fascial tunnels and between muscles.

TUNNEL SYNDROMES: Upper Extremity, Lower Extremity and Trunk

UPPER EXTREMITY

- Thoracic Outlet Syndrome
- Suprascapular Nerve Syndrome
- Musculocutaneous Nerve
    - Shoulder region
    - Elbow
- Dorsal Scapular Nerve Syndrome
- Long Thoracic Nerve Syndrome
- Radial Nerve Compression
    - PINES
    - Supinator Syndrome
    - Wartenberg's Syndrome
- Ulnar Nerve Compression
    - Cubital Tunnel Syndrome

- Guyon's Cannel
- Median Nerve
  - CTS
  - Pronator Teres Syndrome
  - AINES

LOWER EXTREMITY

- Lumbosacral Tunnel Syndrome
- Gluteal Nerve Syndrome
- Iliacus Muscle Syndrome
- Obturator Muscle Syndrome
- Post. Fem. Cut N Syndrome
- Piriformis Muscle Syndrome
- Meralgia Paresthetica
- Saphenous Nerve Syndrome
- Popliteal Entrapment Syndrome
- Peroneal Tunnel Syndrome
- Superficial Peroneal N Syndrome
- Sural Nerve Syndrome
- Anterior Tarsal Tunnel Syndrome

- Tarsal Tunnel Syndrome
- Morton's Metatarsalgia

TRUNK

- Superficial Cervical Plexus
- Rectus Abdominus Syndrome
- Iliohyphogastric N Syndrome
- Iliolinguinal N Syndrome
- Genitofemoral N Syndrome

In these tunnel syndromes, nerves pass through narrow anatomical spaces where they are vulnerable to compression and tension forces and subsequent damage. In these areas, they pass through bony, fibrous, osteofibrous and fibromuscular spaces. In these spaces, compression and damage can take place, causing pain and downstream impairment to their innervated tissues. Many of these issues develop from over-use and friction with the formation of fascial fibrosis and muscular hypertrophy.

Other causes must be ruled out, including tumor compression, infection, metabolic, toxic and vascular issues. It is important during the patient history to ask questions about the type of pain.

Sensory problems will appear before muscular weakness occurs. Patients will feel a loss of two-point discrimination or vibration sense, sharp burning, parasthesias, hypalgesia, hyperesthesias, hyperalgesia and pain. The pain can sometimes be vague and blunt, or they may experience pain at night.

Sometimes an EMG can be used to test for nerve damage. A normal or borderline test does not exclude a tunnel syndrome, so often the decision to treat is based on the history of the pain and the physical examination. It's important to question about when the symptoms developed - were they brought on by trauma, surgery or immobilization? What areas are involved? What aggravates the symptoms? What treatments have you tried? What do you do repetitively at work and play? What is your general state of health and do you have other comorbid conditions? What is your surgical and medical history? Are you on any medications or supplements?

A good physical exam should be performed to look for any physical signs of nerve impairment. With the skin, look for temperature changes, scars, sweating ability and hairless areas. The nails are important to examine for thickness and quality. Muscles should be tested focusing on tone, bulk and strength. The skeleton is examined looking for deformities, anomalies, range of motion and crepitation. The area is then palpated looking for pain in the distribution of nerve, as well as focusing on putting pressure over the different anatomical tunnels. With a thorough history, physical and knowledge of the different tunnel syndromes and the anatomy of the nervous system, a subsequent treatment plan can be formulated.

For treatment, there are two types of injections used when treating neuropathic pain. They are both called perineural injections (PNI), which means they are injected around the nerve. There are perineural deep injections (PDI) and perineural subcutaneous injections (PSI). The deeper injections are done at the site of compression where the nerves are being compressed between muscle, fascia or bone. These injections are done with ultrasound guidance to ensure accuracy and aid in hydro-dissection of the fascia that is compressing the nerve.

The goal with the deeper injections is to free the area of compression, release areas of fibrosis and scarring around the nerve, and also deliver the TRPV 1 antagonist solution around the nerve. This approach will free the nerve from the compressive and restrictive forces as well as turn off the TRPV 1 ion channel and stop the destructive defects of CGRP and Substance P.

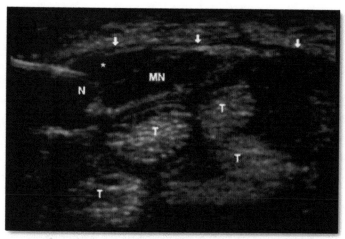

Hydro-dissection of the Median Nerve in Carpel Tunnel Syndrome.

Perineural subcutaneous injections (PSI), also known as the Lyftogt technique, are injected just under the skin and subcutaneous layers, with the goal of delivering the solution on top of the fascia where the terminal nerve branches run. The goal is to block TRVP1 effects the peripheral nerves have on the surrounding tissues. A study in New Zealand on Achilles tendinosis looked at this technique for Achilles tendon issues. Injections were done targeting the terminal nerve branches around the Achilles tendon of the peroneal, tibial and sural nerves. The study was effective at decreasing pain and also reversing the degenerative findings found at the initial ultrasound evaluation. Results are shown in the following graph.

Another study looked at an epidural injecting 5% dextrose in the epidural space. It examined the effects of delivering a TRPV 1 antagonist to the lumbar nerve roots that cause severe back and leg pain. It was a successful study in two ways. First, it showed that 5% dextrose is safe in the epidural space without any side effects. Next, it showed a significant decrease in pain for a sustained period after the procedure. This procedure has been coined the "sweet caudal".

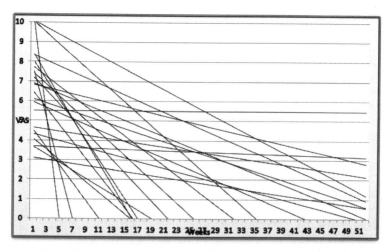

One Year Linear Recovery of 25 Patients after Achilles PSI

In the *Journal of Bone and Joint Surgery* in 2013, a study was done looking at the side effects on the spine from a standard epidural steroid injection. They compared 3,000 patients receiving a standard dose steroid epidural injection to 3,000 who did not receive a steroid injection and analyzed spine fractures afterward. The study showed that, for every epidural steroid injection, there was an increase in the risk for spinal fracture by 29%.

Unfortunately, many patients come to see me after receiving 3 to 6 more of these types of steroid procedures done into the spine in one year. There is no unique risk reported with dextrose epidurals and an equal or better relief in pain, compared to steroid epidurals. An epidural using 5% dextrose instead of steroid or cortisone will offer an alternative for those patients who don't want the negative side effects or for whom steroids are contraindicated.

NERVE HEALTH TREATMENT OPTIONS

With patients who suffer from neuropathic pain or from pain in a structure that that nerve innervates, we need to treat the **mechanical interface,** or the structures the nerve runs through, the **nerves** themselves and also the **innervated tissues** that are breaking down from the negative effects of compressed or strained nerves.

MECHANICAL INTERFACE. The mechanical interface is the muscle, bone and fascia structures that the nerves run through. There are different treatment options for the mechanical interface of the nerve. First, physical therapy is implemented to correct muscle imbalances focusing on posture, strength and flexibility. Manipulation and alignment can also be performed to decrease abnormal forces coming from the mechanical interfaces. Sometimes we use taping as well as unloading braces release or unload the areas. Weight loss and fitness are always part of the goals to decrease the stress and strain of the mechanical interface on the nerves.

NEURAL STRUCTURES. The neural structures are the nerves as they course deeply through muscles and fascial planes, and also the superficial branches that course on top of the fascia under the skin. We can perform hydro-dissections to the deeper compressed fascial tunnel areas as well as superficial nerve blocks to the peripheral branches. Epidurals can be performed for spinal nerve impingement using the "sweet caudal" dextrose-based epidural, avoiding the degenerating side effects of steroids. Topical compounded creams containing elements like vitamin D, dextrose and/or mannitol can be used to treat the superficial nerve branches as well. There are also some supplements that are helpful to decrease inflammation around the nerves and improve nerve function, including omega-3 fats and B vitamins.

INNERVATED TISSUES. As we've seen, the innervated tissues can break down because of the effects nerves have on either healing or degenerating them. When these tissues are breaking down, we can use treatments like Prolotherapy, PRP and Stem Cell treatments to initiate a healing response and regenerate those areas. Physical therapy is also important to strengthen the structures themselves and the supporting structures around them.

Ultrasound, cold laser and infrared heat can be used to augment the healing response and increase blood flow to the area. Supplements are often given to maximize healing responses, including amino acids like glutamine and arginine, vitamin D, optimizing anabolic hormones, and antioxidants like resveratrol and vitamin C. Optimizing nutrition with whole, healthy foods is also important for the cell health of the innervated tissues.

To summarize optimal healing, the umbrella that covers all other aspects of health is **CELL HEALTH.** This includes optimizing fitness, nutrition, avoiding food sensitivities, hormone optimization, avoiding medications with degenerative side effects, controlling stress in the body, maintaining adequate hydration, and avoiding environmental and food toxins.

While you are optimizing your cell health, that is a good time to work on **FUNCTIONAL MOVEMENT.** This is the time to work on strength, balance, posture, fascial health and joint and spine stability. After functional movements and cell health has been restored, a good examination of any pathologic function of spinal and peripheral **NERVES** needs to be done to make sure those don't have to be treated before focusing on the articulation regeneration.

Finally, the **ARTICULATION,** or joint, can be addressed with the goal of avoiding surgery or joint replacement and focusing on treatments that can restore function and regenerate the degenerating area. Treatments include Prolotherapy, PRP and Stem Cell procedures. Through the implementation of the above **C.F.A.N.** plan, we truly can regenerate our bodies, optimize our health and restore ourselves to a level of activity and function we once enjoyed.

Cheers to your health! Take charge and regenerate.

SECTION THREE

TIME TO MAKE LASTING CHANGE

CHAPTER 13: FOOD ADDICTIONS - BREAK THE CYCLE

Action is the foundational key to all success. —**Pablo Picasso**

Pizza, pizza, pizza... I NEED PIZZA! Sometimes I feel like I am the cookie monster but, for me, it is less for the sweet and more for the savory. I crave them. I want them. I desire them. It's more than just a crush, it's an infatuation. Last year, I was getting dialed in with the Rejuv4LIFE plan. I was three days into it and I thought I was doing pretty well. I rushed home from work to make the end of my sons 12th birthday party.

Everyone was out back, having fun in the yard after devouring some pizza. The problem was they left all the leftover pizza in the kitchen, piping hot and calling my name. I was alone in the kitchen - just me and that savory pizza. I walked past the boxes many times, with each pass getting just a little closer as I smelled its spicy seductive aroma. With one pass, I slowly opened up the box lid, with the intention of just looking and admiring. This courtship dance lasted about ten minutes with me closing the lid but then circling back, only to be tempted again. I walked to the backyard window to ensure no one was around. I was still alone. I almost tripped running back to the box as I opened it up to grab the gooey, cheesy, oily piece of deliciousness. I attacked it. Round one goes to the pizza.

Now, it is okay that I took a break from my healthy mission, but it's the way I did it that was not the healthiest. It's okay to take breaks but, when you do, celebrate it and enjoy it. That evening, I got back on the bandwagon of health and continued on my journey of healthy eating. Food is addictive. Let's examine why it can have such control over us and learn techniques to overcome its power to increase our healing and health.

With pleasurable experiences, the brain releases dopamine. This also happens when we eat food that is pleasurable. Because of this release of dopamine and other opioid-like substances by the brain in response to food, we often will find ourselves self-medicating, eating when we are bored or using food to enhance the pleasure of a social experience. Studies show that overweight people have fewer dopamine receptors and often will overeat to get the dopamine stimulation that they lack. Decreased dopamine receptors has also been seen in alcoholics and smokers. Food is meant to be enjoyed, but we need to be in control of the experience and what it is that is entering our mouths. Different foods can act like drugs on the brain, making us crave more of them to get that "high".

CHOCOLATE. When chocolate is digested, it releases an opioid-like compound that has effects on the brain similar to morphine. It also releases amphetamine and marijuana-like compounds that encourage addiction and feed addictive cravings. Chocolate on occasion is okay, but it does contain a lot of extra calories from fats and sugars. One study showed that if you block chocolate's opioid effects, the cravings for chocolate dropped by 90%. Chocolate can be addictive. If you have control over your chocolate, dark chocolate can be a good option.

MILK. Milk contains the protein casein. During digestion, casein breaks down into opioid-like substances that give the pleasurable feelings that we crave. That's why we need that ice cream "fix". It is a difficult thing to drive by a Dairy Queen and not pull in for a creamy Blizzard.

Casein is also very concentrated in cheese. Similar opioid-like compounds are released to a lesser amount in milk. Studies show that those who cut out cheese and dairy have greater weight loss, decreases in prostate cancer and decreases in migraines and arthritis pain. The prostate cancer study showed men who avoid dairy have a 30% reduction in their risk of cancer.[82] Many people take dairy for its vitamin D. But the vitamin D added to dairy is in an inactive form and not utilized by the body well.

SUGAR. Sugar releases opioids in the brain and it stimulates the appetite. A high sugar load causes a spike in insulin, creating an environment for weight gain. Remember, this sugar effect takes place with any refined processed foods, like high glycemic index foods, soda, candy, junk food and fruit juices and sports drinks. Sugar has been linked to diabetes, high cholesterol, hypertension, obesity, cancer growth, tooth decay, kidney stones, constipation, free radical formation, decreased tendon repair, headaches, depression and children being cranky with anxiety issues. As you can see, in the end, sugar is not very "sweet".

MEAT. Meat also has opioid-like effects on the body. Research shows that a meat break can stimulate weight loss. I tell my patients to do a vegetarian day at least once to twice a week. It is also important to realize you don't have to have meat with every meal. There are plenty of other protein sources to utilize that will not have the same long-term effects as the over-consumption of meat.

FOOD ALLERGIES AND ADDICTIONS

We discussed how food allergies and sensitivities can cause the gut to leak larger, partially digested food particles into the bloodstream. This then causes a low-grade systemic inflammatory reaction which leads to degeneration in the body. The same foods we have allergies and sensitivities to are also the foods that our body craves because of the stimulatory effect of the inflammatory reaction. We need to break the addiction cycle as early as possible to avoid chronic inflammation and further disease and degeneration.

There are four stages of reaction with a food allergy or sensitivity as follows.

ALARM	ADDICTIVE	ADAPTIVE	DEGENERATION
Body reacts with symptoms	Body now craves with endorphin rush	Person eats it at regular intervals to avoid withdrawal (chronic stress)	Body breaks down with exhausted survival systems

4 Stages of Reaction with Food Sensitivities and Allergies

During the alarm phase, you may have vague symptoms, like headache, diarrhea or drowsiness. This is the body saying, "stay away". During the addictive phase, if you eat the food again, the body will start to crave it and want it repeatedly to get an endorphin rush. During the adaptive phase, you will eat the food at regular intervals to avoid withdrawals. This creates chronic stress in the body. Eventually, degeneration will set in and the body breaks down with an exhausted survival system. This is analogous to the stress cycles we looked at earlier where, eventually, the adrenal glands can no longer keep up, cortisol drops, and you are left feeling wiped out and fatigued.

With food allergies, you have two options to try to avoid them. First, you can take a food sensitivity or allergy test, which will give you very specific foods to avoid and a plan to slowly bring them back in. You can also try an elimination diet taking out sugar, dairy and wheat/gluten foods – the three most common foods that can create sensitivities, addictions and degeneration - first to identify which foods you may be sensitive to, and then slowly adding them back in while watching symptoms closely.

We all have times in our lives where our will is weakened, and we are more vulnerable to the temptations of eating unhealthy. With unhealthy eating patterns, you are more prone to have cravings with sugar spikes, followed by sugar crashes. Avoid the yo-yo diet with sugar highs and sugar lows. Also, constant dieting impairs the appetite-controlling hormone leptin. With lower leptin levels, you have less control over your appetite and will have more hunger and food cravings. The menstrual cycle will also increase cravings as well as being stressed and fatigued. Be aware that you are vulnerable during these times and have a plan to deal with the cravings when they tempt you. It's time to break the addictions. Following are some tools you can use to help you break the negative food patterns.

1.   **Steady your blood sugars**. Say NO to sugar.

Strive to practice habits that steady your blood sugars and avoid sugar crashes. This will also decrease those crazy sugar cravings. Eat enough nutrient-rich food with each meal. Choose high-fiber foods, as research shows that increased fiber intake leads to a lower body fat. Choose low glycemic index foods to decrease sugar spikes and crashes. Examples include beans, vegetables and fruits - except for watermelon and pineapple that have a high glycemic index. Choose early fruits over ripe fruits as the riper they get, the higher the glycemic index. If starting with R4L

Foundational Nutrition, pastas are better than breads as they have a lower glycemic index and have a steadier effect on blood sugars. If having trouble losing weight, try to drop all sugar, pasta, bread and even grains and see if you can start burning fat. Avoid the bad fats like vegetable oils and trans fats. High-carbohydrate diets require more insulin to get the job done and, with higher insulin levels, you have more fat storage.

2.   **Do things to boost your appetite-suppressant hormone - leptin.**

Higher leptin levels will suppress your appetite and decrease your cravings. Fat cells secrete leptin when there is enough nourishment in the body. Higher leptin levels increase your metabolism. Dieting and calorie restriction make the body think it is starving. The body will then decrease leptin levels to increase your cravings for food. You want your leptin levels to be as high as possible.

To better understand what your calorie needs are, it might be helpful to get a metabolic test. This will tell you your calorie needs over a 24-hour period. You can also try the rule of 10 - eat 100 calories for every pound of ideal body weight. That is your **ideal** body weight - not your current weight. If your ideal body weight is 160 pounds, the minimum number of calories per day would be around 1,600 calories. If you consistently eat below that level, you will slow down your metabolism and decrease your leptin levels, which will increase your cravings and addictions.

Foods low in bad-type fats boost leptin levels. The consumption of healthy fats and omega-3 type fats will not have this effect. Also, exercise increases the body's sensitivity to leptin. It makes the leptin you have more effective at suppressing cravings and making your feel satiated and full. Exercise not only burns calories, increases metabolism and strengthens muscles, but also leads to better control over the appetite and less food cravings. Did I mention that food is the best medicine?

3.   **Break the crave cycle.**

Cravings will come in set patterns on a daily, monthly and yearly schedule. Be aware of this and break the cycle. Start by eliminating food allergies and sensitivities to help break the cycle. The pattern seen in overweight individuals shows that they consume fewer calories in the morning and noon and higher calories in the evening. They often eat out of habit, when watching TV, and also tend to consume an after dinner "treat" out of habit.

The pattern seen in healthy weight individuals shows that they consume calories evenly throughout the day. They consume 6 to 7 meals a day. They eat a small meal before bed to keep the metabolism burning and give them nutrients needed for healing while they sleep. It is helpful to journal to see your pattern and make a choice to change that pattern to the healthy weight pattern.

Here is a checklist to help you break the crave cycle.

DAILY:

- Clean out the cupboards.
  - Don't leave seductive morsels around... they will find you.
- Get to bed an hour early.
  - Rest restores the body, while poor sleep increases cravings.
- Change the people and places that trigger binges.
  - Make healthy, active friends who share your passions.
  - Get out of the house, if needed, to get away from temptations.
    - Walk, library, gym (boot camp)
- Eat a high-fiber, healthy protein good-fat breakfast to give sustained energy through the morning.
- Create a new pattern.

- Stop the mid-morning donut or late-night cereal. Instead, do a brisk walk around office and eat an apple and walnuts.

MONTHLY: Women have monthly estrogen surges followed by a hormone drop. This drop is what creates PMS (pre-menstrual stress). This sudden drop from high to low estrogen levels also creates cravings. There are a few things you can do to tame the high estrogen levels by implementing some dietary changes.

- Lower the bad FATS, lower the ESTROGEN levels (which results in less of a drop).
  - Studies show lower cravings and body weight as well as less PMS mood changes and cramping.
- Increase the FIBER, lower the ESTROGEN levels.
  - The liver filters waste and excess ESTROGEN and empties it in to the gut.
  - FIBER can soak up the ESTROGEN and help to eliminate it.

- Studies show eating high fiber cuts ESTROGEN levels in half.[125]

Also, before your period you may be more sensitive to rises and falls in blood sugars that can happen after eating food with a high glycemic index (fast-acting carbohydrates, such as white bread and sugary drinks). Basing meals and snacks around low GI carbohydrates (vegetables) may help with PMS symptoms by maintaining an even blood sugar level.

This type of a diet may also help reduce food cravings. A low glycemic load (GL) diet, where both the GI and the amount of carbohydrate are taken into consideration, has been shown to be associated with a decrease in inflammation markers which could, in turn, lessen the PMS symptoms.[83]

You can have the power over PMS by practicing these tips consistently. Weight loss and renewed zest and energy await.

ANNUAL: Most people gain more weight from October to December. During this time, there is colder weather, and people tend to be less active and consume more comfort foods with their winter cravings. There are also the holiday temptations that linger during this time.

This is when it is extremely important to have a habit of exercise as well as the knowledge and skills to eat clean. To start exercising and break your sluggish pattern, you may have to go to the gym for group boot camp-type workout or hit the weights and cardio. Head to the mall and don't shop - go for a walk. Get outdoors and enjoy the weather. Start to embrace and get excited when the weather man says, "snow is on the way." Pick up some outdoor activities, like cross-country skiing and snowshoeing. With the right gear, you can always get outside and go for a walk or a run. Once you start to exercise, maintaining healthy nutrition will be easier as you increase leptin levels and strengthen your motivation for healthy habits during this challenging time.

4.   **Exercise.**

Exercise blocks appetite swings and cravings. It increases the appetite-taming hormone leptin. Exercise also resets the mood and your sleep cycles. Exercising during the day will help with sleep. It also lifts your mood by releasing natural endorphins, the same endorphins that are released when we consume our craved comfort foods. Substitute your exercise "high" for your sugar "buzz". Exercise will also increase insulin sensitivity and reduce chronic disease risk by decreasing the need for high insulin levels. With lower insulin levels, there will be less fat storage.

5.   **Get Enough Sleep.**

Good sound sleep decreases stress and leads to fewer cravings. Studies show being tired and having a lack of good sleep leads to a lack of motivation, fatigue and increased food cravings.[84] Studies show we need around eight hours of sleep to be fully rejuvenated. Sleep is when the body heals and recharges, and studies confirm that poor sleep leads to chronic disease and degeneration. Here is a checklist of things you can do that can help with sleep.

- Engage in exercise or some type of physical activity during the day.
    - Tired muscles trigger sleep so they can heal.
- Stretch and yawn on purpose to start shutting down the mind and body.
- Sleep in complete darkness.
- Cortisol is released with any amount of light and can wake you from sleep or cause you to sleep anymore superficial state.
- Keep it quiet.
    - Use ear plugs to decrease and sound that can wake you.
- Nap if you need it.
    - Napping actually relaxes you and helps with better sleep in the evening.

Here is a checklist of things that may be hindering your sleep.

- Caffeine.
  - Limit consumption in the afternoon and evening as it has 6-hour half-life and can keep your awake six hours after consumption. Remember, decaf is not truly decaffeinated.
- Alcohol.
  - When consumed, it is broken down into aldehydes. They can be very stimulating and interferes with deep sleep.
- Exercising too close to bedtime.
  - Exercise can stimulate cortisol levels, which will impair your body's ability to fall asleep. Try exercising earlier in the day so cortisol has a natural ability to fall to a lower level prior to sleep.
- Other activities that are not sleep.
  - Try to avoid watching TV, checking your phone or reading in bed. The bed should be reserved for sleep.

6.   Get Support.

Most people have difficulty with food addictions and cravings as well as binge eating. You are not alone, and you need to get support to ensure success. Join a group, like a church Bible study, sports league, fitness club or workout group. Enlist family and friends to join you on this journey. When you do it together, it is much more fun, and you can be accountable to each other at any time.

As said previously, have that person whom you can call at any time. They are your lifeline and can be very truthful and honest with you to help your stay away from the things that bring you down. Let people know about your journey so they can be supportive and encourage you along the way. You could be that person who is posting on Facebook about their healthy recipes, workout of the day, and become an inspiration to your family and friends. You can also get them to join you in this healthy adventure.

After you have the knowledge to change yourself, you then have the responsibility to help others. You become the inspiration who can teach others the skills you have learned as your pass your knowledge about health and healing on to your family, communities and world.

CHAPTER 14: CHANGE YOUR MINDSET, NOT WHO YOU ARE

There are two primary choices in life; to accept conditions as they exist or accept the responsibility for changing them. — **Denis Waitley**

Now that you know the truth about the body's ability to regenerate, you have a decision to make. You can continue to live the way you are now, or you can take steps to make positive changes in your life. If you feel you want more out of life, that you want to live with less pain and inflammation, and you want to decrease your risk of chronic disease, now you have the power to do something about it. It starts with a decision.

Grab a pencil and get ready to think through some questions. In this chapter, you will find out your **WHY**. Your "why" is the fuel that will keep you going in this journey to health. When you are struggling, facing barriers, and want to give up, you will return to your why and it will re-inspire you to keep going.

There are three critical steps you need to work through before your journey to health and healing begins. The first is to understand the truth about who you are – which is much more than you might think. The second is to find your core reason for making a change. The last thing you need to do is to make that decision. Once you have made the decision, you have the momentum to take that first step.

After you work through these three steps, you will have the fuel needed to start your journey. You will have many obstacles, barriers, setbacks and challenges but, if you refer back to the answers of these three steps, you will find yourself back on track.

First let's talk about **TRUTH**. What is the truth about your existence? The first thing to know is that you are a powerful creation, created from a powerful source. You are not a product of chance, but a beautiful masterpiece infused with the ability to live, love and make a difference in your life and the life of others. The same creator that made you also made the universe that you live in. You were given the potential to live a life full of vitality and purpose. Every day is a gift to live amongst others in this wonderful world. **THAT IS THE TRUTH!**

You were not created to fail but created to be SUCCESSFUL. You are amazing and have the power to make meaningful change and live a joy-filled life full of purpose. Write down the truth about yourself here. Make it personal based on your convictions and beliefs. Include your source of inspiration and strength. I personally believe in a God that created me. I believe He has a purpose for me and it is my responsibility to examine my gifts and purpose and live a life driven to fulfill my purpose.

My truth would read, "*I am special. I was created to be successful and to utilize my gifts that were uniquely given to me from a powerful Creator, to change people's lives for the good. I have a responsibility to use my unique gifts to make the world I live in a better place and to create health and healing in the patients I* serve. I have been given the gift of an amazing of a loving, beautiful family and I vow to love, honor and protect them. Every day they will know how special they are to me and that they, too, have a unique purpose and are wonderful perfect creations."

Now write your truth.

_____

_____

The next step is to find your why, or **CORE REASON,** for creating change. What is the core reason you want to change? This core reason must have a deep personal meaning to you. Is it to be healthy? To feel more useful? Do you want less pain and more energy? Do you want to avoid the chronic medical conditions your parents may have suffered from? Do you want to feel energy zest and passion again? Do you want to be a great and inspiring spouse, friend or parent? Once you have answered that question, start to visualize yourself exactly as that, write it down and say it out loud in the form of an "I am..." statement.

"I am healthy!"

"I am free of pain and inflammation!"

"I am youthful and full of energy!"

"I am a healthy and inspiring parent!"

Write your **CORE REASON** now.

I am:

_____

_____

Let that core reason be the fuel for your change. After you have written it down, put in a place where you will see it every day. On the mirror where you wash your face and brush your teeth is a great place to tape it. When you see it, read it out loud to yourself and believe it! Your truth can be written right above it.

The next and final step is to make the **DECISION**. You must make the decision to leave behind your habits from the past. Let go of the baggage holding you down. You must start fresh and new. Become a new creation. To be rescued from the unhealthy decisions of your past, all your need to do is say, "I will start right now." This is the day you take that step to become healthy and inspire those you love most to be the best they can be as well. Remember, you cannot depend on someone or something outside of yourself to make the decision for you. You need to rescue yourself and make the decision for positive change.

Just relax and be who you truly are. You were created to be the perfect you. Anything else that you think or perceive about yourself that is not based in the truth just blocks you from being who you are and sets you back in your journey of health and discovery. It's time to get rid of any negative thoughts and remember they are not you, but they are what holds you back from becoming the truly amazing, beautiful, wonderful and perfect YOU. Only you can change your life, but you must start by making that decision to change. If you want to make that decision now, write it down and read it to yourself out loud. Tell someone close to you about the decision you have made because they will be vital to supporting your success. Write down who you want to tell as well as your decision statement

Mine would read:
"*Today (today's date), I will make the decision to change my life. I will take the steps needed to become healthy, using the knowledge I have gained. I will be a positive influence to my family and friends. I am amazing. I am powerful. I am loved. I am needed. I have a purpose. I am healthy.*"

Write yours now.

_____

_____

5 STAGES OF CHANGE

To get you to the first step, let's talk about the five stages of change. You will be able to see where you are and make the steps needed to walk through the five stages. By doing this, it will increase your ability to be successful in any decision your make.

Here are the 5 STAGES of Change.

- Pre-Contemplation - "I won't..."
- Contemplation - "I may..."
- Preparation - "I will..."
- Action - "I am..."
- Maintenance - "I still am..."

PRE-CONTEMPLATION. During the pre-contemplation phase, you don't feel you are ready for a change. You say "I won't because... I don't have time... I don't have a problem... I don't have the energy... I don't care." Or you say, "I can't." You might like to change, but don't believe it is possible. This is where your need to focus on what the truth is - your need to ignore false beliefs and start to believe that you have the ability to overcome.

CONTEMPLATION. In the contemplation phase, you say, "I may." You start to think about making a healthy change in your life. You realize you are not satisfied with the present and want to make a change to make your life better or improve your health. You begin to weigh the benefits change may bring against the effort it will take to start that journey. The keys to change to the next phase is to focus on your strengths and compelling reasons to change. It is vital to develop a clear vision of what you want in life. Create, write it down and focus on small goals to build confidence. Believe in the truth that you can do it!

PREPARATION. You say "I will." Your insecure feelings and ambivalence are overcome and you start to feel that you can change. You plan to take action within the next month. This is the time when you start to develop a plan of action. The key to bring about change and move on to the next level are to first develop a plan of action. Write out a statement with details of **what** you want to accomplish, **where** you will do it and **how** you will get it done. Establish your WHAT, WHERE and HOW now by writing them down.

WHAT_____

WHERE_____

HOW_____

ACTION. This is the phase where you can probably say "I am!" You have identified the change you desire, and you are doing it. You are motivated in planning your next level goals. This phase lasts up to around six months.

During this time, you are building new healthy relationships, behaviors and good habits. This is an essential time to change your behaviors from what they were into new habits grounded in the new knowledge you have developed. If you can do something consistently for more than two months, it will become part of who you are every day - your new way of doing things.

Here, the keys to change and getting to the next level include setting realistic and achievable goals so you can feel you are making progress and then to celebrate those accomplishments. Continue to develop new healthy and positive relationships with others who share your similar goals. Use the mistakes and relapses, which will inevitably happen, as learning experiences to refine your process and improve your plan for success. Think about potential high-risk situations and have a plan for when those situations arise.

MAINTENANCE. "I still am." This new behavior has become a habit at around 3 to 6 months. You feel confident that you can maintain your new behavior. Keys to maintaining your success during this time include keeping yourself challenged with interesting and achievable goals. Develop a deep social and environmental support system to keep you on track. Review your original motivators that brought about your decision to change and remember your WHY.

As you progress, develop new goals and new motivators to keep your energy high. Become a role model for others to follow and share your story. This will keep you accountable because you are now becoming a role model for others. Realize that relapse may happen and get back on track quickly - don't judge yourself. Have your plan of action ready for those times of relapse and roleplay it so you are fully prepared.

Congratulations! When you have set your goals, worked through the five stages of change, and maintained high motivation, you are on your way to a life where you can - and will - fulfill your destiny and purpose. Roadblocks, relapses and barriers are sure to happen along the journey. It is expected and, when you get through them, you will be a stronger individual with more resilience and wisdom that you can use to help others. To ensure that your change is long-lasting, let's look at some steps you can take to ensure your success.

Steps to Lasting Change

There are five steps that you can use to ensure that a change you have decided to make is a lasting decision. At the top of the pyramid above is "ME". Once you have worked up the pyramid, you have become the real you. It is the truth that has been inside you all along.

To get to the top of the pyramid, you must start at the base and work yourself up. The base is a large part of your success and the vision must be fully understood, as it will be your strength and foundation.

VISION. In this step, you must have good self-awareness of your strengths and your weaknesses and choose to take responsibility. It is you who is in control and can make the change. Focus on your strengths and what you do well. Look at your unique gifts and abilities and how they have helped you with success in the past. Figure out what your core values are as they become the compass to your higher purpose and deeper meaning for change.

Your core values are the principles you live your life by and may be represented by words like HONESTY, INTEGRITY, DILIGENCE, CREATIVE, HARD WORKING. Also remember your core purpose - your WHY which you discovered previously. During this time, you need to gather as much information as possible and expand your knowledge base. Become emotionally connected to the benefits that will happen when you apply this knowledge to your life.

PREPARATION. After your vision is set and you know your core reason and purpose, you understand why this change needs to happen. You can then become emotionally connected to those goals and are motivated by the benefits. You are then ready for the next step of preparation. During this time, you need confidence, commitment, support outside yourself, and a written plan.

First, your **confidence** needs to be high during this time to ensure sustained success. You need to rate your self-efficacy at least an 8/10. If you don't have this type of confidence, you need to figure out why you are feeling insecure and focus more on your vision to get the motivation and confidence you need for successful change.

Next, you need to be fully **committed** to the process. Take a pencil and write a written commitment to yourself on why you are doing this change. Engage a friend, spouse or coach to hold you accountable to that written commitment. This person will also be someone you can call at any time when you have an "emergency", like when you are about to eat a box of donuts.

Write your written commitment and share it with someone your trust.

_____

_____

You need to have **support** along the journey. Have a person or group who can ask you the deep questions and keep you accountable to your goals. Again, have that someone you can call on at any time of the day or night when you need some motivation, accountability or just a good talk.

I have only a few people in my life who I trust that deeply - my wonderful wife and probably two close friends. These people are extremely valuable in my life and are needed to keep me motivated, on-track and balanced. They share my values and understand my strengths and weaknesses. They pull me up when

I am frustrated, and they keep me focused when I am off- track.

Write down your core support here.

_____

_____

Finally, you need a **plan**. We previously established your what, where and how. You need to write this plan with specific detail as it will be the map you will use to achieve and sustain your goals.

Expand here on your what, where and how with details - include weekly, monthly and yearly goals you have for yourself.

_____

_____

ACTION. After your preparation has been laid on your firm vision and foundation, it is time to take action. You must take some **behavioral steps** in order to be successful. You have chosen, refined and committed to very specific goals. Now it's time to plan specific actions to meet those goals. They should be specific and measurable, like "I will work out four days a week," or, "I will follow the REJUV4Life meal plan for three months." You should set up weekly, monthly and yearly goals. By having smaller goals within your larger goals, it enables you to taste a little success along the journey and gives you more reasons to celebrate your accomplishments.

Next, you need to develop your **problem-solving** skills. Obstacles will happen, so you need to be ready with a plan. Use this as a time to learn, grow, improve and sharpen yourself. Brainstorm and think about potential obstacles that may come to create a plan of action for when they do happen and, finally, take prompt action when the obstacles arise. List some obstacles you may face and your plan of action that you will take to hurdle over them. For example, "*When I feel like eating that pizza, I will eat and apple and go for a walk.*" Or, "*When I feel tired and want to skip my* *workout, I will call my friend and meet to work out together."*

_____

_____

RESULTS. During this step, you are starting to create lasting change. After six months, the change becomes a part of your new behavior. This new behavior is becoming part of who you are and what your stand for in your life. The change is becoming naturally you. You crave good nutrition and a workout. During this step, where you are getting results and achieving success, you need to continue to plan for relapse prevention.

To do this, you need to view your new self as a role model for others – doing so will keep you motivated and accountable. Join a gym, a support group, a running club or bring together a bunch of your friends and establish a "healthy network." You are only as strong as the people you surround yourself with so choose to spend time with people who have your same motivation and goals in mind. Choose not to spend time with those who bring you down, deflate you or pull you back into past habits.

ME. Congratulations - you have made it to the top of the pyramid! You have laid the foundation for success by taking the essential steps needed to ensure you will stay on top. Change has occurred and is now part of you. The baggage of your old physical and emotional stress is now gone. The "real me" is revealed. You are confident in who you are, but thankful for the journey and the lessons it has taught you. It is time to celebrate and be proud of who you are and have always been, knowing you have just set yourself free.

Continue to take time to grow personally. Always seek to better yourself and to be an inspiration and positive influence on those you care about - start helping others climb their pyramids so you can celebrate the peak together.

You now have the roadmap to successful change. You understand the five stages of change and where you are in those stages. You also understand the five steps to lasting change. If you are ready, then it's time to take the first step. Let's take some time to answer some questions.

The first question to answer is, why do I really want to change my behavior? Before you answer the following questions, take about ten minutes. Find a quiet place, put on some relaxing music and connect with your subconscious using guided imagery. Refer to the guided imagery techniques described in chapter 8 of this book. By taking this time, you will develop more powerful and meaningful answers to the questions below.

Take a few minutes and list out all the pros to making a positive change.

PROS:

_____

_____

_____

Next, answer the question, why shouldn't I try to
change my behavior? What are the cons?

CONS:

_____

_____

_____

Do your pros outweigh your cons? If you have more
cons, ask yourself what would it take for me to
change my behavior and overcome my cons?

_____

_____

_____

Answer this next question. Can you really do it?

_____

_____

Next, circle what stage you think you are in:

- Pre-contemplation
- Contemplation
- Preparation
- Action
- Maintenance

Now, go back and read through your stage again and make the decision to move from that stage and into the next stage. If you are ready, now is the time to make it happen.

Take the next few minutes to dig deep and answer the next seven questions.

1. The goal or behavior I want to work on first is:

_____

_____

_____

2. My reasons for wanting to accomplish this goal is:

_____

_____

_____

3. The strengths, aptitudes, values and resources that I can draw from include:

_____

_____

_____

4. The main challenges I will face while changing this behavior are:

_____

_____

_____

5. My strategies to move forward changing this behavior are:

_____

_____

_____

6. The efforts I made toward changing this behavior are:

_____

_____

_____

7. My goal for next week with respect to my behavior is:

_____

_____

_____

You can refer back to and answer these questions over again as you progress through your journey to health. You may often have to redefine your goals and continue to develop new behaviors that reinforce your new values and desires for health. You truly have the ability to create health and prosperity in your life.

Once there was apathy, loss of interest and motivation, painful aging joints and arthritis. Now you can live with confidence, love of yourself, enjoy life and the adventures of living, and celebrate your ability to **REGENERATE**. Body Heal Thyself.

"Our deepest fear is not that we are inadequate. Our deepest fear is that we are POWERFUL BEYOND MEASURE. It is our light, not our darkness that most frightens us. We ask ourselves, 'Who am I to be brilliant, gorgeous, talented, fabulous?' Actually, who are you not to be? You are a child of God. Your playing small does not serve the world. There is nothing enlightened about shrinking so that other people won't feel insecure around you. We are all meant to shine, as children do. We were born to make manifest the glory of God that is within us. It's not just in some of us; it's in everyone. And as we let our own light shine, we unconsciously give other people permission to do the same. As we are liberated from our own fear, our presence automatically liberates others."

— **Marianne Williamson**

CHAPTER 15: NOW THAT YOU ARE HEALTHY - RECRUIT!

If you want to travel swiftly, go alone. If you want to travel far, go together. —**African Proverb**

Congratulations! You have taken that powerful first step on your journey to health and healing. You understand the wrong trend that is happening in the United States as obesity rates are increasing in our adult and child populations, which is paralleling the increase in chronic disease, pain and arthritis that our populations are suffering. This is not just a local or national problem, but a global epidemic.

Healthy cultures from around the world that used to teach us the secrets to longevity and health are now being diseased by the over-consumption of foods that don't heal as well as the loss of physical activity that can strengthen and protect. You know that healthcare is not going to be fixed by more medications, cover-up procedures or surgeries. Trillions of dollars are being spent, yet our population suffers from more chronic disease and degeneration than ever before.

You know what needs to happen. We need to change our focus to disease prevention utilizing what we know to be true -that we can regenerate. Change is not easy, but it is essential. With your knowledge, motivation and unique abilities, you are in a position to create needed lifestyle and behavioral changes not only in yourself but in your family and community. You now have options to create a healthy and healed body.

SELF

Let's review what you need to do with yourself first. Remember to find your true reason - your WHY. This is needed for deep inspiration to fuel your journey as you change your life for the good. Next, create a plan for success. Write out your weekly, monthly and yearly goals and make sure they are achievable. Celebrate your accomplishments. Plan for your obstacles. It is important to have trips and holidays to decrease your stress, but make sure that you plan to make them healthy getaways for the mind, body and soul. Surround yourself with friends who support you on the journey and are also are motivated to join you on the adventure. Here is your checklist of things to focus on to improve your **SELF**:

o NUTRITION - Start Rejuv4LIFE Foundational Nutrition.

o EXERCISE - Exercise at least 5 days, preferably most days of the week.

o WATER - Drink half your body weight in ounces daily.

o SLEEP - Get eight hours of restorative sleep per night.

o STRESS - Avoid stress and implement relaxation techniques into your life.

o AVOID TOXINS – Environmental, physical, with your work and in your relationships.

o OPTIMIZE YOUR HORMONES - See a provider who can help you.

○ EDUCATION - Continue to read books and educate yourself.

FAMILY

It is now time for your to be the leader and inspire your family to join you as you create long-lasting health together. One of the most important things you can do as a family is eat together. On average, this only happens about three times a week and only lasts around 20 minutes. Many times, dinner is eating while watching TV and not interacting with each other. There is more time spent watching the FOOD NETWORK and Cup Cake Wars than preparing actual food together.

Studies show that children who eat together with their family have better grades and healthier relationships, and hey, get in less trouble during and after school. They are 42% less likely to drink alcohol, 50% less likely to smoke cigarettes and 66% less likely to smoke pot. Eating together as a family can protect girls from bulimia, anorexia and diet pills. There's also a decrease in childhood obesity in families who consume their meals together. The dinner table is a time where you can talk, laugh and catch up on the happenings of the day.

It is important to make dinner special. Plan for healthy, tasty and fun meals. Use this time to educate your family with your new-found knowledge of healthy food and nutrition. Find a special place to eat, set the table and light a candle. Use dinner as a time to share, reflect and have a lot of fun. Just try not to laugh with a mouthful! An important rule is to have no toys, games or phones at the table. This is a sacred and special time for the family only. Eliminate any distractions. Make sure you plan for enough time before events and activities and eat slowly and drink water throughout the meal.

The next thing you can do as a family is to learn together. Find healthy topics that your entire family can enjoy. Each week let somebody different pick a new topic. You can discuss nutrition, health and the good and bad effects of food choices. Go to a museum, see or create art and attend a play or concert. We all have skills and things we are good at, so take an evening and teach each other a new skill or hobby. Have your kids teach you karate, dance, hockey or - if you are brave - gymnastics.

The family that plays together, stays together. Make time to play, adventure and move together. Set an example for your family with your own personal fitness. Children tend to model after the activities of their parents. Schedule weekly times to work out together. You can do team sports, swimming and water activities, hiking, tennis, running or just get out and go for a walk around the neighborhood. To increase your kid's excitement about this, let them bring friends to your activities.

As you know, friend time is important, so why not combine it with family time? It is also important to get everyone's input on what activity, sport or workout you all will engage in together. You must choose activities that everyone can do to make sure it is fun and age-appropriate. Try to avoid coaching or putting pressure to perform - just make it fun and make games out of it. By doing this, you will create lifelong fitness habits that can have payback for generations to come.

Teach your family about the environment, recycling and conservation. The outdoors is your playground and we all have the responsibility to keep it clean, functional and safe for our families and our community. Collect and recycle cans, paper, bottles and plastics. Teach them about the importance of recycling. Get them their own bottles for water and teach them about filtering water. Get them excited about water and energy conservation.

Do yardwork together. This pays back two-fold. First, you get a nice-looking well-trimmed yard and, second, you all get a good workout doing it. Learn to compost

Get Free Recipes and Meal Plans at www.JoelBaumgartnerMD.com

and teach your kids how to help. Kids who learn to respect their environment will grow up and pass it on.

COMMUNITY AND FRIENDS

It is time to engage in your community and connect with friends who share your same values about health. Join or organize a small group to get together and have some fun, relax and de-stress through a healthy connection. Use this group to be accountable to each other and to dig deeper into each other's core reasons and "why". Develop profound friendships and have conversations that matter.

It is also important and helpful to connect in other already-established community activities. Join a sports league, like softball or volleyball. Take dance or healthy cooking classes. Sign yourself – or, even better, your family - up for a 5K or 10K running event. Sports clubs like running, triathlon and biking groups can be a good source of friendship, accountability and fun. One thing I like to do is get together with about eight of my closest friends and do a monthly healthy eating dinner club. In our group, the host makes the main course and the others bring healthy sides, appetizers and drinks. The host picks a unique theme, like Asian fusion, Caribbean, German or backyard barbecue. It is a good time to connect, have some fun and eat healthy doing it.

This truly is an incredible time to be alive. Innovation has given us the ability to integrate healthy lifestyles to optimize our bodies. We have regenerative procedures like PRP and Stem Cells, so we don't have to live with the pain of degeneration and arthritis. You now have the knowledge and the steps it takes to create long-lasting change in your life that will have a positive effect on yourself, family, friends, community and world. If you want it, it is yours. Open your mouth, inhale, exhale and take the first step. It is now time to REGENERATE.

Go to *www.JoelBaumgartnerMD.com* for additional information including a detailed recipes book and meal plans.

ABOUT JOEL JAY BAUMGARTNER, M.D.

Joel Baumgartner, M.D., is the Founder of Rejuv Medical and HealthOvators and a Leader in Regenerative Healthcare.

"Nine years ago, the large traditional healthcare system he was working for changed and he either had to follow them to a new city, find a new job or start his own practice. At the time, he was unhappy and frustrated with relying on prescriptions to mask symptoms and 5-minute appointments in trying to keep up production.

So he started his practice, using all his savings and risking his financial future. It paid off. He needed a system to get his patients healthy. He needed to restore health in his patients through movement and mindful eating to have even better outcomes while regenerating the body. He needed to create a healthcare model that would be the solution to the healthcare crisis. His goal was to combine the science of medicine with the physiology and endocrinology of the body to develop a healthcare model that creates permanent change and regeneration in his patients.

And he did it. He's built the practice of his dreams, seeing patients as a healer, and is now teaching others how to build next-level success in their healthcare practices. He's walking his talk and changing the face of healthcare globally.

Living in Minnesota with his wife, Debbie, and three children, Teddy, Corrielle and Faith, he joyfully shares his life story, skills and experience to make a bigger difference in his community and around the world.

You can reach Dr. Baumgartner at:

Office / Phone: 320-217-8480

Clinic Website: rejuvmedical.com

Personal Website: JoelBaumgartnerMD.com

Facebook: facebook.com/JoelBaumgartnerMD/

LinkedIn: linkedin.com/in/joel-baumgartner-a67a2149/

REFERENCES

1. Foot Ankle Int. 2009
2. Acta Orthop Scand 2006
3. Int J Sports Med. 2010
4. JAAOS. 2010
5. PMR. 2011
6. Center for Blood Research. APR 2001
7. Stem Cell Research & Therapy 2013
8. Orthopedic Journal of Sports Medicine, March 2016
9. EMBO J. May 2004
10. Arthritis Research and Therapy. 2013
11. Cell Transplant. 2014
12. Nephrol Dial Transplant. August 2012
13. Annals of Family Medicine, June 2013
14. Int J Adv Res Biol Sci. 2016
15. Anesthesiology and Pain, 2016
16. PMR, November 2015
17. Anatomy Trains. Myers. 2014
18. Fascial Dysfunction. Chaitow
19. Vitamins, Minerals, Herbs and More. Smith
20. Regenerative Injections. The Art of Healing. Baumgartner
21. Tunnel Syndromes. Pecina
22. Osteoarthritis Cartilage. 2015
23. Orthopaedic Journal of Sports Medicine, May 2015
24. Cortisone and lateral epicondylitis. JAMA 2103
25. N Engl J Med. July 2013
26. Osteoarthritis Cartilage. 2016
27. Ann Rheum Dis. 1999
28. Ann Int Med. 2005
29. Spine. 2004
30. Pain. 2005

31. BMJ. 1999
32. Cochrane Library. 2005
33. Curr Op Clin Nutr. 2004
34. Acta Physiol Scand. 1990
35. Scientific American. 2011
36. Am J Clin Nutr. March 2008
37. STEM CELL. May 2012
38. World J Gastroenterol. 2009
39. J Clin Endocrinol Metab. 1988
40. Ann Clin Biochem. 1983
41. Medicine & Science in Sports & Exercise: 1999
42. Gen Pharmacol. 1989
43. J Bodyw Mov Ther. 2012
44. Podiatry Today 2004
45. Glob Adv Health and Med, March 2013
46. Am. J. Sports Med. May 2006
47. AJSM 2010
48. Injury 2009
49. Clin Exp Rheumatol 2008
50. Am J Sports Med 2012
51. Am J Phys Med Rehabil. 2012 May
52. Patel et al, Am J Sports Medicine 2013
53. Knee Surg Sports Traumatol Arthrosc. 2014
54. Arch Phys Med Rehabil. 2014
55. Rheumatology 2012
56. LANCET. 2010
57. Annals of Family Medicine. 2013
58. J Stem Cells and Reg Med. 2016
59. Transplantation. 2013
60. Pain Physician. 2008
61. J Bodyw Mov Ther. 2012
62. Podiatry Today 2004
63. Glob Adv Health and Med, March 2013
64. Am. J. Sports Med. May 2006
65. AJSM 2010

66. Injury 2009
67. Clin Exp Rheumatol 2008
68. Am J Sports Med 2012
69. Am J Phys Med Rehabil. 2012 May
70. Am J Sports Medicine *2013*
71. Knee Surg Sports Traumatol Arthrosc. 2014
72. Arch Phys Med Rehabil. 2014
73. Rheumatolog. *2012*
74. LANCET. 2010
75. Annals of Family Medicine. 2013
76. J Stem Cells and Reg Med. 2016
77. Transplantation. 2013
78. Pain Physician. 2008
79. Amino Acids. 2006
80. Nature. 1988
81. J Clin Sleep Med 2014
82. Am J Clin Nut. 2001
83. Medhealth. 2012
84. Nature Communications. 2013
85. Hypertension. 2001
86. Am J Clin Nutr. 2010
87. N Engl J Med 1990
88. J Food Lipids. 1994
89. Br Med J. 1965
90. Br J Nutr. 2010
91. J All Clin Immun. 2006
92. BMC Med. 2012
93. Lipids. 2004
94. Psychosomatic Medicine. 2007
95. Pediatrics. 2007
96. Nutr Metab. 2008
97. Curr Athrosclero Rep. 2003
98. Prostaglandins Leukot Essent Fatty Acids. 2004
99. Nutr Metab (Lond). 2004
100. Am J Clin Nutr. 2008

101. Diabet Med. 2007
102. Adv Exp Med Biol. 2009
103. Nutr Metab. 2005
104. Ann Int Med. 2005
105. Nutr Clin Prac. 2008
106. Nutr Metob. 2007
107. J Neuros Res. 2005
108. Transl Res. 2014
109. J Clin Invest. 2008
110. Am Clin J Nutr. 2005
111. Autophagy. 2010
112. Ageing Res Rev. 2006
113. Am J Physio. 1988
114. Obes Rev. 2011
115. Free Rad Bio Med. 2007
116. Am J Clin Nutr. 2009
117. Teratog Mutagen. 2002
118. Ann Rev Nutr. 2005
119. Neurobiol Dis. 2007
120. Gerentol. 1982
121. Am J Physio. 1990
122. Am J Clin Nutr. 1987
123. J Clin End Metab. 2011
124. C hronobiology Int. 2013
125. Endocr Rel Cancer. 2013
126. J Clin End Met. 2006
127. J Diabetes Res. 2017